Theories of Crime and Punishment

Claire Valier

with a Foreword by
Loraine R.R. Gelsthorpe

Longman

An imprint of **Pearson Education**

Harlow, England · London · New York · Reading, Massachusetts · San Francisco
Toronto · Don Mills, Ontario · Sydney · Tokyo · Singapore · Hong Kong · Seoul
Taipei · Cape Town · Madrid · Mexico City · Amsterdam · Munich · Paris · Milan

Pearson Education Limited
Edinburgh Gate
Harlow
Essex CM20 2JE

and Associated Companies throughout the world

Visit us on the World Wide Web at:
www.pearsoned.co.uk

First published 2002

© Pearson Education Limited 2002

ISBN-13: 978-0-582-43792-0

British Library Cataloguing-in-Publication Data
A catalogue record for this book is available from the British Library

Library of Congress Cataloging-in-Publication Data
Valier, Claire.
    Theories of crime and punishment / Claire Valier.
        p.   cm. – (Longman criminology series)
    Includes bibliographical references and index.
    ISBN 0–582–43792–X (PPR)
    1. Crime–Philosophy.   2. Criminal behavior.   3. Punishment–Philosophy.   I. Title.
II. Series.
    HV6018+
    364–dc21   2001029665

10 9 8 7 6 5 4 3 2
06

Typeset in 10/12pt New Baskerville by 35
Printed in Great Britain by Henry Ling Limited, at the Dorset Press, Dorchester, DT1 1HD

Theories of Crime and Punishment

Longman Criminology Series

Series Editor: Tim Newburn

Titles in the series:

Contents

Foreword

As we have witnessed a growth in certain types of crime and the development and discovery of new crimes in recent years, we have also seen a growth in Criminology courses. There has been rapid publication of a number of theory texts to accompany the increasing fascination with crime in both political and academic discourses. Some of these books have become classic introductions to the principal theories of crime and social deviance in the European and North American context; some portray the theoretical terrain as a battlefield – charting both the entrance and demise of critical ideas about deviance; other authors set theorising about crime in a context of movements between modernity to postmodernity.

There are different layers to this new book by Claire Valier: it offers a description of core criminological theories, provides a critical exegesis of those ideas and theories, and surpasses other texts in its engagement with postmodern criminologies and consideration of what have become known as 'cosmopolitan theories' of crime and punishment reflecting the optimism of those writing about global civil society and the potentiality for non-hostile sociability in late modernity. But the special contribution of this book to my mind is not only that it is wonderfully rich in detail, but that it explores the development of theories of crime and punishment in specific cultural contexts. Theories about crime and punishment reflect fashions in broad ideas about social science, and about what counts as knowledge. More than this, notions and representations of crime and criminals at any one time are telling of changing social orders. As Valier describes, theories of crime and punishment are linked to notions of 'the good society'. The designation of the criminal is inextricably linked to processes of defining the good citizen.

This is an intelligent, insightful and eminently readable text which looks set to be at the forefront of texts about theories of crime and punishment. To coin a phrase which is fast becoming central to 'change philosophies', this book reflects a stance of 'appreciative enquiry'; it sets out to understand the shape and context of ideas and theories and thus contributes to a growing body of sophisticated and subtle analyses of theories and theorising about crime and punishment.

Loraine R.R. Gelsthorpe

Series Editor's Preface

Our society appears to be increasingly preoccupied with crime and with criminal justice. Despite increasing affluence in the postwar period, crime has continued to rise – often at an alarming rate. Moreover, the pace of general social change at the beginning of the twenty-first century is extraordinary, leaving many feeling insecure. High rates of crime, high levels of fear of crime, and no simple solutions in sight, have helped to keep criminal justice high on the political agenda.

Partly reflecting this state of affairs, the study of crime and criminal justice is burgeoning. There are now a large number of well-established postgraduate courses, new ones starting all the time, and undergraduate criminology and criminal justice degrees are also now appearing regularly. Though increasing numbers of individual textbooks are being written and published, the breadth of criminology makes the subject difficult to encompass in a satisfactory manner within a single text.

The aim of this series is, as a whole, to provide a broad and thorough introduction to criminology. Each book covers a particular area of the subject, takes the reader through the key debates, considers both policy and politics and, where appropriate, also looks to likely future developments in the area. The aim is that each text should be theoretically informed, accessibly written, attractively produced, competitively priced, with a full guide to further reading for students wishing to pursue the subject. Whilst each book in the series is designed to be read as an introduction to one particular area, the Longman Criminology Series has also been designed with overall coherence in mind.

It is undoubtedly 'theory' that scares students the most. There is a ghastly tendency for scholars interested in theory to write in arcane and impenetrable prose. As a consequence many are frightened away from important ideas and debates. In this book Claire Valier breaks away from this mould in an attempt to provide, as she puts it, an appreciative and critical approach to theories of crime and punishment. *Appreciative*, in that she introduces readers to the key features of different theories in an accessible and entertaining manner; *critical* because she is clear about both their uses and their shortcomings.

Though a volume such as this cannot hope to cover everything, it is enormously broad-ranging in scope. The reader is taken on a journey that begins with Bentham and Lombroso, and proceeds via Durkheim and the Chicago school, Robert Merton, Erving Goffman and Howard Becker, to critical criminology, the 'new criminology' and the impact of feminism, before arriving at Michel Foucault, and recent theories of globalisation and late modernity.

Theories of crime and punishment are important because they help illuminate the nature and organisation of current practices and discourses. In addition, as Claire Valier points out, treated and used critically they can also help challenge the 'assumption that social order, or social solidarity, is an unproblematic good'. This book provides a superb guide to a broad sweep of social and criminological theory and will be an invaluable resource for undergraduate and postgraduate students and teachers for many years to come.

Tim Newburn
London, May 2001

Preface

This book provides an introduction to the principal theories of crime and punishment advanced by scholars from the late eighteenth century to the present day. I have very much enjoyed reading the books and essays discussed within these pages, and hope that something of this pleasure comes across to readers. My thanks are due to a number of people whose assistance and encouragement I have benefited from.

I am grateful to the President and Fellows of Queens' College, Cambridge, for electing me to the Munro Scholarship. This provided marvellous bed and board, but more importantly gave me the collegial support of deep thinkers and kindly souls. The librarians at the Radzinowicz Library in Cambridge have always been exceptionally helpful as well as pleasant and friendly (I promise to return to keep on giving an airing to the books that nobody else reads). The discussion of theories in this book owes something to the lectures and seminars that I have conducted over the last six years with students in Cambridge, Lancaster and Leeds. I have been fortunate to have had plenty of enthusiastic, intelligent and amusing pupils among whom Lieut. Kat Astley stands out. Tony Jefferson and Loraine Gelsthorpe made very useful comments on the proposed outline of this book. I am indebted to both of them and to Tony Bottoms for their assistance in practical and inspirational ways.

I would like to take this opportunity to thank my family for all their support, both moral and practical, over the years. Without an imaginative and inspiring mother who fostered my love of the written word, and an encouraging father who keeps me up to date with the newspapers, this book may well not have been written. My wonderful little sister kept me smiling with terrible jokes and lent me copies of novels. I would like to express my gratitude to M. and Mme de Fonds-Montmaur for their kindly and splendid hospitality at Lamothe and in Spain during the time that I was writing this book. Mr John and Mrs Ghislaine Grant kept us in game and potatoes!

My friends have kept me dancing, shopping, wining and dining, so cheers to you Simon, James, Rupert, Clare, Guillaume and Philippe. I would like to thank Annabel for fantastic cooking, making sure I have plenty of sun, sea and skiing, and tirelessly reading the manuscript.

Finally, many thanks to an excellent and friendly editorial team at Longman, and in particular Pat Bond, Natasha Dupont and Jill Birch.

Introduction

The approach taken by this book is one that aims to be both appreciative and critical. I have set out to elucidate how the different theories may be related to one another, as well as describing the key features of the cultural and political context from which each work emerged. I remember being frustrated as a student by oblique references to political events that I had little idea of. I have hoped to give some insight into events with which readers may not be acquainted. My sincere apologies go to those who, whether by reason of direct experience or historical study, may find some of this detail unnecessary. This contextualising gesture is important because theories are embedded within the cultures from which they arise, as well as sometimes provoking changes to those cultures. Theory is not just a reflection on the world; it also shapes that world.

Theories of crime and punishment have, from the outset, been linked to visions of 'the good society'. Ways of understanding crime and punishment have carried within their carefully structured arguments, and key concepts, ideas about the kind of society that it would be desirable to live in. The designation of the criminal is bound up with the process of defining the good citizen. Theories of crime and punishment have never just been ways of solving the 'crime problem'. They have involved, whether explicitly or implied within their concepts and arguments, a normative view of what acts *ought* to be crimes and what the criminal justice process *should be* for. Sometimes theories have undertaken a directly normative style of analysis, for instance the classical jurisprudence discussed in Chapter 1 took this form. At other times, the normative assumptions of a theory have remained relatively unspoken, and have later been subjected to critique on this basis. The tradition of theorising crime and punishment has played an important part in a series of projects that have sought to order and govern society in certain ways. Theories don't come from nowhere. Representations of criminals in both public opinion and scholarly discourse can be related to the changing social orders within which they emerged (Melossi, 2000). Ways of thinking about crime and punishment are embedded within specific cultural contexts, hence studying these theories can tell us a great deal about a society.

Because theories are not ahistorical, they do not produce timeless concepts and arguments. One implication of the historical specificity of theories is that their generalisability might be negated for that reason. Are they so tied to the problems and ways of thinking of their times that they are soon outmoded? This question is not a simple one to answer. I vigorously deny the idea that earlier theories are obsolete and can be resigned to the dustbin. We need to foster a sophisticated understanding of earlier theories because many of their features linger on in the theories of today, both overtly and covertly. The genres of theory covered in this book all continue to exercise an effect on contemporary thought about crime and punishment. However, the applicability of a theory that was popular even a decade ago, to changing social, political and cultural milieux, merits serious thought. Major transformations suggest that theories cannot be retained *in toto* and without substantial qualification and modification. Some scholars insist that changing times merit new concepts and forms of reasoning. That said, these arise in a dialogue with the older theories, as well as drawing upon other disciplines. There are important respects in which new scholarship takes its bearings from the perceived shortcomings of existing theories. However, this process does not support a belief in the progressive sophistication of theory. While the organisation of this book is largely chronological, it is not intended that later theories are assumed to be better than earlier ones, nor that they iron out earlier problems.

A commitment of this book is to convey the extent to which theorising is a contested activity. There are divergences between academics that can go as deep as the very point of undertaking scholarship on crime and punishment. One rather polemical dispute is that which has taken place between 'theorists' and 'researchers'. This has tended to erect a false dichotomy between the two. Those who express allegiance to empirical research have tended to depict 'research' as practical, realistic and systematic, and 'theory' as mere armchair-theorising which is obscurantist and ill-disciplined. On the other hand, theorists have seen empiricists as simplifying what constitutes reality, hiding their subjective investments behind a methodology which conceals personal interests and opinions, and being too beholden to the research-funder. It seems to me that theorists and empiricists have been talking in incommensurate registers. They simply cannot understand each other (which is somewhat like swearing at somebody in a foreign language).

It is not the case that empirical research has a set of methods which can be learned and carried out systematically, whereas theorising is a speculative activity with no obvious reference points. Neither is it the case that being tested by empirical research is, or should be, the principal way of judging a theory. Theory has its own purposes, as well as its own ways of establishing its validity. Theories of crime and punishment have from the first made claims about the kind of knowledge that they give rise to, as well as the status of this knowledge. This book therefore describes the epistemologies underlying theories of crime and punishment. An epistemology is a theory of knowledge, and the kind of questions that epistemologies address include the following:

- What is the purpose of the knowledge produced? What is the knowledge for? Is knowledge an end in itself, or should knowledge be directed at some ultimate purpose, for instance, social change?
- What relationship is there between knowledge and knower, theory and theorist? Is the scholar a detached and neutral observer? If unbiased knowledge is impossible, how can we tell which knowledges are more authentic, or more emancipatory? How do we adjudicate rival knowledge claims?

The different epistemologies give rise to distinctive methodological approaches, which relate the kinds of principles mentioned above to particular processes through which knowledge is produced. A key theme of this book is the tension that has existed between the objectivity of knowledge and its moral-political commitments.

In addition to epistemological disagreements, scholars writing within the same theoretical perspective sometimes disagree on the interpretation of particular texts. For instance, there is simply not one Durkheim: he is different things to different people. This recognition means that I cannot hope to authoritatively state what Durkheim *really said*. I do hope, however, to be able to convey something of the principal ways in which people have understood what Durkheim may have been saying. This does not suggest that his work was unintelligible, but rather that it was complex and can support a number of different readings. To demonstrate how these readings arise, I have provided my own critical commentary on some of the key texts published by theorists of crime and punishment. I hope to inspire readers to undertake a detailed reading of these texts themselves, many of which are by now seen as classics.

A book of this kind is necessarily selective. To give any depth of coverage, decisions have to be taken about its scope, as well as choosing which works to discuss in more detail than others. A number of points may be made in this respect. Firstly, this book only claims to engage with the Western criminological tradition. Within this tradition, the principal works covered are American, French and British. A further point is merited concerning accessibility. Today students encounter theories of crime and punishment at all levels of academia, both undergraduate and postgraduate. This book has been designed as a multi-levelled text. It aims to enable readers of all abilities to improve their critical thinking around questions of crime and punishment. The book is hence not a rudimentary one, and some parts of it will require more reading than others. A final word about critical scholarship: each of the chapters of this book challenges the assumption that social order, or social solidarity, is an unproblematic good. The chapters also make apparent the costs of certain attempts to achieve social control. I hope to stimulate and guide critical thinking, by interrogating ways in which we can question the role of the scholar, as well as interrogating the key assumptions of concepts and perspectives that continue in one way or another to animate our thought.

Chapter 1

From Enlightenment jurisprudence to the born criminal

The Count is a criminal and of criminal type. Nordau and Lombroso would so classify him, and qua criminal he is of imperfectly formed mind.

(Stoker, 1897/1993: 439)

Theories of crime and punishment express the manner in which the exercise of power and the nature of social relations are construed at any given time. The eighteenth century, commonly known as the 'age of Enlightenment', brought the first systematic theorising about crime and punishment. Enlightenment jurisprudence, also known as the classical school of criminal law and penal policy, emerged at a time of major changes throughout Europe, which revolutionised the institutions of power. The transition from feudalism to capitalism transformed social, political and economic relations. Economies shifted from being primarily based in agriculture towards commercial market forms. The ascendancy of the landed aristocracy was challenged by the rising bourgeoisie. In feudal societies, law had been maintained by appeal to notions like the 'divine right' of monarchs, this phrase denoting the idea that monarchs ruled by God-given right. At this time, there was no idea of rights as common to all; instead there were privileges commensurate with social rank. The workings of the justice system were haphazard, and reflected the personal ties of the powerful. The Enlightenment brought a revolt against the unquestioning acceptance of traditional forms of authority. Through bloody revolutions in some countries, or more gradual transition in others, the absolute power of the monarch was circumscribed or eliminated. The concept of individual rights began to replace that of customary bonds, as the new capitalist class called for the extension of rights instead of a regime based solely on hereditary privilege. Before the courts, the ideal was enshrined that all were transformed into abstract legal subjects, to be treated equally. The work of Enlightenment thinkers profoundly influenced the reform of criminal codes, and set out a number of assumptions about crime and punishment that persist today.

Enlightenment thinkers sought a rational and humane social order in contradistinction to the arbitrary power of absolute monarchy. The Enlightenment was a project which especially sought to create its actuality through law; the law reflected and condensed Enlightenment thought in practice (Fitzpatrick, 1990). The quest for a rational system of criminal justice was based in a vision of social life as calculable, rulebound and efficient. For thinkers like Beccaria in Italy and Bentham in England, the rule of law would be central to the constitution of a new society. This project rested in a view of controlling the individual in their capacity as a thinking person able to make decisions and choices. The legal subject at the foundation of modern law was very much the Enlightenment's 'man of reason'.

A century later, the theoretical principles and political ambitions of classical jurisprudence were rejected outright by the criminal anthropologists as mere abstract philosophising. They too professed their faith in reason, but took a different view of scientific method. Criminal anthropologists opposed the classical vision, which they saw as built out of vague speculation, with a biologically deterministic view of the criminal as destined to crime by bad heredity. The biocriminologies of the late nineteenth century were a thinly veiled way of imagining a purified racial and national identity. The approach of the Italian and French schools of criminal anthropology assumed 'an apartheid model of society' (van Swaaningen, 1997: 32). The theory of the born criminal type made the identification of criminality part of the process of constructing an Italian national identity by fixing and excluding those deemed outside the sphere of orderly and civic society (Pick, 1989). A fatalistic picture of the criminal doomed to crime on account of his bad blood was produced, and circulated in the form of popular images like that of Count Dracula. The shady and monstrous figure was depicted as a degenerate being who carried the stigmata of his criminality on his body. The marks of crime were believed to be written on the body in deformed ears, overdeveloped jaws and other visible characteristics. Criminal anthropologists aimed to construct laws explaining criminal behaviour, that could be used to predict and hence to control future events. Crime for them was only a symptom, an outward sign that pointed to the pathology of the individual. They looked beyond the offender to the criminality inherent in him, to his individual predispositions and their causes. To make this pathological essence visible, the criminal anthropologists conducted post-mortem examinations and anthropometric studies to investigate the physical characteristics that would differentiate criminals from noncriminals. They dissected the brains of executed criminals and took bodily measurements of prisoners, from which they derived average values. Their books are filled with tables of numbers, anatomical illustrations, and sketches or photographs of criminals' heads and faces. These drew on popular conceptions that character could be read from facial features, and gave them a new scientific authority as well as an exclusionary and racist tenor.

Reasoned justice, the rule of law and the Enlightenment

What was the Enlightenment? This burgeoning of critical thought during the eighteenth century is commonly associated with the work of a small number of philosophers and men of letters, whose activities are thought to have inspired the American War of Independence and the French Revolution. But the Enlightenment was much more than this. It was a new way of seeing which 'should be viewed not as a canon of classics but as a living language, a revolution in mood, a blaze of slogans, delivering the shock of the new' (Porter, 2000: 3). As Roy Porter explains, it embraced the introduction of new moral values, standards of taste, and views of human nature, as well as their embodiment, in urban renewal, hospitals, schools, prisons and factories.

Classical jurisprudence sought to develop rational and efficient means of delivering justice.[1] Thinkers like Montesquieu, Voltaire and Beccaria made a plea for ending the injustice of prejudiced, arbitrary, corrupt and immoderate forms of punishment: 'The classical postulate of law is that of a pure legal system, free of political influence. The classical principles aim to offer the individual citizen a safeguard against arbitrary state interference' (van Swaaningen, 1997: 30).

What were these classical principles? They may be summarised as follows:

- The law should restrict the individual as little as possible.
- The law should guarantee the rights of the accused at all stages of the criminal justice process.
- Punishment is only justified to the extent that the offender has infringed the rights of others or injured the public good.
- The severity of the criminal law must be drastically curtailed. Penalties should be proportionate to the crime committed, and no more than what is necessary to deter both the offender and others from committing crimes.
- The written law should clearly advertise what acts were forbidden, as well as the different sanctions imposed for committing each crime.
- Punishment must be inflicted swiftly and with certainty, in order to create a close association in people's minds between a crime and its inevitable penalty.
- The infliction of punishment upon an offender must be free of corruption and prejudice.

These principles were not fully translated into reality, but criminal codes aspired to follow them in a number of ways.

Among the arbitrary and corrupt aspects of criminal justice procedure, *lettres de cachet* were regarded by enlightened opinion as particularly invidious. A *lettre de cachet* was a sealed administrative order signed by the monarch containing a command that an individual be detained. It was to be executed swiftly, secretly and with no recourse to the courts. The order gave no explanation, there was no trial and no legal mechanism for appeal, and release was dependent upon the monarch's pleasure. A *lettre de cachet* could be granted to a private person for action on another individual. The comte de Mirabeau, a politician during the early phase of the revolution, had seventeen *lettres de cachet* issued against him during his dissolute youth. He later published a book criticising the practice. The Marquis de Sade, a libertine author, was imprisoned in the Bastille on a *lettre de cachet* requested by his mother-in-law. The diabolic universe of sadistic cruelty depicted in the books that he penned while in prison demonstrates the excesses to which the abuse of aristocratic privilege might lead. He drew an imaginary world in which the virtuous were the victims of kidnapping and seemingly unending tortures. A frequent complaint in the seventeenth and eighteenth centuries was that the use of *lettres de cachet* was corrupt, used by those in favour with the king to dispose of their personal enemies. However corrupt, the practice was an unpopular expression of monarchical power independent of the law. During the French Revolution, the Constituent Assembly abolished them in 1790. For the Enlightenment thinkers, the machinery of justice must answer instead to the rules of due process.

Charles, Baron de Montesquieu (1689–1755) published his *Spirit of the Laws* in 1748. He wrote that in a despotic government, where the ruling principle was fear, punishments were severe. In more moderate governments, legislators had a greater interest in preventing than in punishing crimes, aiming to inspire good morals. This led Montesquieu to argue that in countries where liberty was favoured, a dimunition of penalties would be seen. He strongly opposed the use of torture in the criminal process. Enlightenment jurisprudence also found an advocate in Italy. In *On Crimes and Punishments* (1764/1995), Cesare, Marchese de Beccaria (1738–94) addressed his criticisms of the violent barbarism and the irregularity of eighteenth-century criminal justice to 'the disciples of reason'. Proclaiming the equality of all before the law, Beccaria insisted that the laws ought to be the 'compacts of free men', and urged the establishment of general principles curbing the unbounded force of ill-directed power. These would identify and provide a basis for, the right to punish, beyond which all else was abuse. This right to punish was hence sited by Beccaria in the need to protect individual rights and freedoms from usurpation by others. On his view, the rule of law could protect people from the violence of the powerful. A fixed code of laws must be laid down which were not subject to petty tyrannies. Beccaria defined crimes as actions contrary to the public good. This made them injuries to the society rather than the abstract sovereign. He wrote that punishments should be equal to the injury done to society.

During the 1760s, Voltaire (1694–1778) campaigned against the use of the law as an instrument of religious persecution. In *Traité sur la tolerance à l'occasion de la mort de Jean Calas* (1763/2000), he sought to rehabilitate the reputation of a man who had been tortured and executed for the murder of his son. It was alleged that Jean Calas, a Protestant, had killed his son to prevent him from becoming a Catholic. The son had probably committed suicide, and Voltaire was deeply disturbed by the frenzied reaction to the crime by the people of Toulouse. The case of Calas was to Voltaire an example of bigotry. That of La Barre in 1766 indicated the extremes to which intolerance could go. La Barre, a youth aged nineteen, was tortured and executed for blasphemy. He had refused to doff his hat to a religious procession and mutilated a wooden crucifix. Voltaire wrote that the sentence imposed on him was execrable, absurd, and a disgrace to France. He famously wrote in 1768 that 'if God did not exist, it would be necessary to invent him', by which assertion he meant that the belief in the existence of God helped maintain social order. However, he also vigorously attacked the abuses of the Catholic church, and appealed for the tolerance of other faiths.

Whether it emphasised the individual or society, classical jurisprudence employed a voluntaristic view of human nature, that is, it emphasised individual choice. Classicists held that individuals were responsible for their actions, and hence for the consequences arising from them. Crime was viewed within the classical approach as a product of rational free will. In the work of Jeremy Bentham, this voluntarism took the form of a number of fairly crude psychological assumptions about what motivated people to act.

Bentham, utilitarian rule and punishment

One of the most important figures of the later British Enlightenment was the philosopher Jeremy Bentham (1748–1832). Bentham insisted that the discourse of natural rights associated with the writings of the Enlightenment *philosophes* and the French Revolution was anarchical, and foregrounded the importance of society. The utilitarian movement with which he is associated can be seen as a project aimed at securing effective forms of rule for the new industrial era. With increasing industrialisation and urbanisation, finding a means of disciplining the masses of workers emerged as an urgent concern. Bentham, infuriated by irregularity, sought the rational codification of the law, where, as he put it, 'all is darkness' (Bentham, 1776/1948: 29). He insisted that government must be made transparent and accountable, arguing that the light of publicity would protect people from corruption and misrule. Bentham was a committed individualist, holding that the government must interfere as little as possible in the liberties of its people. His primary maxim was 'the greatest happiness of the greatest number', which produced the principle of utility:

> By the principle of utility is meant that principle which approves or disapproves of every action whatsoever, according to the tendency which it appears to have to augment or diminish the happiness of the party whose interest is in question.
>
> (Bentham, 1789/1970: 2)

Bentham thought that the happiness of the community was augmented if the total of the pleasures of all its members increased to a greater extent than the sum of their pains. He believed that his 'felicity calculus' would give precision to this principle, a simple way of measuring pleasure–pain, which provided a means of estimating the goodness or badness of acts. This would supply a basis for morality and legislation. Simply put, in deciding upon a course of action, people followed their self-interest, avoiding pain and seeking to maximise their pleasure:

> Nature has placed mankind under the governance of two sovereign masters, pain and pleasure. It is for them alone to point out what we ought to do, as well as to determine what we shall do.
>
> (Bentham, 1789/1970: 1)

Government that maximised happiness would therefore guide people by rewarding some conduct and punishing other actions.

Bentham claimed that all law and punishment should be founded in the utilitarian calculus of pleasure and pain. For utilitarians, all punishment was in itself an evil, and could only be justified in any specific instance if it prevented some greater evil. Put differently, the pain of punishment must not only be compensated, but indeed outweighed, by its good consequences. For Bentham, any law should be judged by reference to its consequences for human happiness. He believed that if sanctions were well advertised, and crimes were always punished, people would be deterred from offending. His disciple Samuel Romilly agreed that the absolute certainty of punishment would act as a powerful deterrent, although he also noted that due to 'human imperfection' total efficacy was unlikely: 'no crime, therefore, could exist, if it were infallibly certain that not good, but evil, must follow, as an unavoidable consequence to the person who committed it' (Romilly, 1810: 20–1).

But what of those who did commit crimes? Bentham's 'Panopticon Plan' of 1791 applied his voluntaristic philosophy to this problem. He designed an inspection house, which could function as a prison or a factory. Although the Panopticon Plan itself was never built, it exercised an important influence on the design of penitentiary prisons during the nineteenth century. The Plan proposed a particular arrangement of architecture, which would put into practice Bentham's inspection principle.

A central observation tower was to be surrounded by a ring of cells, which were backlit so that the activities of their occupants could be seen from the tower. The tower must have a special arrangement of screens so that the prisoners could not tell whether they were being watched by the inspector or not. The inspection principle required both that inmates conceived themselves to be potentially visible at any moment, and that they actually were under the view of an inspector for as long as possible. According to Bentham, the greater the chance of actually being under inspection, the more intense the feeling that one might be so. He explained the principle at work as 'the *apparent omnipresence* of the inspector . . . combined with the extreme facility of his *real presence*' (Bentham, 1995: 45). The desired overall effect of the inspection principle was that inmates be assured that all their doings were known, and hence were convinced that 'in this house transgression never can be safe' (Bentham, 1995: 105).

Enlightenment, domination and control

The critical thought of the Enlightenment, its enshrining of the rule of law, and its modernised institutions, have an ambiguous legacy. As the words of the historian Eric Hobsbawm make evident, critiques of the Enlightenment have been varied:

> These days the Enlightenment can be dismissed as anything from superficial and intellectually naïve to a conspiracy of dead white men in periwigs to provide the intellectual foundation for Western imperialism.
> (Hobsbawm, 1997: 254)

Two of the principal forms that this critique has taken are:

1. The argument that reason and the rule of law have been instruments of exclusion.
2. The argument that the discourse of Enlightenment provided a cloak under cover of which new forms of power and control spread throughout society.

These critiques rigorously deny the claim that the Enlightenment was emancipatory, and draw attention to its 'dark side'.

Critics of Enlighenment jurisprudence have pointed out that classical theory masked the reality of widespread discrimination. The observation has often been made that purportedly universal human rights are systematically denied to vast numbers of people. Critics have pointed out the effective exclusion from the social contract of distinct individuals according to group identities along the lines of class, race, religion, sex and sexuality. The *Déclaration des Droits de L'Homme et du Citoyen* (1789) proclaimed the 'natural, inalienable and sacred rights of man'. It stated that all men were born equal and asserted that the very reason for any form of political association was the preservation of liberty, property, security and resistance to oppression. The *Déclaration* opposed tyranny with the promise of emancipation. However, despite elevating the natural rights of the human being, its actual use involved the exclusion of women, aliens and blacks from political rights. In practice, the abstract human nature referred to in the *Déclaration* took the concrete form of a white, property-owning French citizen. Furthermore, the political individual was taken to be both universal and male (Scott, 1996).

As we will see in Chapter 7, during the 1970s feminists undertook a damning indictment of the law and the criminal justice system as replete with damaging sexist ideologies. In 'Rape: An Act of Terror', Barbara Mehrhof and Pamela Kearon presented a strong criticism of the idea of the rule of law as a protective force:

> We are given to understand that in Western society the rule of law operates in contradistinction to the rule of men. This implies that society is built upon principles derived from Nature or God which are generally assented to by the governed. By its nature law deals in generalities; the governed are viewed as equal and indistinguishable.
>
> (Mehrhof and Kearon, 1973: 228)

They argued that women had traditionally existed outside of this rule of law due to their relegation to the private sphere, in which they existed as servants to the male, cancelling out any 'paper rights' they might have.

Slaves and the colonised also had little reason to trust in the rule of law. The aggressive project of Empire used the law to dominate invaded countries, although it claimed to give the colonised the gift of Western law, which it depicted as a linchpin of civilised culture. Peter Fitzpatrick (1990) depicted law as an important mode of legitimation of imperialism. He also argued that the experience of imperialism was central and enduring in the making of modern law. Instead of seeing imperialism as incongruous, as a failure of Enlightenment, he saw it as emblematic of the Enlightenment project. Law, Fitzpatrick wrote, was part of a new system of the scientific administration of society. He commented that the Enlightemnent project could only relate to those it excluded by envisaging them as of a qualitatively different nature, writing that it placed 'the enslaved and colonised beyond the liberal equation of universal freedom and equality by rendering them in racist terms as qualitatively different. . . . As a universalistic project imperialism, like Enlightenment, made all that stood outside it provisional and strange' (Fitzpatrick, 1990: 97–9). He also argued that the excluded and alien Other was central to the making of the disciplined, liberal individual of Western societies.

The violence of this process of rendering other can be seen in France's domination of Algeria. Algeria had been annexed to France in 1830, despite intense popular resistance. French colonials looked upon the Muslim populace as an inferior underclass who must be tightly controlled. Algerians were hence subjected to a much harsher penal code than existed in France. Although they were French subjects, Muslims could not become French citizens unless they renounced Islam. The National Liberation Front (FLN) was founded in 1954, declaring war on the French. The populist guerrilla war that ensued paralysed the country, and 400,000 French troops were sent in, employing a brutality that shocked many people. The use of concentration camps, torture and the mass execution of civilians suspected of aiding the rebels, were widely denounced. Franz Fanon became Head of the Psychiatry Department at an Algerian Hospital. He was horrified by the stories of torture recounted by his patients, and in 1956 resigned his post, setting out to work for the Algerian cause. Fanon's *The Wretched of the Earth* (1961) announced the end of the Rights of Man. He wrote that to turn the scale and call the world to question, absolute violence was necessary. *The Wretched of the Earth* closed with a call to action, and an indictment of Europe's proclaimed elevation of man:

> When I search for Man in the technique and the style of Europe, I see only a succession of negations of man, and an avalanche of murders. . . . Let us try to create the whole man, whom Europe has been incapable of bringing to triumphant birth.
>
> (Fanon, 1961/1990: 252)

Colonial rule was, according to Fanon, a persistent denial of the attributes of humanity, forcing the colonised to constantly question their very identity.

It has been argued that the Enlightenment quest for reasoned justice enabled the arrival of a new and insidious form of control. As we will see in Chapter 8, Michel Foucault famously stated that the Enlightenment, which brought the liberties, also brought the disciplines. He argued that the discourse of rights served to disguise the proliferation throughout society of disciplinary practices that brought a new kind of subjection to power. Foucault's critique of classical jurisprudence is exemplified by his approach to the work of Jeremy Bentham. Foucault famously drew upon the Panopticon to depict the new regime of disciplinary power. Punitive practices that appeared to be more humane and civilised were linked by Foucault to the proliferation of forms of surveillance and correction that exercised a subtle and insidious effect over people's lives. He also saw nineteenth-century criminologies that advanced a science of the causes of crime as part of the exercise of disciplinary power. Over the nineteenth century, a number of forensic psychiatrists and prison doctors published studies claiming that criminality was caused by hereditary degeneracy.[2] Enlightenment jurisprudence constructed those to be ruled as alien and other. Criminal anthropology and eugenics were genres of a scientific racism that developed processes of othering suited to the new social and political conditions.

Criminal anthropology, difference and Italian unification

The most famous of the criminal anthropologists was Cesare Lombroso (1853–1909), a professor of psychiatry. He stated that the born criminal was an atavistic throwback to a more primitive developmental stage of the species. This, according to Lombroso, meant that crime was a reversion to brutal and animalistic behaviour, quite out of place in civilised times. The term 'atavism' designated those cases in which a species reverted spontaneously to what were presumed to be long-lost characteristics. It hence denoted the reappearance of physical or mental features supposed to have been possessed at one time by remote ancestors (the term 'atavist' is derived from the Latin *atavus*, meaning ancestor). Lombroso described an anomalous feature in the brain of a famous Italian brigand called Villella, in a publication of 1871. This is how he retrospectively described the figure that came to life through his 'discovery' of this abnormality in Villella:

> an atavistic being who reproduces in his person the ferocious instincts of primitive humanity and the inferior animals. Thus were explained anatomically the enormous jaws, high cheek bones, prominent supercillary arches, solitary lines in the palms, extreme size of the orbits, handle-shaped ears found in criminals, savages and apes, insensibility to pain, extremely acute sight, tattooing, excessive idleness, love of orgies, and the irresponsible craving of evil for its own sake, the desire not only to extinguish life in the victim, but to mutilate the corpse, tear its flesh and drink its blood.
>
> (Lombroso, 1911: xiv–xv)

Lombroso asserted that in the countryside, as well as in urban slums, atavistic individuals were breeding criminal offspring. These people might have been eminently suited to the conditions of living in primitive societies, but they were hopelessly adrift in civilised times. In coming to this view, he drew upon a melange of evolutionary and anthropological theories. Lombroso argued that the born criminal could be spotted from the observation of physical anomalies, though some of these might only be apparent to the trained eye of the expert observer. His approach assumed that crime was something essential to the nature of the individual. It was premised on the idea of a fixed relationship between biologically-determined character and conduct.

The school that was set up around Lombroso became known as the *'scuola positiva'*. Italian positivists argued that the nineteenth-century criminal law was fundamentally flawed in its very outlook, and redundant because it failed to offer clear guidance for social action. Criminal anthropologists accused the theorists of classical jurisprudence like Beccaria and Bentham of having produced vague and unfounded ideas. Against the voluntarism of the Enlightenment thinkers, they insisted that criminal behaviour was determined by biological abnormalities, and was not freely chosen conduct. This approach was in clear opposition to

Enlightenment conceptions of criminal law, which were reliant on abstract universal ideas about freedom, social responsibility and duty. Criminal anthropologists argued that born criminals could not escape their inherited taint, being under the sway of natural laws, and not the criminal law. They claimed that progress could only be achieved by treating all activities as events occurring in the material world. For them, observation, experimentation and quantification, would reveal the truth. Science could disclose the objective reality of the social world, just as it did the natural world. This led criminal anthropologists to call for the preventive detention of those who could be identified as tainted with atavism. Their fatalism also supported the use of the death penalty:

> You have shown us lubricious and ferocious orangutans with human faces; certainly, being such they can act no other way; if they rape, steal, and kill, it is invariably on account of their nature and their past. The more reason for us to destroy them as soon as one is sure that they are and will remain orangutans. On this account I have no objection to the death penalty if society finds profit in it.
>
> (letter of Taine to Lombroso, cited in Pick, 1989: 109)

On occasion, Lombroso acted as an expert to the court. However, with their doctrines of free will and responsibility, lawyers were reluctant to accept the ideas of criminal anthropology. Lombroso's positivism expressed great confidence in the natural sciences as the key to social advancement. Yet this claim about objective, value-free methods for producing theories was actually dependent on specific ways of looking, that constructed particular images of the criminal. Patrizia Guarnieri's essay 'Alienists on Trial' (1991) described the involvement of Lombroso in the case of Vincenzo Verzeni in 1873, in which the professor depicted a young man on trial for murder as being of criminal type. We can see that this assessment of Verzeni required particular ways of looking, which were quite a disappointment to those who expected to see a monstrous figure:

> Who would have guessed to look at him that this was the 'hyena', the 'monster'? Professor Cesare Lombroso, however, sought for and naturally found that there was something severely abnormal, though barely evident, in the physique of Vincenzo Verzeni. First of all he was to demand that the defendant's head be entirely shaved, after which his knowledgeable fingers would have felt it all over; measured the distance from certain points to others . . . comparing the resulting data with averages and percentages for criminals, normal persons and the insane. Next he would have gone on to more complicated examinations. . . . It was thus that he noted, or rather hypothesised, that in Verzeni's brain the right cerebral lobe was smaller than the left, concluding that other stigmas would not be lacking, revealing a form of hereditary pathological degeneration. . . . This diagnosis, which implied that Verzeni could not be held responsible for his crimes, was unacceptable to public opinion. It was held up to

> ridicule by the Public Prosecutor and given scant consideration by the
> judges.
>
> (Guarnieri, 1991: 394–5)

Hepworth Dixon's (1850: 137) study of London prisons perceived a 'monotony and family likeness' in the faces of criminals, from which he posited that there must be a common cause of criminality. He saw the ugly faces of prisoners as the external impressions of the uglier minds beneath, revealed to him by their 'low, misshapen brows . . . animal and sensual jaws'. Others like Mayhew and Binny (1862) and Archer (1863) denied that any such features existed. Michael Davitt (1972: 15–16) wrote that the physiognomy of Charles Dickens' 'man-brute' Bill Sykes was not often met with in convicts. Arthur Griffiths (1894: 17) took a dim view of this purportedly 'new type of man, the criminal who is vowed to evil courses by his inalienable birthright', and insisted that the distinctive features of the inmate were produced by the prison environment. The French judge Louis Proal (1892: 62–3) rejected Lombroso's photographs of criminals as any real proof of the existence of a criminal type, stating that 'it is impossible to see in these physiognomies what M. Lombroso claims to see in them'.

The demarcation of the other as degenerate involved an extensive pictorial representation, in which prostitutes, gypsies, Jews, homosexuals, lunatics, artists as well as criminals figured. Behaviour, speech, appearance and the comportment of the body became visible signs, stigmata that marked degeneration on the body of the Other. This science of bodies set out to ground and locate difference. These processes of othering took different forms within specific national contexts. In *Faces of Degeneration* (1989), Danny Pick related the work of Lombroso to the project of Italian Unification. At the beginning of the nineteenth century, Italy was separated into a number of states and a movement to secure its unification, known as the *Risorgimento* (which can be translated as 'resurgence' or 'revival') began. Through a series of political and military events, Unification was achieved by 1871 but it did not bring stability to the country. Nationhood had been formally achieved, but the realities of division and fragmentation were evident. The territory was politically and economically diverse, and regionalism hampered the centralisation of government. It has been estimated that only eight out of a thousand Italians spoke the national language at the time of Unification. Voting restrictions stipulated that a voter must be over twenty-five, literate and tax-paying. This amounted to only 2 per cent of the population. Pick saw Lombroso's theories as important to an active process of constituting a national identity, writing that:

> The chimera of national unity was the implicit concern of much of
> Lombroso's research. Criminality was part of the problematic of 'making
> Italy'. . . . His work sought to settle the definition of the political subject, by

fixing more clearly and inexorably those who were beyond the pale of polity and society.

(Pick, 1989: 119–20)

In his earlier career, Lombroso charted the racial variation of the Italian population, attesting to the savagery of peasants. Later, he constructed a narrative that deployed images of crime, insanity, anarchism, peasantry, brigandage, prostitution and crowds as figures of disorder. Calabria, in the toe of the Italian peninsula, was one of the poorest southern provinces, and was associated with backwardness. There were frequent protests by Calabresian peasants over the burden of taxation, and anarchists were active in the region. Lombroso had served in the military campaign against brigandage in Calabria in 1862. Brigandage was a term that referred to banditry, but was also loosely used to designate insurrection, for instance violent local opposition to the laws of Italy. Villella, the purportedly atavistic man who first catapulted Lombroso to fame, was a Calabrian peasant who had been incarcerated for brigandage. In him, the figures of criminal, brigand, Calabresian and atavist were condensed by Lombroso, who wrote from Pavia, a northern literary centre blessed with an ancient university. His theory drew upon a racialised narrative to demarcate a primitivism within the national body that must be expunged:

> Northern Italians sometimes said that Calabria evoked Africa. . . . The South was cast as a form of other world, socially different, a space to be explored, penetrated, contained, colonised. . . . The white races represented the triumph of the human species, its hitherto most perfect advancement. But then inside the triumphant whiteness, there remained a certain blackness. . . . Each region had its cultural, economic, and political forces threatening the state. Enemies were without and within, dispersed everywhere. Lombroso's criminal anthropology sought to help contain the threat: to comprehend it scientifically and hence exclude it politically.
>
> (Pick, 1989: 114, 127–8)

According to the Italian positivists, due to a morbid deviation the brutish atavist was incapable of fulfilling their functions in the world. A unified Italy must eliminate the counterproductive. As van Swaaningen (1997) explained, the ideas of Lombroso were used to legitimate the cruelly low standard of living in southern Italy, by attributing it to the mental inferiority of its people.

The notion of *homo criminalis* was wholly discontinuous with normal people because criminal anthropology isolated criminality within certain identifiable individuals. Lombroso's work can hence be seen as the somatic transfiguration of profound cultural difference. It also sought to ground sexual difference in biological notions, producing notions of women's crime that were deeply sexist. Foremost in the pantheon of misogynistic criminology indicted by feminist scholars from the late 1960s was Lombroso and Ferreros' *The Female Offender* (1895). In this text, Lombroso and Ferrero held that woman was atavistically closer to her origin than man. They described women as 'big children' who had more numerous evil tendencies than men, as well as a deficient moral sense. Their point was that women criminals showed fewer signs of degeneration because all women were less evolved than men, so the criminals among them would stand out less. Instead of erecting firm boundaries around the transparent pathology of the criminal woman, what emerged was 'the barely legible potential dangerousness of the normal woman' (Horn, 1995: 109). This made all women risky.

The notions and images of criminal anthropology were circulated in popular culture in a number of different forms. Lombroso's work inspired Max Nordau's *Degeneration* (1893/1993), which argued that physical and moral degeneracy were linked. In America, Richard Dugdale's *The Jukes* (1877) and Arthur MacDonald's *Abnormal Man* (1893) popularised hereditarian notions of crime. However, it was Bram Stoker's *Dracula* (1897) that presented the most enduring image. His Transylvanian vampire was depicted as having massive eyebrows, sharp and protruding teeth, red lips, a cruel mouth, pointed ears, broad and squat fingers, and long sharp nails. It seemed to Jonathan Harker that the Count was neither animal nor human, crawling down the castle wall like a lizard, and driven by obsessive blood lust. Minna Harker explained Dracula's condition in the scientific terms of her day as follows: 'The Count is a criminal and of criminal type. Nordau and Lombroso would so classify him, and qua criminal he is of imperfectly formed mind' (Stoker, 1897/1993: 439). Readers were told that the criminal predestinate to crime was clever and resourceful, but 'has not full man-brain' (Stoker, 1897/1993: 439), this deficiency explaining the selfishness driving his deeds.

The eugenics movement, probabilities and the power of the norm

Another genre of scientific biocriminology that emerged during the late nineteenth century was eugenics. In England, the idea of the born criminal type was not received with enthusiasm. However, a eugenic approach developed, which related criminality to bad breeding.[3] The science of eugenics was based in the rise of probabilistic statistical thinking. This made the power of enumeration and of the norm a new control strategy (Hacking, 1990). Hacking argued that by the end of the nineteenth century, Western societies had become statistical, taking the normal as their model. He described what he called an 'avalanche of printed numbers' produced by new enumerating and classifying technologies, which operated as a new mode of social control.

It was Francis Galton (1822–1911), a cousin of Charles Darwin, who first coined the term 'eugenics', defining this new discipline in his *Inquiries*

Into Human Faculty (1883) as 'the science of improving stock'. Eugenics posed the problem of racial decline, which it saw as due to the differential rates of reproduction achieved by different sectors of the population. The abundant fertility of the unfit was contrasted with a lower birth rate of the better classes:

> the core of the eugenist argument was that there was a grievous 'fertility differential' between the well-off and healthy, who limited their births, and the diseased and destitute masses of the poor, who bred like rabbits.
>
> (Nye, 1985: 65)

Galton was an independently wealthy gentleman scholar of conservative leanings, who believed that mental qualities owed more to nature than to nurture. He was the first individual to hold that intelligence was a scientifically meaningful concept that could be measured. By the use of biographical encyclopaedias, Galton found that leaders of opinion and originators tended to come from families of reputation. Instead of saying something about the rigidity of the British class structure and the exclusivity of elite education, this indicated to him that heredity governed talent and character. His theories were based on statistical analyses, and particularly used the normal distribution, which is represented in graphical form as a bell curve. For Galton, the normal was the mediocre. He expressed his opposition to charity, philanthropy and reforms in health and education, as suspensions of natural selection. His interest was focused on the propagation of better stocks. However, later eugenicists concentrated on preventing the propagation of the 'unfit'.

The eugenics movement reached its peak in the period from 1900 to 1930. Targets of the eugenics movement included the alcoholic, the syphilitic, the immigrant, the feeble-minded and the prostitute. Galton wrote that, 'it is unhappily a fact that fairly distinct types of criminal breeding true to their kind have become established, and are one of the saddest disfigurements of modern civilisation' (Galton, 1883: 15). He described the 'ideal criminal', who he claimed was possessed of a hereditary deficiency of conscience and a lack of self-control. Clouston, a member of the Eugenics Education Society, wrote that 'if there is no absolutely marked criminal type that all will agree on, there can be no doubt that criminals fall far below a high or ideal anatomical and physiological standard of brain, and body and mind' (Clouston, 1894: 219).

Charles Goring's study *The English Convict* (1913) was a product of the eugenics movement. Goring opposed the anatomical method of the Lombrosians with the statistical method, advising that 'we must build upon measurements and upon measurements alone' (Goring, 1913: 29). Goring insisted that the criminal differed not in kind from the law-abiding person, but in their degree of possession of certain characteristics, writing that:

> There is no such thing as an anthropological criminal type. But despite this negation, and upon the evidence of our statistics, it appears to be an equally

indisputable fact that there is a physical, mental, and moral type of normal person who tends to be convicted to crime . . . the criminal of English prisons is markedly differentiated by defective physique . . . by defective mental capacity . . . and by an increased possession of wilful anti-social proclivities.

(Goring, 1913: 370)

The influence of eugenics is seen in the Mental Deficiency Act of 1913, which recognised the condition of moral imbecility and allowed for the detention of people diagnosed with it. The link between the collation of information and the new project of social regulation is evident in this kind of legislation. The violent consequences of eugenicism are seen in the majority decision written by Judge Oliver Wendell Holmes Jr in Buck v Bell (1927). In this case the Supreme Court upheld the State of Virginia's right to involuntarily sterilise a poor woman:

It is better for all the world, if instead of waiting to execute degenerate offspring for crime, or let them starve for their imbecility, society can prevent those who are manifestly unfit from breeding their kind.[4]

The power of reason and positivist epistemologies

The contrast between classical jurisprudence and the biocriminologies of the late nineteenth and early twentieth centuries has been neatly expressed by the following aphorism: 'The classical school exhorts men to study justice, the positivist school exhorts justice to study men' (cited in Radzinowicz and King, 1977/1979: 75). Yet despite major divergences of purpose and perspective, the classicists and the positivists share a fundamental orientation. Both classicists and positivists expressed their faith in rational methods of inquiry. The writings of Enlightenment thinkers are seen as emblematic of the emergence of distinctively modern ways of thinking because they emphasised the power of reason to produce a better ordered society. Lombrosian criminal anthropologists dropped the normative vision of classicism in favour of the paradigm of the natural sciences, adopting the term 'positivist'.

It would be a mistake to think that positivism was restricted to biological criminologies. A number of socially orientated positivisms have emerged. Positivism was a broad movement of thought that became especially popular during the second half of the nineteenth century. The term 'positivist' was introduced during the early nineteenth century by the Comte de Saint-Simon (1760–1825), and was further developed by Auguste Comte (1798–1857). In A General View of Positivism (1848/1865), Comte wrote that intellectuals should not interfere directly in the practice of government, because this was the province of the politician. Instead, the sociologist should endeavour to define and amend the principles upon which politics could be conducted. These principles, he claimed, would spring from the discovery of sociological laws. Theology and speculative philosophy were outmoded according to Comte. He insisted that laws derived from scientific observation would answer the questions of society, and thus solve pressing social problems. Comte explained that the political motto of positivism was 'order and progress'. His work can be seen as a reaction to the French Revolution of 1789, the principles of which he saw as anarchistic. Comte called for a 'sociocracy' presided over by scientists, a hierarchical and orderly society ruled by specialists knowledgeable about the scientifically advisable courses of action.

Positivists treat their work as if it were wholly unconnected with any value orientation other than a dispassionate interest in 'objective knowledge'. For them, the goal of knowledge is simply to describe phenomena, hence the scholar should restrict their attention to what can be observed and measured. The primary concern is to secure the accuracy of facts. Facts are depicted by positivists as irreducible units of truth that are waiting to be discovered by the social scientist. This implies that social reality exists independently from the positivist scholar's own way of perceiving things. It is believed that facts are open to verification, as well as being objectively measurable. Given the assumption that emotional involvement produces biased judgements which invalidate results, there is an aspiration to achieve a disinterested attitude towards crime. The scholar takes up a posture of sober judgement. Yet the sharp distinction drawn between fact and value has not always been easy to sustain. As we will see in the following chapter, this was a problem with which Émile Durkheim wrestled. Danny Pick (1989) contended that Italian positivism was an expression of insecurities, and social anxieties, at a time of profound political confusion and disorientation. Émile Durkheim also wrote in a time of social and political instability, when notions of Frenchness were hotly contested. With the advent of the Dreyfus affair, as we will see in the following chapter, he found himself writing in a storm.

Notes

1. On classical criminology, see Morrison (1994: Ch. 4) and Beirne (1993).
2. On late nineteenth-century criminology, see Harris (1990), Leps (1992), Garland (1985, 1994) and on theories of degeneracy, see Gilman (1985) and Pick (1989).
3. On the eugenic approach, see Garland (1985: 142–52) and McLaren (1990).
4. Buck *v* Bell 274 US 200 (1927). On American eugenic criminology, see Hahn Rafter (1997).

Chapter 2

Durkheim, the Dreyfus affair and the passion of punishment

What we need to know is what the religion of today should be.

(Durkheim, 1898/1969: 25)

The influential French intellectual Émile Durkheim (1858–1917) initiated a tradition of relating the phenomena of crime, law and punishment to the creation and regeneration of consensus in society.[1] His theories suggested that the criminal law does not simply exist to prohibit and punish crimes. More importantly, law and its enforcement functions to shore up group values. Writing that 'moral ideas are the soul of the law', Durkheim (1909/1987:150) argued that law expressed all that was fundamental in the morality of a society. He took this view because for him law expressed important shared beliefs. This chapter discusses an important series of reorientations and shifts in Durkheim's work on law and punishment, from around the time of his involvement in the Dreyfus affair. In one of the most infamous miscarriages of justice of French history, a Jewish military officer was convicted of treason. The affair unleashed a political storm, and is still remembered today as symbolic of conservatism and anti-Semitism. The case revealed and exacerbated bitter divisions within French politics and society. Following a number of other scandals, it seemed to some to suggest the immanent collapse of the young republic.

Writing in France at the end of the nineteenth century, Durkheim's work was animated by an interest in the emergence of new sources of social cohesion at a time of major instability. Unsurprisingly his principal concern was to theorise what kind of bonds hold a society together. Profound social and political upheavals had taken place. Following defeat in the Franco-Prussian War, the revolt of the Paris Commune in 1871 brought about a major civil war, and its bloody repression left bitter class conflict simmering. Some commentators claimed that society was breaking down, while others emphasised the need for comprehensive social reconstruction. Durkheim tended towards the latter view, and partook of the reformism of the Third Republic. Supporters of the republic strongly criticised the reactionary stranglehold of the Catholic Church on French society. Republicans also opposed what they saw as the danger of revolutionary socialism, especially where it was prepared to secure utopian aims through the use of violent means. For the adherents of the Third Republic, universal rights and economic justice were important aims, but they must be pursued by democratic means. Durkheim insisted that increasing social complexity need not inevitably produce class conflict.

Over the last century, a number of divergent readings of Durkheim's work have been developed. Some critics have emphasised Durkheim's 'functionalism', meaning that he interpreted phenomena in terms of how they related to the preservation of social stability. Yet it would be a mistake to write Durkheim off as a conservative figure (as did Coser, 1960 and Bottomore, 1981). On the contrary, he was a forward-looking thinker with a deep interest in social change. Durkheim saw himself as a moderniser, and linked the rise of sociology to the decline of traditionalism, explaining that:

> Wherever the religious, political, and legal traditions have retained their rigidity and their authority, they restrain all inclination to change and by that very fact prevent the awakening of reflection; when one is raised to believe that things should remain in the state they are in, one has no reason to wonder what they should be or, consequently, what they are.
>
> (Durkheim, 1990, cited in Bellah, 1973: 21–2)

A number of scholars have recuperated a 'radical Durkheim', teasing out the most challenging aspects of his work and arguing for its continuing relevance (Pearce, 1989; Gane, 1992; Meštrović, 1992). This does not, however, mean that Durkheim's ideas are wholly unproblematic. Indeed, his work can be criticised in a number of important ways. Durkheim advocated a specific approach to intellectual enquiry. How did he envisage the processes through which knowledge should be produced? As Roger Cotterrell (1999) explains, Durkheim's work shifted from a positivist orientation towards a stance of the critically engaged intellectual. In his early methodological treatise *Rules of Sociological Method* (1894), Durkheim saw social phenomena as objective data to be discovered, and the route to acquiring knowledge of them as one of detached observation. He gave the following injunction:

> Treat social facts as things. . . . To treat phenomena as things is to treat them as data, and these constitute the point of departure of science.
>
> (Durkheim, 1894, cited in Thompson, 1982: 101)

This meant that social science must be based on objective realities that existed independently of the consciousness of the observer. The positivist scholar must eliminate the impurities of the subjective, which Durkheim construed as the ideas of the imagination.

The insistence that science concern itself with the observable paid scant attention to the notion that there are different ways of looking at things, which may be equally valid. Durkheim's scientific outlook was dismissive of other perspectives as mere mysticism or irrationalism. He particularly railed against the dogmatic character of religion. The doctrine of papal infallibility was announced by the Vatican Council in 1870. This stated that the Pope's statements on religion and morality were infallible. This authoritarian measure was anathematic to Durkheim's views of the eminence of science:

> That which science refuses to grant to religion is not its right to exist, but its right to dogmatize upon the nature of things and the special competence which it claims for itself for knowing man and the world.
>
> (Durkheim, 1917, cited in Bellah, 1973)

Durkheim took the view that socialism was disruptive and reckless, preferring his own model of rational social analysis to what he saw as socialism's irresponsible sloganeering:

> Socialism is not a science, a sociology in miniature – it is a cry of grief, sometimes of anger, uttered by men who feel most keenly our collective malaise.
>
> (Durkheim, 1928, cited in Thompson, 1982: 159)

Later, Durkheim tended to the view that the sociologist could not in fact remain neutral in delineating moral necessities. The explanatory process, it seemed, inevitably involved validating some ideals and depicting others as aberrant. However, Durkheim did not generally engage in purely abstract reasoning, still insisting that sociology must give speculation an empirical grounding in 'social facts'. Despite the sense of instability or even crisis found in some of his work, Durkheim maintained an optimistic belief that a rational sociology could provide an accurate knowledge base to equip those in power to direct society. But could a scientific approach rise above partisanship so easily? Certain difficulties in his position of politically engaged positivism are seen in Durkheim's involvement with the Dreyfus affair. A discussion of Durkheim's principal ideas about punishment and society will prepare us for an examination of his activities as a supporter of Dreyfus.

Durkheim, Third Republic France and social solidarity

As Roger Magraw (1987) explained, Third Republic France saw a resurgent new Right, which vigorously rejected the liberal and democratic character of the republic. Catholic hostility to the 'godless' republic constituted one major strand of right-wing politics. In the 1880s, this anger melded with the bitter discontent of other groups. Military defeat in the Franco-Prussian War had aroused xenophobia and an obsession with revenge. Those on the political Right claimed that France's defeat could be attributed to its 'excess of democracy'. One of the most vocal and violent pressure groups was the *Ligue des Patriotes*, numbering 30,000 members, worshipping the army and trading populist rhetoric. It drew on a volatile mix of authoritarianism and wounded nationalism. Right-wing groups of this kind were composed of Catholics, workers disillusioned by unemployment, and members of the petty bourgeoisie whose hatred of big business had taken a xenophobic form. As Magraw explained, anti-Semitism was particularly functional to the consolidation of a mass movement against the 'liberal' Republic:

> Only an ideology utilizing common hatreds could unify any such alliance of disparate groups and traditions. Anti-semitism alone offered the possibility of achieving this, because the multifaceted stereotypes of 'the Jew' were sufficiently elastic to provide a target for all the disaffected and, thus, to paper over the new Right's internal contradictions.
>
> (Magraw, 1987: 263)

Maurice Barrès, a right-wing novelist and politician, insisted that instinctive hatreds and not rationalist tolerance would regenerate France. Biological stereotypes were circulated, and in criminal anthropology, science made prejudice respectable (Magraw, 1987: 169). Most French Jews were assimilationist with weak religious ties, fervently loyal to France, and professed their faith in French justice. However, the new Right promulgated a politics of paranoia. The militant Catholic daily *La Croix*, with a circulation of 180,000, was the biggest selling Catholic publication. In vehement rhetoric, it blamed the decline of Catholic influence on the Jews. The aggressive scapegoating of Jews made visible the extent of dissensus between the groups in French society.

Durkheim anticipated the advent of a new form of shared values, departing from the static and locally rooted beliefs and customs of the past. He thought that this new kind of consensus was necessitated by an increasing social differentiation, with the shift away from simple forms of social organisation. Durkheim was hence concerned to discover the sources of social solidarity; the fundamental conditions of collective life and social cohesion. He believed that society and its patterned forms of mutual interaction required a shared framework of meanings and moralities. He had a clear idea of what a society was. For him, society was made up of the distinctive thoughts and actions of individuals, taken collectively. Collective representations were the constitutive stuff of society itself: 'by continually uniting, acting, and reacting with one another, individual consciousnesses (*consciences particulières*) combine to create a new consciousness (*conscience collective*) which is society' (Tole, 1993: 5).

Durkheim defined the concept of the *conscience collective* in *The Division of Labour in Society* as 'the totality of beliefs and sentiments common to the average citizens of the same society [which] forms a determinate system which has its own life' (Durkheim, 1893, cited in Thompson, 1982: 60). Simply put, for Durkheim, social cohesion arises from shared moral beliefs and ideals.

What changing forms of social solidarity emerged as societies underwent change? It was generally believed in Durkheim's day that the increasing diversity of beliefs and values threatened to destroy society, because they could only produce social conflict. Durkheim, however, argued that the chief threat was not the increasing differentiation of societies, which was both necessary and inevitable, but the threat posed to society by an amoral unbridled individualism. He believed that individualism must become altruistic. Durkheim saw religion as a vital unifying force, defining it as an authoritative body of collective beliefs, rather than a set of symbols and rites accompanied by priests and temples. He contended that modernisation entailed religion's transformation. For him, the new religion suited to industrial societies was the 'cult of the individual' or 'religion of humanity'. He believed that the *conscience collective* was slowly becoming more secular, rational and individualistic. This required active adherence to the values of individual dignity, civic ethics, reason and tolerance. In this vision, the individual was the prime repository for society's most cherished ideals, symbolising the moral beliefs upon which social order rested.

The cult of the individual suggested a new kind of patriotism, for instance Durkheim wrote that:

> As long as there are states, so there will be national pride, and nothing can
> be more warranted. But societies can have their pride, not in being the
> greatest or the wealthiest, but in being the most just, the best organised,
> and in possessing the best moral constitution.
>
>   (Durkheim, 1950, cited in Thompson, 1982: 154–5)

In the incendiary climate of Third Republic France, he appealed for a new kind of *amour patrie*, resting in the fundamentally sacred character of the individual. The need for this new altruistic and civic nationalism was vividly demonstrated to Durkheim by the turbulent Dreyfus affair. One side cast their opponents as anti-republican and hostile to the rights of man. The other depicted their enemies as traitors to the 'true France'. The Catholic journal *La Croix* depicted the Dreyfus affair as a 'race war', orchestrating outrage against those intellectuals who spoke up for Dreyfus. As Roger Magraw explained, this case 'revealed the susceptibility of the public to the prejudiced distortions of the mass press' (Magraw, 1987: 275). This signalled to Durkheim the urgent need for new values that might transcend factional dispute. What might these new values consist in?

From mechanical to organic solidarity

Social commentators and political scientists had noted the development of a more complex division of labour (the increasing specialisation of work tasks), as well as the decline of universal adherence to a single religion, long before Durkheim began writing. Some of them saw these processes as a necessary part of the progress from primitive to modern society. Others warned that individualism and secularisation were great evils which could only tear societies apart.

Durkheim stated that pre-industrial societies had been composed of small groups, in which solidarity was attained through the sharing of an all-encompassing set of norms and values. The cohesion of these groups was based on the similarity and likenesses of the individuals within them, so Durkheim termed their characteristic kind of solidarity, 'mechanical solidarity':

> The social molecules that cohere in this way can act only in so far as they have no action of their own, as with the molecules of inorganic bodies.
> (Durkheim, 1893, cited in Giddens, 1972: 134)

Within societies of mechanical solidarity, reactions to nonconformity had been harsh. Durkheim argued that modern societies would eventually develop forms of what he termed 'organic solidarity'. What might the sources of organic solidarity be? At first, Durkheim suggested that in modern industrial societies, social integration would be derived from the functional interdependency arising from an extensive division of labour. On this view, with the specialisation of activities, people would be dependent on others who performed different tasks from them. Durkheim thought at first that the increasingly complex division of labour would destroy mechanical solidarity through processes of individuation. An unstable transition period would ensue, in which he thought French society currently found itself. This was a time of excessive individualism, rife with social problems.

Yet eventually organic solidarity would arise: 'Organic solidarity means that differentiated, specialized individuals are integrated with each other and regulated by each other, because they must engage in cooperative productive interactive processes and because they must exchange the products of their labor' (Lehmann, 1995a). In organic solidarity, Durkheim suggested, people are attached to one another through their differences. The tension between individuation and the need for new sources of social cohesion makes Durkheim's writings on crime, law and punishment fascinating reading. Durkheim saw individuation as a central feature of modern societies, freeing the individual from the rigid constraints of earlier times. In the *Rules of Sociological Method* (1894/1964), Durkheim explained that with the more flexible and tolerant values of modern societies, the resulting diversity of behaviour would include some forms that would be sanctioned as criminal. Interestingly, Durkheim also claimed that crime had an important function in introducing new ideas into society and hence preventing its stagnation. The argument was that a certain rate of crime was healthy for a society, indicating a flexibility that meant that it could accommodate individual originality. This led Durkheim to depict some criminals as innovators who had ideas ahead of their time. He argued that some of those whose beliefs were repressed by criminal sanctioning were actually visionaries. Durkheim offered Socrates as an example, the Athenian philosopher who was executed for the independence of his thought. Yet how could one tell which acts and beliefs were visionary and progressive? Durkheim's work offered little advice.

Durkheim's notion of organic solidarity involved a number of problematic arguments about race and gender. In his account of the transformation from primitive to modern societies, Durkheim argued that the category of race became obliterated as a result of the emergence of differentiated individuals (Lehmann, 1995a, 1995b; Fenton, 1980, 1984). This theory of the disappearance of race was an intervention against nineteenth-century scientific racism (Lehmann, 1995b). However, Durkheim retained a notion of biological caste in the form of the hereditary transmission of general levels of potential occupational ability. He contended that general abilities of an indeterminate nature were inherited by individuals, although the specific manner in which these were developed during life differed. He even countenanced the possibility of a 'general' hereditary predisposition to crime (Durkheim, 1893/1933: 316). He believed in the continuing existence of natural inequalities of talent, which would be reflected in unequal standards of living. Furthermore, while acknowledging the possibility of vertical individual mobility, Durkheim also saw as damaging the excessive aspirations of the working class. He argued that organic solidarity would occur spontaneously as long as the division of labour was a natural one (following natural abilities). He hence opposed the inheritance of wealth, contending that it forced individuals into unfair contracts and debased them.

Durkheim's understanding of sex was based on a theory of sexual dimorphism (that men and women compose two wholly distinct biological groups), as was regrettably the case with a large number of the thinkers of his day. He posited that this rigid difference was the natural basis of the functional specialisation whereby men occupied the public sphere and women the domestic. Durkheim did not simply describe the unequal position of women in his society, but rather saw the persistence of dichotomous natures and separate spheres of activity as beneficial (Lehmann, 1995a, 1995b). Overall, Durkheim saw neither race nor gender differences as divisive forces within the system of social relations. He did not present any analysis of racism or sexism, even when his views on the division of labour had undergone substantial revision. While the division of labour was initially construed by Durkheim as both necessary and beneficial, in his later work it became another divisive force. Rather than giving rise to cooperation, he came to see the division of labour as a source of conflict. He then looked to the emergence of a modern set of shared values and ideals rooted in the 'cult of the individual' for the sources of social order. What might this mean for his views on law and punishment?

The passion of punishment

Durkheim's work offered a number of forceful and original arguments about the enraged passions seen in social reaction to certain crimes. For Durkheim, moral conduct was essentially to be understood in terms of its underlying emotions, and in attending to these, he emphasised their irrational aspect. As Tole (1993: 7) explained, morality was not construed by Durkheim as a set of abstract propositions to which the individual deferred out of fear of punishment or rational argument. It was something which moved people quite profoundly, inspiring in them feelings of positive attachment as well as enraged fury. Penal sanctions were taken by Durkheim to furnish a visible index of the moral order of society, a tangible example of the *conscience collective* at work, both expressing and regenerating society's values (Garland, 1990). Durkheim hence emphasised the moral content of instrumental action. Punishment was primarily construed by him as symbolic of group values and not as merely instrumental (that is, for a specific purpose, for instance deterrence or rehabilitation).

In *The Division of Labour in Society*, Durkheim contended that 'passion is the soul of punishment'. Punishment was depicted in this text as an intense collective phenomenon driven by irrational forces. Its practices were seen as rituals expressing the furious moral outrage of the group against those who had violated its sacred moral order. Durkheim believed that crimes were unsettling because they were attacks on the *conscience collective*:

> We must not say that an action shocks the conscience collective because it is criminal, but rather that it is criminal because it shocks the conscience collective. We do not condemn it because it is a crime, but it is a crime because we condemn it.
>
> (Durkheim, 1893, cited in Giddens, 1972: 123–4)

In response, 'all healthy consciences' came together to reaffirm shared beliefs, actively constructing a 'public wrath':

> [W]e have only to notice what happens, particularly in a small town, when some moral scandal has just occurred. Men stop each other on the street, they visit each other, they seek to come together to talk of the event and to

wax indignant in common. From all the similar impressions which are exchanged, and the anger that is expressed, there emerges a unique emotion, more or less determinate according to the circumstances, which emanates from no specific person, but from everyone. This is the public wrath.

(Durkheim, 1893, cited in Giddens, 1972: 127)

A number of other approaches have also theorised powerful punitive emotions. From around the 1930s, psychoanalytic theories emphasised the importance of hostile punitiveness to the constitution of self-identity, rather than to the maintenance of group values. Durkheim had seen punishment as the expression of dutiful moral outrage. For him, punishment was part of a 'virtuous circle' or 'functional spiral which helps create and recreate social cohesion' (Garland, 1990: 33, 34). Psychoanalysts like Edward Glover (1931), a founder of the British Society of Criminology, took a different view. He argued that punishment was sadistic and a displacement activity. Glover contended that punishment was an act by which individuals indulged in a concealed manner emotions that they could not own, indeed which might not even be known to them. Punishment was not construed by Glover as a matter of collective communication, but rather as a means of experiencing something while hiding what one was really feeling. Durkheim (1893/1933) believed that punishment 'serves to heal the wounds made upon collective sentiments'. However, instead of producing social solidarity, psychoanalytic approaches suggested that legal punishment was inherently divisive. On the basis of these views, psychoanalysts opposed the use of corporal punishment in prisons and schools, and participated in the campaign for the repeal of the death penalty.

Roger Cotterrell (1999) explained that Durkheim had equated mechanical solidarity with repressive law and harsh punishment. This condemned the wrongdoer and marked him as an outsider to be cast aside. Organic solidarity was associated by Durkheim with restitutive law, which acted to restore the status quo. Cotterell pointed out that Durkheim related punishment to a one-time harsh and monolithic *conscience collective* which he claimed was passing away:

[W]hile Durkheim is very ready to recognise moral diversity and difference of attitudes, sentiments and beliefs in considering the conditions of organic solidarity and restitutive law, he will not do so in considering repressive law and punishment . . . the idea of crime and punishment is tied to the concept of a uniform, all-embracing collective consciousness. Restitutive law in *The Division of Labour* represents social complexity and differentiation – it points towards the rich moral diversity of modern societies, and the need to balance and negotiate different outlooks, sentiments and values. But repressive law and the whole of Durkheim's thought around crime and punishment revolve around the idea of social homogeneity.

(Cotterrell, 1999: 66)

Durkheim never elaborated a theory of punishment under the criminal law in societies of organic solidarity. However, some indication of what form this theory might have taken can be found in his work.

Durkheim condemned physical punishment as a degrading affront to the dignity and sacredness of humanity. He declared his opposition to oppressive appeals to punishment, seeing these as distractions from the urgent need for fundamental reforms (Miller, 1996: 269). In *Moral Education*, Durkheim discussed punishment in schools, but his understanding of it is still of interest. Punishment was construed as a form of communication, signalling disapproval, and was rehabilitative.

> Punishment's role in enforcing morality is a central focus of Durkheim's early work, but, significantly, in *The Division of Labour* this is presented as of declining relative importance among law's functions. As Durkheim's view of morality moves from its early stress on coercion and duty to its later equal concern with attachment to groups and individual autonomy, law is presented as facilitative and liberating rather than repressive . . . this emphasis even colours Durkheim's later writings on punishment. Thus, his perspective on law is, in general, non-authoritarian and relatively non-censorious.
>
> (Cotterrell, 1999: 238)

In 'Two Laws of Penal Evolution', Durkheim (1901/1992) accounted for the replacement of brutal bodily punishment by imprisonment as a sign of the transformation of the *conscience collective* towards the hallowing of human dignity. It was just this kind of view that Michel Foucault was to critique in *Discipline and Punish* (1975/1991), as we will see in Chapter 8. For Durkheim, the slow evolution of the *conscience collective* brought changing sensibilities towards physical forms of punishment. However, angered reactions to crime persisted, and Durkheim did not theorise public wrath in societies of organic solidarity. Even if some shift from repressive to restitutive law could be discerned, angry emotion remained evident in responses to crime and the practice of punishment.

George Herbert Mead (1918) posited a link between punishment and social solidarity, but thought that the hostile response to a criminal had the effect of 'uniting members of the community in the emotional solidarity of aggression' (Mead, 1918: 591). Durkheim had contended that 'crime brings together honest men and concentrates them' (Durkheim, 1893, cited in Giddens, 1972: 127). Mead did not see this intense emotion as 'dutiful moral outrage', and pointed out various of its deleterious effects. Following this line of argument, the spirals of rage emanating outwards from a heinous crime were traumatising rather than healing. What Mead didn't discuss was the constitution of rival aggressive communities, having a different yet equally passionate response to a particular crime. Societies could be deeply divided on the question of the punishment of a particular offender.

Shifts in Durkheim's work

The principal shifts in Durkheim's work around the time of the Dreyfus affair can be summarised as follows:

- Objective positivism → Politically engaged positivism
- The division of labour is a source of solidarity → The division of labour is a divisive force
- The law is constraining → Law is an object of attachment
- Hostile punishment is beneficial → Hostile punishment is counterproductive. Punishment must not degrade the individual.

Some clues as to why Durkheim's thought on law and punishment might have developed in this way can be found in his article on the Dreyfus affair, which is discussed later in this chapter. Reading this article also brings certain problems with the new orientation and theories to light. Before talking about this article, the main contours of the Dreyfus affair are described.

The Dreyfus affair

The details of the basic events of the Dreyfus affair tell of a spy-story that turned into a frame-up. In September 1894, French counter-espionage services retrieved a letter from a wastebasket in the German embassy in Paris. This was a memo addressed to the German military attaché, referring to the sale of military information. Captain Alfred Dreyfus, an Alsatian Jew whose family had moved to Paris when the Germans had annexed Alsace in 1871, was accused of authoring the memo. A secret military court martial found him guilty of high treason, without producing in court the incriminating memo. Dreyfus was sentenced to deportation and life imprisonment on Devil's Island, a penal colony off the coast of South America. Following the customs of military ritual, his punishment began with a humiliating ceremony in which he was stripped of his rank in front of the assembled troops on the court of the École Militaire. During this official rite of degradation, his braid and buttons were struck from his uniform and his sword was broken.

The political right, whose strength was increasing at this time, cited Dreyfus' alleged espionage as evidence of the failures of the republic. The right-wing and nationalist press intensified their denigration of Jews, portraying the incident as evidence of Jewish treachery. Editorials expressed violent hatred and pseudo-scientific stereotypical representations of Jews were promulgated. A tide of anti-Semitism swelled, with attacks being made on Jewish businesses and synagogues desecrated. In hostile marches and demonstrations, large numbers of people shouted 'Death to the Jews'. Dreyfus' defence counsel was shot in the back on his way to court.

Dreyfus seemed destined to die in disgrace. However, in 1896 French counter-espionage found a telegram from the German embassy addressed to another officer. Lieutenant-Colonel Picquart investigated and became convinced that this man had authored the memo which had been attributed to Dreyfus. The chiefs of the army did not want to hear this information, being more interested in preserving the image of the army than in rectifying their error. Fauré, President of the French Republic, also disregarded this new information. When Picquart persisted in trying to reopen the case, the army transferred him to Tunisia.

Incensed by this injustice, the novelist Émile Zola published a letter to Fauré in the newspaper *L'Aurore*, which has become famous. It commenced with the headline, 'J'ACCUSE . . . !', and denounced the army's cover-up. Zola gave a point-by-point description of the entire affair, and concluded with a number of serious accusations against the chiefs of the army. Within two hours the edition had sold 200,000 copies. Zola wrote in 'J'ACCUSE . . . !':

> It is a crime . . . to whip reactionary and intolerant passions into a frenzy while sheltering behind the odious bastion of anti-Semitism. France, the great and liberal cradle of the rights of man, will die of anti-Semitism, if it is not cured of it. It is a crime to play on patriotism to further the aims of hatred.
>
> (Zola, 1898/1996: 51)

Zola's article sparked off anti-Semitic rioting in sixty towns, which continued sporadically for eighteen months (Wilson, 1973). Parliament debated a bill excluding Jews from public service. Although this was defeated, it did win 158 votes. Zola was convicted of slander for defaming the army, and received the maximum sentence of a year's imprisonment and a huge fine. He fled to Britain, where he remained until he was exonerated. Public passion became more aroused than ever as the political right and the leadership of the Catholic Church declared the case to be a conspiracy of Jews and Freemasons determined to discredit the army and hence destroy France.

In June 1899, an appeals court annulled the conviction of Dreyfus. He was tried before the Council of War at Rennes, found guilty again, but with 'extenuating circumstances' and sent back to Devil's Island. German officials repeatedly approached the French minister of war, to make statements clearing Dreyfus, but these were refused. The affair assumed international significance, with outraged comment in the American, British, Italian and other newspapers. Later in the year Dreyfus was pardoned and returned to Paris. It was not until 1906 that a civil appeal court overturned the Rennes decision and exonerated him, twelve years after the case had begun. On the day after 'J'ACCUSE', *L'Aurore* carried the 'Manifesto of the Intellectuals', in which artists, men of letters, scientists, lawyers and professors protested against the violation of judicial procedure. The Right mobilised its intellectuals to denounce this as an unpatriotic interference in politics.

The responsibility of the intellectual and the cult of the individual

Durkheim, who was himself Jewish, joined the campaign on the side of the Captain. He was active in the Dreyfusard *Ligue pour la Défense des Droits de l'Homme*, acting as secretary to its Bordeaux branch. Durkheim's father, grandfather and great-grandfather, had been rabbis. The young Durkheim attended rabbinical school, but after arriving to study in Paris, he put his Judaism aside (Pickering, 1994). Both Dreyfus and Durkheim rejected the traditionalism of their ancestors in favour of a faith in a secular and all-inclusive community. To Durkheim, the Dreyfus affair represented a moral crusade in defence of a new vision of collective values.

Durkheim's 'Individualism and the Intellectuals' (1898) was published as a response to an article by the literary scholar Ferdinand Brunetière, who belonged to the right-wing *Ligue de la Patrie Française*. Brunetière had defended the army as crucial to security, prosperity and democracy, which he felt were threatened by individualism. He asserted that this malign individualism was primarily to be found in certain intellectuals, and objected to their use of science to support their opinions. He depicted the mental malaise of Dreyfusard intellectuals as a manifestation of an individualism which he described as 'the great sickness of the present time. . . . Each of us has confidence only in himself, sets himself up as the sovereign judge of everything' (cited in Lukes, 1969: 17). For Brunetière, the self-infatuation of the intellectuals rapidly approached anarchy. Catholic polemicists accused the Dreyfusard intellectuals of 'corrupting souls' and being 'enemies of the social order' (Lukes, 1969). Maurice Barrès called them 'the anarchists of the lecture platform' (Lukes, 1973: 335).

The use of the term 'anarchist' was particularly derogatory at this time. Anarchist attacks saw the use of dynamite to convey a political message. At the official level, anarchists were defined through their acts, which were considered to be aimed at 'the destruction through violent means of all social organisation' (Jensen, 1981: 327). They engaged in a planned campaign of violence, had detailed rationalisations of their acts, and both mocked and attacked the criminal justice system. There were violent re-prisals when fellow anarchists were executed, this sanction being seen as legalised murder. Anarchists profoundly questioned the meaning of the criminal act. They used crimes as a means of attack and also of propa-ganda, denying the validity of differentiating between theft and 'honest labour' in a system where as producer or consumer daily transactions positioned people as stolen from or stealing. Pini, for example, declared that his thefts of over 300,000F were a legitimate expropriation by the oppressed. After Émile Henry had bombed the Café Terminus, he told the court that since the bourgeoisie lived off the exploitation of the unfortunate, there had been no innocent victims of his attack. Furthermore, anarchists rejected the rule of law as part of the bourgeois system of oppression. In 1894, the year of Dreyfus' conviction, Sadi Carnot, President of the Republic, was assassinated by anarchists. Brunetière's comment that the Dreyfusard intellectuals were akin to Nietzsche's 'superman', who was not made for laws but rather to rise above them, can be read in this context.

Brunetière's article provoked Durkheim to publish a spirited defence of individualism. He insisted on the responsibility of intellectuals to apply the principles of rational judgement in defence of the rights of man in the face of angered popular opinion:

> Accustomed by the practice of scientific method to reserve judgement when they are not fully aware of the facts, it is natural that they give in less readily to the enthusiasms of the crowd and to the prestige of authority.
>
> (Durkheim, 1898/1969: 25)

Durkheim firmly rejected the claim that individualism was nothing but an inexhaustible source of discord and division. He derived individual rights from the overriding principle of respect for persons, stating that the human person is sacred. He also argued that simply having political liberties was not enough; one must know what to do with them. His answer to this question was that they should be used to further economic and social justice.

Durkheim firmly distanced his individualism from that of Herbert Spencer. Spencer (1820–1903) was a prominent British social philosopher, who as a laissez-faire liberal opposed state regulation and interference. In *Social Statics* (1851/1868), his first principle was that every man may claim the fullest liberty, provided that he does not infringe the equal freedom of others. This led him to oppose measures like the Poor Laws and state-supported education. Durkheim denounced what he saw as the moral poverty of Spencer's philosophy, commenting that social life would be impossible without the existence of interests superior to those of individuals. He located his own contribution in the tradition of the ideas that the Declaration of the Rights of Man sought to give form to, seeing this as deriving moral ideas from the notion of the human condition:

> The human person, whose definition serves as the touchstone according to which good must be distinguished from evil, is considered as sacred. . . . It is conceived as being invested with that mysterious property which creates an empty space around holy objects, which keeps them away from profane contacts and which draws them away from ordinary life. And it is exactly this feature which induces the respect of which it is the object. Whoever makes

> an attempt on a man's life, on a man's liberty, on a man's honour inspires
> us with a feeling of horror, in every way analogous to that which the believer
> experiences when he sees his idol profaned.
>
> (Durkheim, 1898/1969: 21–2)

Durkheim asserted that because the individual was perceived to be sacred, the rights of man must be vigorously defended. He wrote that humanity was higher than the individual, hence the 'religion of man' type of individualism did not legitimate the indulgence of egoistic interests. The cult of man, Durkheim argued, glorified the individual in general, being motivated by pity for suffering and misery and the desire to alleviate these, as well as a thirst for justice. The religion of humanity, he contended, rose far above individual concerns and thus served as a rallying-point for them. On this view, social cohesion resulted from the members of a society looking towards a common end and being united in a singular set of beliefs.

Durkheim claimed that his kind of individualism was particularly functional to the situation of Third Republic France. He wrote that as societies become more populated, their traditions and practices had to adapt to constantly changing circumstances, and so they admitted more individual variation. Instead of seeing the division of labour as a cohesive force, this was now understood by Durkheim to be a further force of differentiation. He asserted that society was moving towards conditions in which the only thing that the members of a single social group had in common was their humanity, 'there remains nothing that men may love and honour in common, apart from man himself' (Durkheim, 1898/1969: 26). Durkheim argued that in departing from the old conformity, the only idea that persisted above the vacillations of changing opinion was the idea of the human person.

As Durkheim pointed out, France was particularly bound up with the fate of the ideas of individualism. Following this view, to denounce individualism was to denounce Frenchness itself. Durkheim saw it as imperative that his society did not renounce all that constituted the worth and dignity of living for the sake of a public institution. He argued that it was time to move beyond eighteenth-century liberalism, which had emphasised the negative aspect of freeing the individual from constraining political fetters, and had focused on emancipation in the forms of freedom of thought, freedom to write, and the freedom to vote. The times, he insisted, called for moving beyond a negative conception of liberty, and required the use of liberties to 'alleviate the functioning of the social machine' (Durkheim, 1898/1969: 29). This, he claimed, was a matter of using and not stifling the rational faculties. For Durkheim, those who believed in the value, or the necessity, of the eighteenth-century moral revolution must urgently bind together to hold positions already won. His article closed by reaffirming his faith in reason to save the nation from this grave crisis.

Universal human rights and organic solidarity

Durkheim's appeal to a universal human condition which could transcend individual interest can be criticised in a number of ways. His extrapolation from individualism to abstract human rights did not theorise conflict, for instance there was no analysis of racism in his article on the Dreyfus case. While writing in the midst of a social and political storm, Durkheim continued to elevate general principles and to appeal to a singular set of beliefs as the source of social solidarity. He was, however, taking and indeed fuelling, one side of the conflict, as pointed out by Richard Sennett (1977/1986). According to Sennett, the Dreyfus affair fuelled the consolidation of community via confrontation, or, *destructive gemeinschaft.* As he explained, the evidence in the case came to define two communities in conflict, these being old France (the army, the church and the high bourgeoisie) and new France (the heirs of the Revolution). Certainly Durkheim's intervention in the affair depicted the view of the opposing side as archaic. He argued:

> that a morality requiring the preservation of traditional beliefs about the state and nation at all costs (such as the official punishment of a man whose innocence was deliberately obscured for reasons of state) was outmoded and in modern circumstances iniquitous.
>
> (Cotterrell, 1999: 27)

Sennett stated that the supporters of the old France linked its lapses to the work of alien and traitorous elements. For them, Dreyfus became the perfect figure of the fantasy of the Jewish traitor. The affair, Sennett argued, saw the powerful formation of collective personality and destructive communal fantasizing. This pointed to a society in which there were low levels of interaction between members, dominated by ideas of the individual, in which a fantasy of the collective person spiralled out of control. According to Sennett, in an absence of shared actions, the fantasy of the collective person was produced through the vigorous rejection of difference, as a kind of communal purification. Intense hostility to outsiders precariously maintained the language of belonging. Durkheim's quest for a new civic ethics based in a notion of impersonal human rights, however noble in intention, hardly seems to engage with this schismatic situation.

The response of the British establishment to the Dreyfus affair demonstrates how notions of liberties, rights and justice could be the support for attitudes and identifications that were essentially conservative. Robert Tombs (1998) presented an analysis of the kind of Dreyfusard position taken up by the British establishment, and of the reasons for people whose values included patriotism, militarism and respect for traditional authority, to express sympathy for the 'martyr'. He described the vocabulary of horror and indignation used by English diplomats, publications like *The Times,* and even Queen Victoria. Tombs depicted the Dreyfusard position of the Victorian establishment as a means of confirming their own prejudices, an important reassurance as to the rightness of their beliefs and practices at a time of economic and political challenges. He noted that criticism of the French judicial system was especially prominent in discussion of the case, at a time when the impartial rule of law was seen as both an index of civilisation and a central support of a national myth. Comment in *The Times* stated that the affair had brought 'a hideous recrudescence of medieval passions', which demonstrated alarmingly that the forces of progress had not yet triumphed. Tombs' comments indicate that simply expressing sympathy with the plight of Dreyfus did not automatically thereby convey the status of progressive thinker. People entered into the fray on both sides for a variety of reasons and these might be none too commendable:

> What the British reaction to the Dreyfus affair chiefly illustrates is the strength of an insular conservative-liberal tradition, 'Whiggish' in its belief in 'freedom broadening down from precedent to precedent', and patriotic in its assumption of the fortunate benefits of being British, or at least Anglo-Saxon.
>
> (Tombs, 1998: 510)

This confidence was of course inflated, as shown by the case of Oscar Slater, who was called the 'Scottish Dreyfus'. Slater was convicted of the murder of an elderly woman in 1909. The trial occasioned extensive speculation and bitter indignation and hostility, especially among the people of Glasgow and Edinburgh. The eye-witness identification evidence was highly debatable, and the trace evidence had been the source of major disagreement among the experts. When Slater was convicted of the murder and sentenced to death, a petition claiming that there had been insufficient evidence was signed by over 20,000 people and sent to the Scottish Secretary. A reprieve commuted his sentence to one of penal servitude for life. He was finally acquitted on appeal in 1928 on the grounds of misdirection and amidst allegations of misidentification, anti-Semitic prejudice and police corruption.[2]

Taking up a stance of politically engaged positivism, Durkheim reaffirmed his faith in rational methods of enquiry at both the outset and the closing of his essay. Yet it is evident that in his article on the Dreyfus case, Durkheim was not simply descriptive, but overtly prescriptive. Furthermore, a statement that one's method is rational does not thereby elevate one's arguments above those of others. In this respect, Durkheim's writing on the affair has similarities with the novelist Marcel Proust's depiction of it. Proust dramatised the very subjective investments that people had in the case, casting them as limited, while suggesting that only the narrator stood outside of, or above, superficial gossip (Wilkinson, 1992). Durkheim's claim that 'scientific' intellectuals 'give in less readily to the enthusiasms of the crowd' merits repeating here (Durkheim, 1898/

1969: 25). However, Wilkinson also commented that Proust's images of the affair suggested that the truth was multiple, and pointed to the difficulties of judging an individual in an era dominated by newspapers and mass politics:

> In his juxtaposition of different points of view – all limited, blind, and somewhat misguided – Proust suggests that we learn to judge the Dreyfus Affair or any issue in an age of mass politics as a concatenation of representations.
>
> (Wilkinson, 1992: 993)

There was a vast profusion of images that multiplied the meanings of the Dreyfus affair. Proust's and Durkheim's writings on it demand that we read beyond the limited perspectives offered by individual media representations. Durkheim's claim to rise above the fray cannot simply be taken at face value. Neither can we assume that the discourse of universal human rights can unproblematically adjudicate between rival knowledge claims.

Echoes of Durkheim: social solidarity and group values

Over the last century, interest in the elaboration of new sources of social cohesion has been a recurrent concern within theories of crime and punishment. The focus on achieving social order has also been subject to a range of criticisms. During the interwar period, the Chicago School of Sociology took up the quest for a modern urban order which might respect individual difference and further democracy. They hoped to facilitate communication, opposing the racism and xenophobia directed at immigrants. For instance, Harvey Zorbaugh noted the lack of common view and common purpose among city dwellers and depicted the whole city as a place of transition, writing that 'everywhere the old order is passing, but the new order has not arrived. Everything is loose and free, but everything is problematic' (Zorbaugh, 1929: viii). He stated that the American political system was based in the belief that people residing in the same locality had common interests and could therefore be relied upon to act collectively for their common welfare, but the city demonstrated that this premise was in fact invalid. Zorbaugh pointed out the increasing mobility of the urban population in terms of their movements, contacts and the stimulations that they experienced. He thought that this very mobility caused the dissolution of public opinion and the decaying of social solidarity, writing that:

> A large part of the city's population lives much as do people in a great hotel, meeting but not knowing one another. The result is a dissolution of social solidarity and public opinion. Face-to-face and intimate relationships

in local areas are replaced by casual, transitory, disinterested contacts. There arises an extreme individuation of personal behavior that makes of the local area within the city something vastly different from the town or village community. There is within it no common body of experience and tradition, no unanimity of interest, sentiment, and attitude which can serve as a basis of collective action. Local groups do not act. They cannot act. Local life breaks down.

(Zorbaugh, 1929: 251)

He thought that the anonymity, the mobility, the lack of group life and common social definitions of the slum area and the cultural conflicts of the ghetto dweller, explained why these localities were a world of unconventional behaviour, delinquency and crime.

During the 1930s, Robert Merton popularised the work of Durkheim in America. As we will see in Chapter 4, he particularly developed the functionalist aspect of Durkheim's work. From the 1960s, scholars advanced studies of social reaction to crime. These emphasised the importance of differential status, and later, power and class rule. These approaches will be addressed in Chapters 5 and 6. From the late 1980s, John Braithwaite developed the theory of restitutive punishment that Durkheim's arguments seemed to suggest. As we will see in Chapter 9, how well his theory of 'reintegrative shaming' theorises notions of community and conflict is an open question. Can customarily hostile reactions to crime be reconciled with the desire to reform the offender? George Herbert Mead stated that the two were quite incompatible, writing that 'it is quite impossible psychologically to hate the sin and love the sinner' (Mead, 1918: 592). Additionally, the problem of appealing to group collective beliefs while also respecting differences is more evident than ever in the pluralistic and highly differentiated societies of the later twentieth century. At best Durkheim's vision of organic solidarity remains elusive. Others would see it as fundamentally flawed.

Notes

1. See Lukes and Scull (1983), Garland (1990), Vogt (1993) and Cotterrell (1999) for scholarship on Durkheim's theories of crime and punishment.
2. Slater *v* HM Advocate 1928 JC 94; See Roughead (1910).

Chapter 3

The Progressive Movement and crime in Chicago

> It is probably the breaking down of local attachments and the weakening of the restraints and inhibitions of the primary group, under the influence of the urban environment, which are largely responsible for the increase of vice and crime in great cities.
>
> (Robert Park, 1915)

By the first decades of the twentieth century, Chicago was a crowded and sprawling metropolis. Loud and lively, it seemed to symbolise the best and the worst of the American urban scene. The spectacular expansion of the city, sited at the hub of the nation's railroad network, made it a fascinating location for studying the processes of urban development. By 1900, half of the population of Chicago had been born outside of the USA. Waves of the Irish and German poor, southern Italian peasants, and Eastern European Jews arrived, as well as blacks from the south who were seeking a greater degree of racial tolerance. The resulting profusion of languages and cultural traditions made the city a vast and dynamic social laboratory. For others, Chicago's exponential and unchecked growth was the cause of grave apprehension, as seen in one contemporary's impression of the city:

> First in violence, deepest in dirt, loud, lawless, unlovely, ill-smelling, irreverent, new; an overgrown gawk of a village, the 'tough' among cities, a spectacle for the nation.
>
> (Steffens, 1904: 6)

Chicago became thus both the hope of democracy and the crucible of all ills.

The Progressive Movement was a broad liberal reform programme of the early twentieth century, and Chicago was a key location for their activities. Progressives were critical of the human suffering that accompanied

America's unrestrained industrial and urban expansion. They deployed a humanitarian rhetoric, and addressed inequities in the marketplaces and workplaces of industrialising America. However, the Progressive effort to regulate social life can be seen as a new form of governing, involving the extension of state power into areas of life once policed by family, church and community. This reformulation of state power was facilitated by the modernisation of the urban courts, and the development of criminological discourses that advocated interventionism of various kinds. Progressives believed that it was necessary to bring the courts and the police in line with the latest scientific knowledge, which they thought could be used to shape a more orderly society. Specific changes included the centralisation of the municipal court system, the establishment of juvenile courts, the individual treatment of offenders, an increased discretion for judges over the disposition of offenders, and an increased use of professional expertise (of psychiatric, psychological and sociological varieties). Additionally, there was the introduction of new measures like indeterminate sentencing and probation, as well as an expanded use of parole. The reach of the state deep into the lives of urban populations was rationalised by what the jurist Roscoe Pound (1912, 1913) called the 'socialization of law' away from the individualist tenets of the eighteenth century. The law, Pound wrote, must take account of social facts, and only secure individual interests to the extent that they were social interests. The new practices of governing the lives of the urban poor and the alien were especially intense in Chicago, in the wake of decades of mass industrialisation and labour militancy, and a massive influx of foreigners.

The Chicago school of sociology

The first university sociology department was inaugurated in Chicago in 1892, and dominated the discipline in America between 1915 and 1940. Leading figures included Robert Ezra Park (1864–1944) and Ernest W. Burgess (1886–1966).[1] It established a distinctive style of elucidating how the distributive forces of the urban environment gave rise to typical social groupings. For the Chicagoans, mass immigration seemed to illustrate powerfully the shift from an older social and economic organisation based on local affiliations and family ties, to forms based on one's occupation. Furthermore, they noted that control rooted in mores was superseded by control based on law. While Chicago scholars noted the disorganising force of urban expansion, these accelerated transformations were not simply construed negatively, as can be seen from Park's (1928) observation as follows:

[W]hen the traditional organization of society breaks down, as a result of contact and collision with a new invading culture, the effect is, so to speak, to emancipate the individual man. Energies that were formerly controlled by custom and tradition are released. The individual is free for new adventures, but he is more or less without direction and control.

(Park, 1928: 887)

The vitality of the urban milieu suggested an exciting range of new possibilities. Park and his associates were fascinated by the ebb and flow of city life. The Chicagoans drew upon the work of Georg Simmel, who in 'The Metropolis and Mental Life' (1903/1950) had depicted the city as both potentially liberating and a place in which the individual might feel lost. The problem was one of how social cohesion might be maintained in a society with a complex division of labour and a profusion of culturally discrete groups.

Mike Savage and Alan Warde (1993) depicted urban sociology as an enquiry into the condition of modernity itself, writing that the study of urban life was integrally linked to an investigation of the relationship between modernity and capitalism:

> The work of the Chicago School is best seen as an extended empirical inquiry into the nature of social bonding in the modern, fragmented, city. The city interested them for empirical, rather than conceptual reasons. It was where the division of labour was most elaborate and developed, and hence where the fragmentary nature of modern life could most profitably be studied.
>
> (Savage and Warde, 1993: 13)

This is a useful way of thinking about the work of the Chicago school, and will be supplemented in this chapter by a discussion of Chicagoan sociology as an epitome of the Progressive vision of social order and social reform.

Urban ecology, natural areas and the struggle for space

The Chicago school are well known for their mapping of what they saw as the natural areas that comprised the city. They used an evolutionary model to elucidate the processes by which a new social order emerged, and to make change intelligible in order that it might be controlled (Park, 1936: 178). The paradigm of ecology was used loosely to grasp the underlying laws of urban life. This amounted to their making the analogy to the patterns of life and processes of change found in plant life. There was, according to the Chicago school, a 'struggle for existence' over territory. They described how the processes of invasion and succession gave rise to typical constellations of people and institutions in the struggle for space.

Their ecological model was given schematic representation in the zonal hypothesis advanced by Ernest Burgess (1925). In this classic essay, Burgess produced a diagram that was to become well known, showing the patterns of land use, and hence of social segregation, in 1920s Chicago. This was an ideal-type representation of the city's growth. He argued that the typical processes of Chicago's expansion could be observed in its series of five concentric zones with distinctively different land use and residential types. These circles demonstrated the city's tendency to expand radially outwards from the Central Business District, in rings of increasing affluence, from the middle to the periphery. He identified what he termed the 'zone of transition' with the residence of the poorest citizens. This undesirable locale received successive waves of migrants, who could only afford to live in what was a run-down area of cheap lodging houses and derelict factories. The zone of transition sustained periodically an influx of different groups of immigrants, and hence had a high degree of racial and ethnic heterogeneity. Additionally, relocation from the poorest areas of the city was the most rapid. Burgess stated that newcomers moved outwards into more attractive residential areas as they became assimilated into the American way of life. Burgess contended that this continuous process of influx and exodus made the zone of transition a place of transience, turbulence and disorder. This was, he claimed, evidenced by the concentration of 'pathological behaviour' in the region. Burgess emphasised that this area of flux was peopled by those who were unaccustomed to one another. The zone of transition was hence the area with the least opportunity to stabilise.

There was more to the Chicagoan interest in the locale than the purely demographic. The idea of distinctive areas was posited on an understanding of the neighbourhood as a moral region. Chicagoans envisaged the city as rooted in the habits and customs of the people who lived there, and described a mutual interaction of the moral and the physical organisation. Their conception of the neighbourhood demonstrates that while they did employ some evolutionary concepts, the perspective went beyond the paradigm of the natural sciences. Chicago scholars believed that over time, the areas of the city took on the character and qualities of their inhabitants, converting mere geographical features into neighbourhoods with sentiments, traditions and histories of their own. Park (1915), for instance, explained that the population segregated according to interests and tastes to form 'moral regions', in which divergent moral codes prevailed. He posited that physical and sentimental distances were mutually reinforcing. As Savage and Warde (1993) point out, we should not dismiss Chicagoan work as mere biological determinism on account of their use at times of concepts from human ecology. They write that Park's work was simply more complex than that, and see the most valuable legacy of the Chicago School as its conception of sociology as the study of forms of interaction and of the sociologist as a promoter of cooperative relationships. A review of the Chiacgoans' methods, key concepts, and a look at a number of their case studies will put this assessment to the test.

Intellectual vagabondage and the ethnographic eye

The Chicagoans undertook statistical research to corroborate and/or qualify Burgess's concentric zone model, which related the distribution of particular populations to the incidence of various social pathologies. Mapping and quantifying were, however, only one way of trying to make sense of the patchwork of differences. The Chicagoans also employed other methods to elucidate 'how life moves' in the areas of the city (Burgess and Bogue, 1964: 9). In addition to their mapping activities, the Chicago school scholars are known for their detailed ethnographies, in which a deep immersion in the life-world of their subjects is seen. For the Chicagoans, a faithful account of the facets of urban life required first-hand experience of their daily existence. Direct observation of 'the ordinary affairs of people' (Baker, 1973: 244) was preferred over complex debate about the grand sociological theories of the day. They undertook extensive participant-observer fieldwork research which sought to gain access to people and to understand their attitudes and motivations. David Matza (1969) termed the approach 'appreciative', on the basis of the close attention paid to the subjective perceptions of the people studied. Park (1927, cited in Baker, 1973: 258) described the process of immersing oneself in the conditions and experiences of those studied as one of 'intellectual vagabondage'. This phrase envisaged the researcher as both a traveller and an outsider, moving between diverse social groups and physical locations as well as estranged from the elite and not welcomed by them.

The Chicagoan approach involved a valorising of the significance of personal experience as a source of accurate knowledge. The researcher's own life experiences were seen as an important part of the ability to see the subject's point of view. Park had grown up in the district of a Minnesota city that was settled by Scandinavian peasant immigrants, with whom he happily associated. He made the comment that 'most that I have learned of the aspects of life in which my interests lie has come out of my personal experience' (Park, 1927, cited in Baker, 1973: 253). He also made much of his experiences in getting to know the life of the American Negro in the South between 1905 and 1912. However, his statement that, 'I became, for all intents and purposes, for the time, a Negro myself', is questionable, as we will see in the course of Chapter 5 when the Becker–Gouldner debate about partisanship in sociology is discussed (Park, 1927, cited in Baker, 1973: 258).

Chicago scholars were committed to the belief that researchers must go out into the city and immerse themselves in the milieu of those studied. They saw talking to their subjects as an important source of information, and hence employed the life history as an integral part of their research. This kind of work can be seen in Clifford Shaw's *The Jack-Roller* (1930), a book which showed how one person became delinquent through recounting in-depth interviews held with him. Shaw apparently identified with his subjects, and the subject of *The Jack-Roller* was one of his best friends (Snodgrass, 1976). Through personal documents of this kind, the Chicagoans strove to get at the subjective aspects of life in the city. They drew on the work of Georg Simmel, who had seen life as based in forms of association and constantly in flux. Simmel's concept of 'sociation' was also an important intellectual resource, designating the informal, ephemeral processes which linked modern urban dwellers, and the moral codes and conventions underlying action. This idea underwrote Park's interest in the life history of the criminal as obtained through informal interviews in which his 'naïve utterances . . . reveal what he assumes is generally understood and taken for granted' (Park, 1930: 451). The everyday conversation of the person studied revealed his outlook on life and the kind of rules and mores in accordance with which he conducted himself.

Nels Anderson's ethnographic study *The Hobo* (1923) demonstrates the Chicagoan interest in the problem of the unattached, and whether they might be forming ties. The hobo of the early twentieth century, Anderson explained, was a migratory worker, who sometimes found himself living in the city among other homeless men. A Committee on Homeless Men had been established in Chicago in 1922 with Ernest Burgess as its director. Its purpose was to obtain the facts necessary for the social agencies to deal with the problems created by the continuous ebb and flow of thousands of homeless men into and out of Chicago. The committee wanted to base their knowledge on the intensive study of cases rather than on statistical investigation, and hence asked Nels Anderson to collect the life-histories of hobos. Anderson had been a migratory worker himself, and was hence able to bring personal experience and empathy to his participant observation research with this group. He explained that Park had instructed him to 'write down only what you see, hear, and know like a newspaper reporter' (cited in Anderson, 1923/1967: xii). Anderson depicted the hobo as 'one of the heroic figures of the frontier' (Anderson, 1923/1967: xxi). He insisted that the hobo's chronic wandering was not a sign of individual pathology, relating him to the tradition of mobility characteristic of American society. For Anderson, the hobo brought a unique type of cosmopolitanism, bringing colour and life. However, he also commented that the congregation of homeless men in Chicago's Hobohemia during the winter was a menace.

Anderson wrote that hobos lived from hand to mouth, perilously close to dependency at all times. He related their situation to the play of economic forces in modern industrial society, seeing unemployment and seasonal labour as maladjustments which disorganised the routine of life and destroyed regular work habits. Anderson also mentioned racial or national discrimination as a factor of adverse selection for employment. He explained that hobos were drawn to the city because it operated as a labour exchange. Anderson wrote that every large city had a district into which the homeless gravitated, finding there those who could understand them. He commented that Chicago had the largest of these 'Hobohemias', a marginal space which had developed as an isolated cultural area. This association of crime and deviance with areas of the city inhabited by the poor and the immigrant meant that while the concept of social disorganisation theorised the negative consequences of geographical mobility and emancipation from tradition, the ethnographic eye of the Chicagoan researcher remained squarely focused on the slum and the ghetto.

The slum and the concept of social disorganisation

The concept of social disorganisation was defined as follows:

> [A] decrease of the influence of existing social rules of behaviour upon individual members of the group . . . during periods of social stability this continuous incipient disorganization is continuously neutralized by such activities of the group as reinforce with the help of social sanctions the power of existing rules. The stability of group institutions is thus simply a dynamic equilibrium of processes of disorganization and reorganization. This equilibrium is disturbed when processes of disorganization can no longer be checked by any attempts to reinforce the existing rules.
>
> (Thomas and Znaniecki, 1918)

The notion of social disorganisation theorised the manner in which in certain circumstances social rules lost their effectiveness. Chicagoans noted that rapid urban expansion was accompanied by excessive increases in disease, crime, disorder, vice, insanity and suicide. Burgess (1925) argued that these phenomena could be taken as 'rough indexes of social disorganization'. On this view, crimes were produced by the inability of the zone of transition to provide integrative mechanisms linking inhabitants to the wider social order. Park (1925) took up this view, claiming that delinquency was caused by the failure of community organisations to function. He (1915) believed that the forces which broke up neighbourhood cohesion included the proportion of floating population, the racial and class composition, and the proportion of nomads and hobos. The zone of transition was the area of the greatest human demoralisation, hence the Chicagoans undertook studies of the gangs, prostitutes, drug addicts and ethnic groups who congregated there. The prevalent association of disorganisation with immigrant areas, and specifically with the slum, can be seen in Harvey Zorbaugh's *The Gold Coast and the Slum* (1929). This book depicted Chicago as a city of striking contrasts, charting the distinctive regions of the Near North Side, in which both the wealthy area of 'high society' and the impoverished and squalid slum were sited.

Zorbaugh wrote that as the Loop, the area of commerce, expanded, the old residents moved out to be replaced by 'a mobile, shifting, anonymous population bringing with it transitional forms of social life' (Zorbaugh, 1929: 3). Within the looming shadow of the skyscraper, which Zorbaugh saw as the visible symbol of the Loop's domination, a zone of instability and change thus emerged. The encroachments of the Loop pushed out the well-to-do, fashionable residential district, and the slum crept in:

> The common denominator of the slum is its submerged aspect and its detachment from the city as a whole. The slum is a bleak area of segregation of the sediment of society; an area of extreme poverty, tenements, ramshackle buildings, of evictions and evaded rents; an area of working mothers and children, of high rates of birth, infant mortality, illegitimacy, and death; an area of pawnshops and second-hand stores, of gangs . . .
> (Zorbaugh, 1929: 9)

Zorbaugh wrote that the slum harboured diverse people, including the criminal, the radical, the bohemian, the migratory worker, the immigrant, the unsuccessful and the unadjusted. It was a distinctive area of desolating poverty and disorganisation, with both dilapidated buildings and human derelicts, a 'jungle of human wreckage' (Zorbaugh, 1929: 129). For Zorbaugh, the mean streets and decaying buildings were characteristic of the slum, but so were distinctive types of submerged humanity. The slum was cosmopolitan, as diverse cultures, languages and creeds coexisted side by side there, but Zorbaugh felt that this proximity led cultures to lose their identity and their traditional social definitions and controls to break down. The slum was hence seen by Zorbaugh as a confused social world, in which no community existed and families were broken, disorganised or ineffective. Immigrant families failed to aid their children to adjust. Zorbaugh did not discuss social change and unconventional or taboo behaviour in high society, even though he wrote in the Roaring Twenties, the decade of the flapper. The significance of this omission will become clearer later in this chapter when the 'thrill-killers', Leopold and Loeb, are discussed.

The gang and the concept of differential association

In his theory of differential association, first advanced in 1924, Edwin Sutherland (1883–1950) argued that criminal behaviour was learned in interaction with other people who violated society's norms.[2] Sutherland held that persons became criminals through intimate association with others who held social definitions favourable to the violation of laws. Crime was hence construed as learned behaviour. The most powerful illustration of differential association was seen in the learning of delinquent values in peer groups. In *The Gang*, Frederick Thrasher (1927) argued that ideas of conduct were passed on down generations of boys on the streets.

John Landesco's *Organized Crime in Chicago* (1929) described how the gangster grew up in the established gang tradition of his neighbourhood, 'in a world where pilfering, vandalism, sex delinquency and brutality are an inseperable part of his play life' (Landesco, 1929/1968: 207). Landesco summarised the picture of the gangster that emerged from his study as 'a natural product of his environment – that is, of the slums of our large American cities' (Landesco, 1929/1968: 221). As the legitimately success-ful moved away from the slums, they left behind the unsuccessful labour-ing foreigner, a quite unattractive model to the youths in their process of Americanisation. The gangster was also left behind, and offered the only other model of success. He presented extracts from the life-histories of gangsters and their acquaintances to explain how the criminal career of the gangster commenced in early childhood. In the course of recount-ing the story of a gangster born to poor Italian immigrants, Landesco explained that 'without the gang, life would have been grim and barren for these children' (Landesco, 1929/1968: 209). Truancy and theft are described by Landesco's subjects as thrilling adventures in an existence of misery and toil in which money for pleasures is sparse.

Sutherland's (1924) theory of differential association foregrounded not only the significance of the learning of techniques, but also that of motives and rationalisations. Landesco presented a picture of the learning of rationalisations for gangster activity, describing how in com-paring getting into a racket with getting a job, practical and not moral considerations predominated:

> He takes as his pattern the men in the neighbourhood who have achieved success. His father, although virtuous in his grime and squalor and thrift, does not present as alluring an example to him as do some of the neighbourhood gangsters. The men who frequent the neighbourhood gambling houses are good-natured, well-dressed, adorned and sophisticated, and above all, they are American, in the eyes of the gang boy. . . . Where the choice of a young man is between a low paid job as an unskilled laborer and good wages for driving a beer truck, a stigma is soon attached to legitimate employment. The conspicuous expenditures and lavish display of the nouveau riche of the underworld confuse and pervert the traditional standards and values of even the law abiding persons in the community.
>
> (Landesco, 1929/1968: 210)

According to Landesco, the typical rationalisation for the criminal career is that 'everyone is doing it' (Landesco, 1929/1968: 212). He wrote that when one youthful criminal was asked about the causes of his own criminality he was baffled at first and then replied 'who around here hasn't a record?' (Landesco, 1929/1968: 212). Another rationalisation noted by Landesco was the comparison between opportunities for success in a criminal versus a legitimate career:

> He contrasts the 'easy money' and the 'good times' of the gambler, beer runner, 'stick-up artist' and 'con man' with the low wages and long hours of the 'poor working sap.' He speaks in flowing admiration of the power,

the courage, the skill, the display and the generosity of the outstanding
gang leaders.

(Landesco, 1929/1968: 212)

The concept of differential association powerfully calls up the image
of the gang of immigrant boys exposed to the alluring patterns of the
criminal tradition. However, Sutherland (1940) was later to employ this
idea of definitions favourable to criminal activity in offering his concept
of 'white-collar crime', which theorised how corporate culture itself could
be criminogenic. Sutherland stated that criminologists principally relied
upon official crime statistics to support theories that crime was caused
by poverty, and that these statistics neglected the criminal behaviour of
business and professional men. He explained that the concept 'white-
collar crime' denoted the crimes of respectable, socially accepted individuals, and stated that this behaviour was found in every occupation.
White-collar crime, Sutherland advised, was found in the leading American corporations and not just among disreputable quacks and swindlers.
Interestingly, white-collar criminals were oriented to legitimate and respectable careers. White-collar crime in business included the bribery of
public officials, the embezzlement of funds, and the use of short weights
and measures. These practices, Sutherland reported, were what the gangster Al Capone had called 'the legitimate rackets'. He argued that white-
collar crime consisted essentially in violations of trust. The financial cost
of white-collar crime, Sutherland contended, far outstripped that of the
actions generally thought of as constituting the 'crime problem'. He
thought that the damage done to social relations was even graver than
the economic losses incurred. He explained that white-collar crimes
created distrust, lowering social morale and producing widespread social
disorganisation.

The marginal man and the concept of culture conflict

The individual produced by the unsettling existential condition of divided
loyalties was illustrated by Park's (1928) essay on the marginal man, in
which he described the inner turmoil and intense self-consciousness of the
immigrant. He saw the stranger as cosmopolitan, but was also aware that
those caught between cultures felt themselves to be in a difficult position.
Park wrote that the marginal man must strive to live in two diverse cultural
groups, the effect being to produce an unstable character. Melossi's (2000:
304) comment that Italian immigrants were called 'the Americans' and
seen as traitors to their original customs and native land by those left in
Italy throws further light upon Park's comments. Park's student Everett
Stonequist (1937) was to further develop the concept of marginal man,
an individual who is freed from the sources of social control through his

mobility, but also finds himself to be vulnerable to internal uncertainties and external stigma. Culture conflicts arose from the differences between two divergent systems of mores. The marginal individual was one who had an uncertain status in two or more groups.

The concept of culture conflict is most associated with the work of Thorsten Sellin. As Sellin (1938a) explained, a 1935 committee on delinquency involving Edwin Sutherland and himself chose the problem of culture conflict and its role in the causation of crime as its object of study. The approach taken emphasised the interdependence of the case and statistical methods of investigation. Culture conflict was taken to refer to the conflict of conduct norms, and Sellin explained that it was assumed to arise when an immigrant group from another country settled in the USA. The committee's approach broadened the understanding of culture conflict as follows:

> [S]uch conflict may arise as a result of a process of group differentiation within a cultural system or area, or as a result of contact between norms drawn from different cultural systems or areas.
>
> (Sellin, 1938a: 98)

The report of the work of the committee was eventually published with the title *Culture Conflict and Crime* (Sellin, 1938b).

Thrill-killers and murder in the Roaring Twenties

Zorbaugh wrote that the society of the wealthy Gold Coast area of Chicago was based on the constant display of affluence. He saw high society as characterised by cliques of very rich young people, but did not have anything to say about crime among the privileged. Sutherland's theory of white-collar crime only referred to crimes within the sphere of business activity. Quite different explanations were required for the Leopold–Loeb case, a murder in Chicago which is known as one of the crimes of the century.

In 1924, Nathan Leopold and Richard Loeb, aged eighteen and nineteen respectively, murdered a young boy named Bobby Franks. They sent a $10,000 ransom note to the father of the deceased, but were apprehended when spectacles inadvertently dropped while disposing of the body were traced to Leopold. Under questioning, the two explained that they had wanted to commit the perfect murder, the thrill of all thrills. The titillating sex, violence and death triplet was an infamous 'cause célèbre' at the time, and has since attained cinematic representation in Alfred Hitchcock's film *Rope* (1948) and Tom Kalin's *Swoon*. The case is a window upon understandings of the origins of crime contemporaneous with those of Chicagoan urban ecology.

Leopold's father was a millionaire box manufacturer and head of large shipping interests. Loeb's father was the vice-president of the Sears Roebuck company. The Leopold, Loeb and Frank families all lived in the exclusive Hyde Park area of Chicago and were 'related to every branch of a little royalty of wealth which Chicago has long recognised' (McKernan, 1925: 54). Attractive, debonair, cultured, some attributed the murder to the unrestrained and luxurious upbringing with which Leopold and Loeb had been indulged. The trial judge meted out sentences of life imprisonment, explaining that the age of the accused had been his prime consideration in refraining from sentencing Leopold and Loeb to death. John Wigmore objected that this ruling was in error because it overlooked the need for punishment to act as a deterrent to others. He complained that 'as everyone knows, today is a period of reckless immorality and lawlessness on the part of younger people' (Journal, 1924: 402).

The 'flapper' was a wild young woman with a certain look: bobbed hair, a short skirt and make-up that aimed to create a debauched look. Her activities included smoking, drinking alcohol, running around in automobiles, playing sports such as tennis and golf, and jazz dancing. In the figure of the flapper, the 'new women' rejected feminine passivity and celebrated a morality of sexual liberation. Jazz music was claimed to have an immoral effect on young people, invoking 'savage instincts' (Shaw Faulkner, 1921: 16). The ethos of pleasure destabilised older relationships between men and women. F. Scott Fitzgerald's *The Great Gatsby* (1926) commented on the moral decadence of the period in the wild extravagance of Jay Gatsby's parties and the shallowness of the guests. Nobody in the novel is able to remain uncontaminated. Tom takes whisky to a hotel suite concealed in a towel but accuses Gatsby of being a bootlegger. The lives of the Buchanans are filled with material comforts and luxuries, but are empty and devoid of purpose. Fitzgerald's novel depicted hedonistic idealism as yielding restless angst: 'A phrase began to beat in my ears with a sort of heady excitement: "There are only the pursued, the pursuing, the busy, and the tired"' (Fitzgerald 1926/1950, 77). Several of Fitzgerald's works depicted the dangers of aesthetic indulgence and pleasure seeking. In *The Beautiful and Damned*, a society couple are driven to destroy each other: 'There was no rest, no quiet. He had been futile in longing to drift and dream; no one drifted except to maelstroms, no one dreamed, without his dreams becoming fantastic nightmares of indecision and regret' (Fitzgerald, 1922/1966: 231).

From the turn of the century, a number of laws were introduced that can be seen as unwieldy and reactionary attempts to oppose change. The Volstead Act is undoubtedly the most obvious of these. The laws created new realms of illicit leisure, in which, as Murphy (1994) shows, relations between the sexes were reconfigured. Before Prohibition, she explains, 'respectable' women did not drink in public. Those women seen in or near the traditionally male space of the saloon were assumed to be either 'loose' or prostitutes. During Prohibition, women flouted the roles traditionally available to them by blatantly breaking the laws. This included drinking in speak-easies and nightclubs, and bootlegging. These actions involved deliberate and self-conscious violation of the conventions defining respectability.

The case raised threatening questions about the sophisticated urbanite's attitude to mores and laws. Leopold and Loeb were the youngest graduates in the history of their colleges, Loeb entering university aged fourteen and Leopold at the age of fifteen. They professed themselves atheists and saw themselves as Nietzschean supermen, far above the confines of conventional morality. They told the detectives and psychiatrists who interviewed them that they believed that the rule of law did not exist for the superman, so they were governed by no code and could not be judged by others. In the press, the initial shocking discourse of Nietzschean ideas and hedonism taken to extremes was soon superseded by one of domestic morbidity and personal pathology (Fass, 1993). The defence lawyer, the famous Clarence Darrow, repeatedly juxtaposed the terms 'abnormal' and 'childish' so as to depict the murderers as sufferers of a retarded emotional development. This rhetorical strategy can be seen in the following quotation:

> [S]omewhere in the infinite processes that go to the making up of the boy or the man something slipped, and those unfortunate lads sit here hated, despised, outcasts, with the community shouting for their blood.
> (Darrow, cited in McKernan, 1925: 232)

This diffused the threat of emancipation run wild by relocating the explanation of the crime in individual pathology. However, this was a risky strategy where it referred to unconscious desires, antisocial and taboo fantasies, and the like, raising the spectre of the uncontrollable.

The pathologisation of Leopold and Loeb did not tie them down in eugenic notions of feeble-mindedness, given their precocious intellectual talents and elite family pedigrees. Indeed, the explanations advanced by the defence team illustrate the shift away from the eugenic jurisprudence discussed in Chapter 1, a mode of governance involving 'the aggressive mobilization of law and legal institutions in pursuit of eugenic goals' (Willrich, 1998: 66). Harry Olsen became chief justice of the Municipal Court of Chicago in 1914, establishing a eugenicist criminological clinic, and producing speeches and publications on the danger of criminal 'mental defectives'. Psychological testing was integrated into daily court practice in the USA, leading Willrich to point up the great coercive power exercised by the allegedly 'natural' categories of eugenic jurisprudence. Tests were used to identify defectives, who were then confined in sexually segregated state institutions to prevent the commission of crimes as well as their reproducing. This dual strategy is seen in Robert Gault's (1925: 583) comment that 'it is not only for the improvement of the race but for the prevention of crime that segregation and sterilization should go hand in hand'. From 1906 to 1930, Chicago judges committed around a thousand people to these institutions, regardless of whether the court found them guilty of breaking any law. During the mid-1920s, Willrich writes, many American 'personal problems' professionals, social scientists and reformers began to oppose the eugenic approach. They replaced the segregationist logic of eugenicism with the therapeutic language of 'adjustment' and 'normal' living:

> The new idiom preserved the optimistic tenor of environmentalism while diverting attention from the socio-economic 'root causes' that had engaged progressive reformers; transforming the social environments that produced criminality, deviancy, and dependency now seemed less important than adjusting the individual deviant's 'personality'.
>
> (Willrich, 1998: 104)

The defence team in the Leopold–Loeb case employed the criminologist William Healy and the eminent American psychoanalyst William White, enabling them to employ Freudian concepts about repressed mental conflict.

William White (1933) contended that lawyers continued to think according to the formulas of yesterday and stated that reactionary measures gave rise to drastic punishments. He explained that criminal conduct had an emotional rather than an intellectual genesis that related to the emotional needs created by early experiences. He saw the 'right and wrong test' of the criminal law doctrine of responsibility as antiquated (White 1920). Healy published *The Individual Delinquent* in 1915, claiming the superiority of the study of each individual as a case, describing conduct as a direct expression of mental life, and relating the problem of crime to poor parental guardianship. Healy was to further develop a psychoanalytic approach in *Mental Conflicts and Misconduct* (1926), emphasising the significance of early mental life and advocating the re-education of offenders. In *Delinquents and Criminals*, Healy and Bronner (1926) stated that no great importance should be attached to the effect of economic status by those wishing to cure delinquency. This line of reasoning was continued in *Reconstructing Behavior in Youth* (1931), in which Healy and co-authors contended that mere improvement of the general environment was insufficient in many cases; delinquents also required psychotherapy. Healy published *Roots of Crime* with Franz Alexander in 1935, which commented that Shaw and McKay's *Delinquency Areas* (1929) 'adds nothing to what we already know by common sense' (Alexander and Healy, 1935/1969: 274). They contended that while the social bases of crime required explication, scholars should not address economic factors alone, but also consider the emotional. This led them to comment that, quite apart from its rational aim, stealing had a symbolic function for the individual. Theft compensated for deprivations that were emotional as well as material. Alexander and Healy hence described criminality as an expressive gratificatory activity, writing that:

[M]achine civilization with its mechanizing and levelling tendencies strangulates individuality and compels the individual to become a part of the collective unit. Criminality remains one of those few outlets left through which the individual can express his spite against this pressure and emphasize his masculine sovereignty. It is a pathological attempt to regain a lost freedom.

(Alexander and Healy, 1935/1969: 283)

They contended that displaying masculinity by showing disrespect for the law compensated for a deep sense of inferiority by engaging in toughness and aggression. Criminality was therefore 'an attempt to regain the lost self-esteem by a kind of pseudo-masculinity' (Alexander and Healy, 1935/1969: 287).

White, Healy and Glueck gave evidence concerning a number of repressed mental conflicts in both Leopold and Loeb. They stated that whatever their level of intellect, the emotional maturation of the boys remained retarded. The language of psychopathy was employed, which served at the time to vaguely designate somebody whose difference was obvious but impossible to pin down (Rafter, 1997: 250). This 'diagnosis' was overtly heteronormative. Psychopaths were often depicted as effeminate, and the sexual relationship between Leopold and Loeb was employed to indicate their departure from the norm of heterosexual masculinity and hence their pathological mental state. Additionally, biological and psychological explanations were merged through the use of endocrinological evidence. Physical examination of the defendants found indications of pathology of the endocrine system. In *The New Criminology*, Schlapp and Smith (1928: 7) contended that there was a criminal imperative driving criminal acts, which was accounted for by physico-chemical laws. In an anti-feminist diatribe, they stated that functional disturbances of the nerves and the glands arose from a glandular malfunction present in the mother at the time of gestation. According to them, it was women who entered into competition with men in a 'revolt against nature . . . [and] absurd quest of equality with a totally different creature' who became the mothers of these defective and criminal individuals (Schlapp and Smith, 1928: 146). In *Emotion and Delinquency* (1928), Grimberg located the organic basis of psychopathology in a defective endocrine system and suggested replacing the idea of the Lombrosian born criminal with that of the constitutional inferior. He argued that delinquency stemmed from a general emotionality produced by a hereditary abnormality of the endocrine system. This line of defence gave the crime a fatalistic tenor quite in contrast with the culprits' explanations of their carefully planned killing.

This was a crime about which the Chicagoan paradigm of urban ecology and the concept of social disorganisation had little to say. The explanations of the crime advanced in court and which proliferated in the mass media located the meaning of the murder in a wholly different set of notions. However, what the Leopold–Loeb case does share with the Chicago school approach is a Progressive outlook. This can be seen in its wish to understand scientifically instead of to punish retributively, and its identification of juveniles as different from adults. Instead of the common-sense approach taken by judges, Progressives favoured scientific modes of explanation. These included psychological ideas of mental conflict as the source of maladjustment which had a conservative tenor:

> Freudian psychology led away from a critique of society, seeking for causes of maladjustment within much narrower boundaries and, in the very use of the notion of maladjustment, making an implicit assumption that society as it stood was worth adjusting to.
>
> (Gittens, 1994: 128)[3]

This scientific outlook explains the urban ecologists' desire to distance themselves from the work of social reformers like Jane Addams (Deegan, 1990: 144). They presented themselves as unemotional observers, and depicted social reform as unsystematic do-gooding.

Democracy and assimilation into multiculturalism

Dario Melossi (2000) depicts the Chicagoan ethos as a quintessential expression of 1920s Progressivism, a period of optimism and experimentation. For Park, while competition produced individuation, communication was integrating, engendering consensus. Park and Burgess believed that social organisation was formed and reformed by changing means of communication. Park saw communication as a matter of overcoming distance. As Melossi (1990) explained, for Park the main problem as well as the hope for modern society was the creation of a sphere of public opinion able to solve the conflicts of democracy. Park was a newspaper reporter between 1887 and 1898, and believed that free communication was the necessary condition for the resolution of conflicts. He described Hearst's *New York Evening Journal*, which was principally read by immigrants, as an important Americanising device, and felt that by making information about the common life cheaply available to all, working democracy might be regained. The newspaper, he thought, might reproduce the conditions of life in the village, in which gossip and public opinion had been the chief sources of social control:

> If public opinion is to continue to govern in the future as it has in the past, if we propose to maintain a democracy as Jefferson conceived it, the newspaper must continue to tell us about ourselves.
>
> (Park, 1923: 278)

However, Park warned against overestimating the power of the press as an instrument of democracy, pointing out that the news was limited and urban society was more complex than that of the village. He was also aware that Hearst's brand of journalism appealed not to the intellect but to the emotions, and that the newspaper functioned principally as a form of entertainment. He contended that an objective look at social and political life was needed.

Park's activities in the newspaper business had convinced him that rather than muckraking, what was needed was 'scientific reporting', which alone could make the press a powerful agency of education and reform:

> John Dewey had made me familiar with the notion that thought and knowledge were to be regarded as incidents of and instruments of action, and I saw in the newspaper, responsible for its mission, an instrument by which this conception might be realized in action, and on a grand scale.
>
> (Park, 1927, cited in Baker, 1973: 254)

Park had originally thought that the newspaper might, merely by accurate reporting, yield changes. But he came to see that the mere dispersal of information was insufficient to mobilise change. This can be seen in Burgess and Bogue's account of Park's move from journalism to sociology:

> Dr. Park had been a newspaperman before he turned to sociology. . . . He was interested in the newspaper, its power of exposing conditions and arousing public sentiment, and in taking the lead against slums, exploitation of immigrants, or corruption in municipal affairs. . . . But Dr. Park found that, while newspaper publicity aroused a great deal of interest and stirred the emotions of the public, it did not lead to constructive action. He decided that something more than news was needed, that you had to get beneath the surface of things.
>
> (Burgess and Bogue, 1964: 3)

Burgess (1928) wrote that new forms of transport and communication like the automobile, the motion picture, the aeroplane and the radio, brought rapid social changes. Prominent among these were the decline of customary neighbourhood controls and a consequent increase in freedom. For Burgess, these new technologies had more profound consequences for society and human nature than the advent of mechanisation in industry because 'the machine and the factory meant routine and repression, but these new devices of communication bring adventure and freedom' (Burgess, 1928: 108). The increase in cosmopolitan and modern influences signalled, he contended, an increasing possibility of participation in democracy. The Chicagoan notion of democracy involved assimilation to a multicultural social order. Sumner (1997: 13) wrote that 'assimilation might have been the watchword for Robert Park's social control project'. According to him, the Chicagoan utopian vision was one of a 'harmonious multi-ethnic community hinged upon co-operation, consensus, participation and individual commitment' (Sumner, 1997: 14). They thought that formal criminal law would not bind citizens together into a corporate community; for this, communication between group members was required. New social control agencies and activities like the juvenile courts, the Boy Scouts and playground associations 'based on reason rather than sentiment and tradition' were required to deal with urban crime (Sumner, 1997: 17). For Park it was important to bring diverse cultures together. He spoke for 'a social control by sympathetic negotiation . . . a voluntaristic integration of citizens into a compact of co-operation, compromise, communication and self-policing' (Sumner, 1997: 17–18).

The Chicagoan concept of assimilation merits some discussion. As Park and Burgess made clear in their influential textbook *An Introduction to the Science of Sociology* (1921), competition, conflict, accommodation (fitting in) and assimilation were types of interaction. Their debt to Darwinian ideas is seen in the insistence that competition is the fundamental form. They explained that accommodation was a temporary kind of adjustment at the level of social organisation, whereas assimilation referred to a deeper and more gradual personality transformation. Accommodation was a matter of changes in habit, transmitted in the form of social tradition. Accommodations were not, they explained, hereditarily transmitted, but instead acquired by the individual in social interaction. They contended that consensus was the product of accommodations, and called for education rather than eugenics. Assimilation occurred when through a process of intimate association, individuals acquired possession of common experiences and traditions. Assimilation, they argued, was not the product of conscious reflection, but of intimate participation in common experiences like the celebration of national holidays.

Park and Burgess stated that the popular conception of assimilation was expressed symbolically in the USA by Israel Zangwill's play *The Melting Pot* (1908/1909), which envisaged it as a natural and unassisted process, in a kind of 'magic crucible' notion of assimilation. Zangwill envisaged America as a crucible of democracy and freedom, in which the separate European nationalities would be transformed into a new race. His play denigrated those who declined to assimilate quickly. The image of melting and merging to produce the American threatened the submergence of separate ethnic identities. Park and Burgess however pointed out that for them, assimilation did not necessarily mean like-mindedness. They emphasised that immigrants also brought valuable contributions from their native cultures to American civilization:

> [T]he unity thus achieved is not necessarily or even normally like-mindedness; it is rather a unity of experience and of orientation, out of which may develop a community of purpose and action.
>
> (Park and Burgess, cited in Truzzi, 1971: 128)

For Park, the solidarity of modern states depended less on the homogeneity of the population than on the intermingling of heterogeneous elements. Social solidarity was based in a working arrangement into which individuals entered as coordinate parts, this producing the corporate character of social groups. Park and Burgess wrote that assimilation was slow, painful and not always complete. They thought that it was most rapid where contacts were primary, and saw the absence of a common language as an insurmountable barrier. Park (1914) wrote that cosmopolitan groups were characterised by superficial uniformity as well as profound differences between individuals as concerned opinions and sentiments. This superficial uniformity, he held, permitted mobility of the individual and facilitated new contacts and free competition. Park asserted that the physical signs of racial difference acted as a barrier to assimilation, writing that the Asian and the Negro 'cannot become a mere individual, indistinguishable in the cosmopolitan mass of the population' (Park, 1914: 611). The vision of a harmonious multi-ethnic community had a number of problems however. Some of these can be seen in criticism of the Chicago Area Project.

The Chicago Area Project

The later work of the Chicago school shifted from addressing the processes of social change in local areas, to taking account of their relatively stable structural features. Furthermore, instead of focusing on primary group relationships, the later work gave priority to pressures emanating from the macro level of the social system. This change can be seen in Clifford Shaw and Henry McKays' *Juvenile Delinquency and Urban Areas* (1942). Shaw and McKay, who were based at the Institute for Juvenile Research, insisted that the relative levels of crime and delinquency rates in Chicago's neighbourhoods remained unaffected by dramatic changes in their racial and ethnic composition. They found that delinquency rates for each nationality remained high only while that group resided in a deteriorated area. Their research found that the distribution of crime was related to social conditions and not ethnic origins. The industrial invasion occasioned by business expansion was seen by them as a primary source of community disorganisation. They argued that with the expansion of the central business district, owners waited for land prices to rise and refrained from spending on new investment or repairs because they expected the buildings to be demolished. Over time, these areas deteriorated and were inhabited by impoverished migrants and immigrants. However, this analysis did not address conflict and the differential distribution of land, property, wealth and power. Ultimately, Shaw and McKay located the cause of deterioration in ecological laws, seeing the processes which gave rise to the zone of transition as an inherent part of the organic development of the city, rather than looking to the role of business elites and dominant institutions.

Clifford Shaw was a social activist, and was involved in the Chicago Area Project (CAP), a delinquency prevention programme initiated in 1932

(Finestone, 1976; Schlossman and Sedlak, 1983). The CAP was a community-based movement, in which the areas identified by research as prone to a high concentration of juvenile delinquency were targeted for a coordinated reform effort. A fieldworker from the Institute for Juvenile Research would enter the community to form councils of local residents. These councils aimed to organise the neighbourhood for civic betterment and delinquency prevention. Activities set up included sports and recreational facilities like playgrounds, summer camps and carnivals. The CAP vision emphasised the importance of maintaining the autonomy of the community, and stimulating community organisation without too much outside controlling. The hope was for local democratic participation in the process of rebuilding communities. Jon Snodgrass (1976) related the rural background of Shaw and McKay to their belief that restoring village life and tradition to the areas of the city would reinstate the natural social control inherent in rural settings. He argued that an agrarian conservatism underlay both Shaw's criminology and the CAP, describing Shaw as 'a folk-idealist waging an imaginary war with urban-industrial reality' (Snodgrass, 1976: 13). The basic model of Shaw's projects was, according to Snodgrass, a mid-Western farm town.

While Shaw was certainly aware of external sources of deterioration, he did not deal with them directly, with the result that the CAP was 'cosmetic rather than surgical' (Snodgrass, 1976: 16). Rather than opposing industrial invasion itself, the CAP approach was a palliative to the ensuing disorganisation, based in the assumption that the expansion and prosperity of business took precedence. Its effect was ameliorative, actually functioning to protect the interests of big business. As Smith (1988) explained, the Chicagoans were bound less by a shared theoretical position than by liberal political ideals, and the wish to base political practice in them. They believed that a properly functioning American democracy would allow people to achieve satisfactions, and hence sought a reformist politics. Snodgrass argued that the CAP was not only reformist; it was also disciplinary. In sum, the CAP evinced more concern with controlling behaviour than with the rights or welfare of the impoverished:

> The Chicago Area Project was first and foremost a disciplinary force, designed to inculcate values, socialise behaviour, and to achieve an accommodation of slum residents to the conventional order. The projects sought fundamentally to force individuals to adapt to American society.
>
> (Snodgrass, 1976: 17)

Snodgrass explained that rather than transforming conditions in the high delinquency areas, the CAP had the effect of lifting nationalities out of them, having a consolatory thrust that implied that the industrious immigrant could escape the slum. However, by the end of the 1930s millions remained unemployed and the ghettos were still racialised.

From democratic corporatism to normative conformism

The influence of the Chicago School began to wane in the 1930s, with the rise of a sociology associated with Talcott Parsons and Robert Merton. The Chicagoan belief in assimilation into multiculturalism can be seen in the social reformer Jane Addams' observations on the importance of respect for variety instead of the imposition of conformity as the source of a new American patriotism:

> The patriotism of the modern state must be based not upon a consciousness of homogeneity but upon a respect for variation, not upon inherited memory but upon trained imagination.
>
> (Addams, 1912: 616)

Addams pointed out that the crowded city could produce the simulacrum of companionship which deluded people into thinking that there was social intercourse. She contended that recreation was a kind of social interaction in which people tended to respect difference, and called for the building of public recreation centres to counter the corrupt training and taste for illicit pleasures received in the gang. Addams saw recreation as the cradle of a new higher type of citizenship based in the establishment of just relationships.

The Chicagoan outlook differed from that of anti-immigrationists. Sumner (1994: 29) writes that whereas the conservative elements wanted to bar the incoming cultures, for instance through restricted immigration legitimated by eugenicist notions, in defence of a 'real America', the Progressives wished to Americanise foreigners through education, training and social work. Burgess and Bogue's retrospect on Chicagoan urban sociology points out that in the 1920s, there was widespread prejudice and discrimination against immigrants, and that the Chicago scholars aimed to dispel malign stereotypes and injustice. Tabloid newspapers proclaimed the criminal inclinations of all Italians in the aftermath of frenzied public reaction to crimes among Italian immigrants. Widespread hysteria saw Italians treated with fear and contempt.

As Sumner (1997: 24) notes, with the dominance of Parsonian approaches, 'assimilation into multiculturalism had been replaced by socialization into a single homogeneous culture'. The cosmopolitan aspirations of the Chicagoans receded. By the 1950s, the methodological precept of explaining phenomena in terms of their contribution to the overall social system supported a view of the status quo as an unquestionable good. Functionalist sociology took on a 'complacent liberalism' (Colomy, 1990: xv). Parsons believed that a crucial feature of societies was homeostasis. The normative functionalism of Merton, Parsons, and their adherents, discussed and criticised in the following chapters, reflected a vastly changed political climate. This shift is prefigured in Robert Merton's depiction of the American Dream as a universal source of aspirations among residents of his country, and a burden to those who were effectively excluded from its satisfactions.

Notes

1. Park's papers can be found in Hughes et al. (1950–55). A bibliography of his writings is presented in Turner (1967).
2. Sutherland's essays can be found in Cohen et al. (1956).
3. On the American psychoanalytic criminology of this period, see Torrey (1992) and on the French, see Donzelot (1979).

Chapter 4

Al Capone, strain theory and the American Dream

Capone represents the triumph of amoral intelligence over morally prescribed failure.

(Merton, 1938)

The 'strain theory' of criminal behaviour was first advanced by Robert Merton, a sociologist at Harvard University, in 1938. Simply put, this theory contended that overemphasis on material success, coupled with a lack of opportunity for achieving this success, led to crime. Merton presented the gangster Al Capone as an illustration of how the disequilibrium of his time gave rise to criminal conduct. This chapter relates Merton's strain theory to the social, cultural and political conditions of New Deal America. 'The New Deal' is a phrase commonly used to designate that period of American politics coinciding with the presidency of the Democrat politician Franklin D. Roosevelt (1933–45). Roosevelt came to power at the height of the Great Depression, a massive worldwide economic slump which followed the prosperity and productivity of the 'Roaring Twenties'. He introduced unorthodox and controversial policies in an effort to revive the American economy, support the unemployed and the failing, and restore hope to Americans.

Roosevelt's New Deal sought to revive Americans' faith through a new vision of the American Dream. The four key elements of the American Dream were the dignity of the common individual, democracy as the guarantee of freedom, the gospel of hard work, and the belief in material progress. By the 1930s, the Dream had taken the tangible form of pecuniary success. Social ascent was read from the display of economic affluence. In *The Theory of the Leisure Class* (1899), Thorstein Veblen introduced the concept of 'conspicuous consumption', by which the wealthy displayed their social superiority. Veblen contended that to acquire social esteem, the mere possession of wealth and power was insufficient. Rather, pecuniary strength must be put in evidence, made visible to others through exclusive leisure pursuits and conspicuous consumption. The consumption of expensive luxuries was an important means of reputability to the gentleman of leisure, Veblen explained, maintaining a distance from the working class as well as an elaborate system of rank within the leisure class. Veblen noted that the wife became a vicarious and ceremonial consumer, the spectacle of her husband's financial potency. He argued that the manner of life and standards of worth of the leisure class provided a norm for the whole society. All social classes, Veblen maintained, observed these standards to some extent. Even the poorest, he noted, could not forgo some customary conspicuous consumption. Veblen also held that in the anonymous city the demonstration of the ability to pay was the only means by which reputability might be judged.

From the turn of the century, the rise of a mass consumer culture began. Over the twentieth century, capitalism shifted decisively from an economy based on production to one based on consumption. Put differently, the 'problem' for capitalism was no longer how to produce enough but rather how to sell the excess produced above market demand. How could people be induced to consume more? The landscape of commerce underwent a striking transformation with the introduction of coordinated methods of distribution, sales and advertising. New ways were constantly sought to expand consumer demand, for instance a multiplication of forms of merchandising and display.

The end of 1937 saw a new and serious recession, and there were still seven million unemployed people in the USA. This was the first depression in an America supposedly strengthened against depressions by the economic control legislation of the early New Deal. A deep contrast was evident between the ideology of the American Dream and the visible reality of harsh social and economic inequality. The promise of an open society had been visibly undermined by the persistence of crushing poverty. The idealism, as well as the practical measures, of the New Deal were placed under massive pressure. In the 1930s, both popular representation and Government rhetoric peddled slogans like 'the forgotten man', and 'the common man', to refer to the hardy struggle of the symbolic worker of the New Deal. Texts such as Steinbeck's *The Grapes of Wrath* (1939/1996) dramatised the doomed flight of the rural poor from the devastation and suffering of the Dust-bowl to the promise of a better life in California. The images of this time reflected the sufferings of a society mired in economic depression. Such images were appealing to people struggling with the incomprehensible and wholly unpredictable forces of an economy in chaos. Roosevelt's programme of reconstruction aimed at easing the suffering of the poor, as well as curbing the worst excesses of economic instability.

Theorists have tended to see Merton's strain theory as Rooseveltian, with its depiction of crime as a normal adaptation to an abnormal and structurally difficult situation (Sumner, 1994; Pitch, 1995). Popular representation of crime at this time condensed contemporary troubles around financial insecurity into sympathetic portrayals of people caught up in circumstances beyond their control. However, the description of Merton's theory as Rooseveltian is not a laudatory one. From the 1970s, revisionist historians have criticised the New Deal for supporting the extant social and economic order. They argued that the moderate reforms of the Roosevelt administration saved corporate capitalism and failed to redistribute income and power. How might theories of crime and punishment have played a part in supporting the status quo? An important feature of New Deal rule was the deglamorising of crime. Merton did not generate images of an alien and pathological type, as the criminal anthropologists had done. His Harvard colleague E.A. Hooton (1939), for instance, described criminals as biologically inferior and deteriorated organisms. Indeed, Merton launched an attack on individualist explanations of crime (Merton and Montagu, 1940). Instead, he depicted criminals as the sad face of American culture during time of economic depression; nothing special or extraordinary at all.

The Roosevelt administration embarked upon a 'war on crime', determined to end the popular heroisation of gangsters (O'Reilly, 1982). FBI officials were encouraged to conduct a media campaign to counter the public's romanticised view of gangsters, whose deeds were sensationalised by tabloid publicity. The FBI exploited dramatic crimes of the 1930s, for instance those of Bonnie Parker and Clyde Barrow, to advance specific legislative objectives. In an annual message to Congress in 1934, Roosevelt called for a stronger public opinion in support of a war against the organised crime that he warned threatened the nation's security. Congress approved a series of bills empowering bureau agents to carry firearms and expanding their jurisdiction and arrest powers. Tough penalties were introduced for violation of a range of federal laws. Roosevelt insisted that 'gangster extermination cannot be made completely effective so long as a substantial part of the public looks with tolerance upon known criminals . . . or applauds efforts to romanticize crime' (Roosevelt, cited in O'Reilly, 1982: 643). The FBI engaged itself upon a PR campaign to make the G-men heroes. Hoover, FBI director at this time, closely monitored comic strips like Dick Tracy. Merton's strain theory accords with the attempt to diffuse the fascinating power of figures like Al Capone. It is very much part of the New Deal's crusade against crime.

Functionalist sociology, consensus and equilibrium

Merton was one of the founding figures of a functionalist school of sociology that flourished in America between the 1930s and the 1960s.[1] This approach dominated the American sociology of the postwar period, before falling into disrepute from the late 1960s onwards. In functionalist sociologies, the notion of equilibrium supplies the analytical reference point for evaluating social systems. This means that rather than seeing social conflict as the defining feature of a society, the theory projects an ideal picture of harmonious social relationships. A theory that is said to be functionalist identifies the requirements necessary to the existence and persistence of a society. Scholars therefore aim to discover the contribution made by the various parts of a society towards the overall condition of stability. Social phenomena are understood in terms of their relationship to a broader system. The ideal society of the functionalist model is relatively stable, well-integrated, and has a social structure based on a consensus of values. This principle of equilibrium is grasped by the idea of the functional unity of a social system: 'a condition in which all parts of the social system work together with a sufficient degree of harmony or internal consistency, i.e., without producing persistent conflicts which can neither be resolved nor regulated' (Radcliffe-Brown, 1935: 397). The functionalist approach is often accompanied by the use of biological metaphors, as though society were a living organism.

The most popular critique of the functionalist treatment of culture interpreted this as 'quintessential consensus theory and as implying both a commitment to social order and the status quo' (Colomy, 1990: xxx). The implicit conservatism of functionalist theory has been seen as a response to a perceived crisis of social order arising from profound social changes such as those associated with industrialisation and urbanisation, and major political changes such as democratisation. Twentieth-century functionalism has been described as 'an essentially American invention', echoing distinctive American concerns around the problem of social solidarity in their emergent society (Hamilton, 1996: 146). What could be more American than a functionalist analysis of the American Dream? Merton's strain theory produced a cautionary tale about its dark side. This 'normative doctrine of universally accessible opportunity' was for various reasons dysfunctional, producing a chaotic dissolution of social order (Merton, 1995: 16).

Anomie, aspirations and moral deregulation

The concept of anomie has exercised a powerful effect upon the sociological imagination, referring to the existence of conditions of relative normlessness in a group or society.[2] This state of normlessness is reflected in a sense of isolation and of the meaninglessness of life and work, as described eloquently by Louis Wirth, one of the Chicago school scholars:

A society is possible in the last analysis because the individuals in it carry in their heads some sort of picture of that society . . . [today] these pictures are blurred and incongruous. Hence we no longer perceive the same things as

real, and coincident with our vanishing sense of a common reality we are
losing our common medium for expressing and communicating our
experiences. The world has been splintered into countless fragments of
atomised individuals and groups. The disruption in the wholeness of
individual experience corresponds to the disintegration in culture and group
solidarity. When the bases of unified collective action begin to weaken, the
social structure tends to break and to produce a condition which Émile
Durkheim has termed anomie, by which he means a situation which might
be described as a sort of social emptiness or void. Under such conditions
suicide, crime, and disorder are phenomena to be expected because
individual existence is no longer rooted in a stable and integrated social
milieu and much of life's activity loses its sense and meaning.

(Wirth, 1936/1964)

As can be seen from this passage, anomie was construed as a property of
the socio-cultural organisation rather than as a trait of the individual.

In *Suicide* (1897), Durkheim thought that anomie resulted from a disturbance in the equilibrium of the regulatory aspect of social order. In
this text, he argued that because the wants of the individual were insati-
able, an external regulative force must limit them. Durkheim argued that
an 'economic ideal' was assigned to each class of individuals in the form
of a regimen which fixed the maximum degree of ease of living to which
each social class might legitimately aspire. The individual with a 'whole-
some moral constitution' respected regulations and adhered to collective
authority, hence he would feel that it was not well to ask more (Durkheim,
1897/1952: 250). In the individual in harmony with his condition, the
acceptance of this relative limitation and moderation would produce an
'average contentment'. Durkheim believed that a time of crisis or abrupt
social change could disturb society such that it was for a time incapable
of exercising this regulatory influence. This disturbance could result in a
state of deregulation. In an anomic society, the individual's consent to
restrict their desires in deference to a respected authority could no longer
be assured, these cravings coming to exert a continual and painful fric-
tion. The controlling influence of society over individual wants and ambitions is no longer effective and people are left without moral guidance
in the pursuit of their goals. The condition of anomie is, according to
Durkheim, not only detrimental to social order but also painful for the
individual because 'to pursue a goal which is by definition unobtainable
is to condemn oneself to a state of perpetual unhappiness' (Durkheim,
1897/1952: 248).

As Simon and Gagnon (1976) explained, Durkheim particularly used
the term 'anomie' to refer to the condition of unlimited desires and
shallow satisfactions among the affluent. They cited his evocation of the
excitable greed of those in the commercial sector:

[R]eality seems valueless by comparison with the dreams of fevered
imagination; reality is, therefore, abandoned, but so too is possibility

> abandoned when it in turn becomes reality. A thirst arises for novelties,
> unfamiliar pleasures, nameless sensations, all of which lose their savor once
> known.
>
> (Durkheim, 1897/1952: 256)

As this passage shows, Durkheim was as concerned about the transience of gratification as he was about the elusiveness of pleasures, and saw both as contributing to anomie. For him, both want and satiation made for the 'futility of an endless pursuit' (Durkheim, 1897/1952: 256). On this view, both poverty and affluence could be anomie-producing. Furthermore, Simon and Gagnon made the point that Durkheim actually saw poverty as a constraint, and considered wealth more potent in inspiring a quest for unending success.

Simon and Gagnon related the Mertonian reformulation of Durkheim to the society of scarcity found in the USA of the late 1930s. Anomic conditions were assumed to be the most profound among the poorest segments of American society by Merton, Cloward, Ohlin and Clinard, and this association continues today. Durkheim related anomie to individualisation. Merton, however, theorized the effects of an injunction to conform that he claimed was universal across American society. Anyway, Durkheim explicitly disavowed a connection between anomie and crime (Besnard, 1987: 224). Merton constructed one. Whereas Durkheim had associated the state of anomie with sudden social change, Merton saw the condition of anomie as arising from the basic values of his culture. Instead of theorising a period of unstable transition like Durkheim had, Merton preferred the idea of a malintegration among the components of his society, and took a strictly synchronic and static view. Instead of the stratified economic ideals described by Durkheim, Merton felt that the American Dream had made aspirations for upward mobility common to all.

Adaptations to the disjunction of means and ends

Merton's theory is summarised in the statement that, 'certain phases of social structure generate the circumstances in which infringement of social codes constitutes a "normal" response' (Merton, 1938: 672). Merton argued for the recognition of two analytically separate elements of the socio-cultural structure: goals and acceptable means. The first of these was a set of culturally defined goals and interests. Merton explained that this set of goals comprised a 'frame of aspirational reference'. The other element of the socio-cultural structure to which Merton drew attention was that of the acceptable means of achieving these goals (Merton, 1938: 673). He stated that every social group invariably accompanied its set of desired ends with regulation of the permissible means for attaining them. Merton posited that there was no fixed relationship between cultural goals and the accepted means of their achievement. This meant that the status of certain goals might be emphasised quite independently of the degree of emphasis placed upon legitimate means. This led him to postulate that antisocial conduct was a symptom of dissociation between cultural goals and socially acceptable means.

Merton theorised five kinds of adaptation to this kind of situation of means–ends disjunction:

1. ritualism
2. conformity
3. retreatism
4. rebellion
5. innovation.

He explained that in ritualism, people feel that goals are no longer of primary significance to them. Means become transformed into ends, as individuals devote themselves to the strict observance of rules and routines. The ritualistic society was characterised by Merton as follows:

> Stability is largely ensured while change is flouted. The range of alternative behaviours is severely limited. There develops a tradition-bound, sacred society characterised by neophobia.
>
> (Merton, 1938: 673)

He offered the occupational mindset of the bureaucrat as an exemplar of the personality produced by this particular kind of cultural malintegration, further developing this figure of 'overconformity' in *Social Theory and Social Structure* (Merton, 1957: 195–206). Another kind of response was that of conformity, which Merton claimed was the most common mode of adaptation in every society, being necessary to the maintenance of its stability and continuity. Indeed, Merton viewed the predominance of conforming behaviour as the very basis upon which a group or society could be said to exist:

> Conventional role behavior oriented toward the basic values of the group is the rule rather than the exception. It is this fact alone which permits us to speak of a human aggregate as comprising a group or society.
>
> (Merton, 1938: 677)

The retreatist adaptation, which involved rejection of both the dominant goals and accepted means for achieving them, was according to Merton the least common of the five modes that he had identified. He depicted people who adjusted in this manner as 'true aliens' who were 'in the society but not of it' (Merton, 1938: 677). He claimed that some of the activities of psychotics, pariahs, outcasts, vagrants, chronic drunkards and drug addicts, could be seen as adaptations of this kind. Merton asserted that Nels Anderson's (1923) description of the behaviour and attitudes of the homeless 'bum' in *The Hobo* could be read in terms of this 'passive rejection' category. This is not, however, the impression that Anderson himself gave of the mobile and cosmopolitan, though suffering, hobo, as seen in Chapter 3. In a later revision of his essay, Merton gave the example of the tramp character played by the movie comedian Charlie Chaplin in over seventy films as a archetypal retreatist, 'always the butt of a crazy and bewildering world in which he has no place and from which he constantly runs away into a contented do nothingness' (Merton, 1949: 251). Merton wrote that retreatism arose when both goals and means had been assimilated by the individual, but the accepted means were not available to them. He stated that this situation produced mental conflict, with the result that the frustrated individual who could not cope dropped out. This 'escape' from social requirements involved an inability to take up alternative means due to the effect of internalised prohibitions.

Merton described the 'rebellion' adaptation as a transitional response, directed at the institutionalisation of new procedures for achieving new cultural goals. He explained that rebellion was an effort to change the existing structure rather than accommodating to it. This was the adaptation about which he had the least to say. Merton associated crime with the 'innovation' adaptation, in which a disproportionate emphasis upon prestigious goals developed along with a slim emphasis upon the legitimate means of achieving them. Merton wrote that the American culture of his day was alleged to tend towards such an emphasis of certain ends over acceptable means.

The pursuit of wealth, anomie and crime

Merton saw the association of wealth with success as particularly characteristic of his society, and set out to explain how it produced anomie. His essay offers a particular argument about the criminogenic character of the American society of the late 1930s. According to Merton, because certain individuals had few legitimate means to acquire cultural goals, they innovated their own, illicit, means. In support of his argument, Merton referred to a study by Joseph Lohman (1937) which had opposed the argument of Walter Reckless (1926) that vice areas were the product of a natural segregation of people on the basis of their interests and attitudes. Lohman had argued that the local opportunities for getting a livelihood were of greater significance. He had stated that unskilled labour was the chief occupational and hence legitimate means for the blacks and Italians of Chicago. The low income levels afforded by this kind of work, he wrote, were opposed to the broader society's standards of success and property. Merton added that the cultural stigmatisation of manual labour, as well as the prestigious status of white-collar work, produced 'a strain toward innovational practices' (Merton, 1938: 678).

Merton stated clearly that the situation in which the innovation adaptation arose had two important features:

> First, such antisocial behavior is in a sense 'called forth' by certain conventional values of the culture *and* by the class structure involving differential access to the approved opportunities for legitimate, prestige-bearing pursuit of the culture goals.
>
> (Merton, 1938: 679)

Illegitimate innovation is the product of both poor integration between the means and ends elements of the cultural pattern, *and* a handicapped position within the class structure. Merton emphasised that the second feature was of equal importance in understanding the high incidence of this response among certain social groups. He explained that advancement towards desired success-symbols through conventional means was both rare and difficult for those who had little formal education and scant economic resources.

Merton pointed out that as well as an objective reduction in opportunities for vertical social mobility, the individual's personal evaluation of the situation was an important factor in their chosen mode of adaptation. This led him to formulate an argument about the cultural pressure towards deviant and criminal conduct:

> The dominant pressure of group standards of success is, therefore, on the gradual attenuation of legitimate, but by and large ineffective, strivings and the increasing use of illegitimate, but more or less effective, expedients of vice and crime. The cultural demands made on persons in this situation are incompatible. On the one hand, they are asked to orient their conduct toward the prospect of accumulating wealth and on the other, they are largely denied effective opportunities to do so institutionally. The consequences of such structural inconsistency are psychopathological personality, and/or antisocial conduct, and/or revolutionary activities.
>
> (Merton, 1938: 679)

This vision of culture, personality and conduct, holds that strain arises from a lack of integration between what a culture calls for and what the social structure permits.

Merton's emphasis upon the cultural pattern of the society made it clear that high rates of deviant conduct were not generated simply by lack of opportunity or by the existence of an exaggerated pecuniary emphasis. He pointed out that the rigid class structure of a feudal or caste society limited opportunities of social mobility far more than the American society of his day. Widespread antisocial behaviour was rather the product of the cultural extolling of certain *common* success symbols for the *whole* population while at the same time the access of many people to legitimate means of acquiring these symbols was restricted or eliminated:

The same body of success-symbols is held to be desirable for all. These goals are held to *transcend class lines*, not to be bounded by them, yet the actual social organization is such that there exist class differentials in the accessibility of these *common* success-symbols. Frustration and thwarted aspiration lead to the search for avenues of escape from a culturally induced intolerable situation; or unrelieved ambition may eventuate in illicit attempts to acquire the dominant values.

(Merton, 1938: 680)

Merton argued for the existence of an inherent trend towards anomie within the American society of his day, that this particular social order necessarily produced a 'strain toward dissolution' (Merton, 1938: 681). He contended that the calculability and regularity of behaviour decreased with dissociation of means and ends, and in the extreme situation 'predictability virtually disappears and what may be properly termed cultural chaos or anomie intervenes' (Merton, 1938: 682). Merton's essay suggested that the condition of anomie that Durkheim had considered to be exceptional became routine. Whereas for Durkheim deregulation led to infinite aspirations, for Merton, inflated cultural goals led to anomie.

Merton commented that in the anomic time in which he wrote, force and fraud became the sole virtues due to their perceived efficiency in attaining goals, making reference to Hobbes' *Leviathan* (1651). According to this seminal text of seventeenth-century political philosophy, when men lived without a common power to keep them in awe, they lived in a condition of 'war of every man against every man' (Hobbes, 1651/1991: 88). In the absence of external security, the competitive nature of man was such that he lived in a state of 'continual fear, and dangerous violent death, and the life of man, solitary, poor, nasty, brutish, and short' (Hobbes, 1651/1991: 89). However, instead of seeing competitiveness as an essential attribute of human nature, Merton pointed out that goals were in his theory culturally derived.

The incompatibility between the egalitarian ideology and social structure of the American society of his day, Merton argued, gave rise to 'exaggerated anxieties, hostilities, neuroses and antisocial behavior' (Merton, 1938: 680). Strain theory transformed the idea of tensions seen in the psychoanalytic theory of mental conflict and crime, into the idea of social structures exerting a pressure on certain individuals. Strain is not an individual problem but a social and cultural one. Merton posited that institutional rules were known to those who broke them, and commented that:

It is unlikely that interiorized norms are completely eliminated. Whatever residuum persists will induce personality tensions and conflict. The process involves a certain degree of ambivalence.

(Merton, 1938: 675n)

Merton referred the reader to the psychoanalyst Karen Horney's *The Neurotic Personality of Our Time* (1937) for a discussion of the psychological aspects of means–ends dissociation. In this book, Horney emphasised the need to understand the influences that a particular culture exerted over the individual. Horney stated that the character structure that recurred in neurotic persons of her time differed only in degree and not in kind from that of the normal person. She wrote that the quest for power, prestige and possession was a common means in American culture of obtaining reassurance against anxiety. She viewed neurotic striving as a protection against feelings of helplessness, insignificance and humiliation. She commented that an irrational striving for possession was widespread in her culture, alluding to the destructive competitiveness of an individualistic culture.

Imagining Al Capone

Portraying the legend of Al Capone as 'the triumph of amoral intelligence over morally prescribed failure' (Merton, 1938: 679), Merton saw his gangsterdom as called forth by the culture and social structure of his society. By the time that Merton published his piece, Capone had been in prison for seven years. The figure of Capone was offered as a symbol of the strain theory on the basis of reducing his significance to the tale of a rags to riches anti-hero. But there was much more to the meaning of Capone than this. In *Inventing the Public Enemy*, David Ruth (1996) depicted the gangster as emblematic of profound changes affecting the lives of millions of Americans, writing that Al Capone was the gangster that Americans found most compelling.[3] Not only did the gangster rebel against the law, but he also threatened conventional behavioural codes, appearing as a particularly troubling figure of the modern urban consumer. In his figure was condensed a multitude of anxieties around the perceived assault of modern society upon traditional restraint:

> Boundaries between law-abiding and criminal, respectable and disreputable, male and female, moral and licentious, individual and group: all seemed at the same time blurry and crucially important.
>
> (Ruth, 1996: 8)

Urbanisation and the expansion of corporate commercialism faced individuals with the difficulties and opportunities of pursuing individual goals within and alongside large business organisations, while simultaneously the marketing of the pleasures and distinctions of consumerism held out new promises of individual fulfilment. Ruth argued that the gangster became a central cultural figure because he epitomised important features of the changing social world and thus symbolically enabled the understanding and mastery of these unstable transitions. Merton's typology of adaptations can be seen as a defence against the blurring of boundaries described by Ruth.

Ruth argued that the figure of the gangster played out anxieties about the precarious character of expanding mass-consumption, signalling that the standards of style confused earlier and supposedly more reliable indicators of social status, especially those of ethnicity and class. Ruth described how the gangster was defined in part by his display of stylish consumption. Old categories of social stratification and of social order were undermined by the promotion of style, in which status no longer depended on the stability of established reputation. Furthermore, the old ethos of hard work and respectability was shaken by the new celebration of play. The worship of purchasable pleasures threatened the morality and docility of groups who now refused to recognise themselves as a lower sort (Ruth, 1996: 76). The gangster represented in thrilling and alarming form the shifting meanings of class in modern urban America. In the representation of gangsters, the criminal was placed in close quarters with those of the most elevated echelons of society, linking the respectable and the disreputable as fellow consumers of the same expensive pleasures. Ruth argued that the gangster also played out confused meanings of ethnicity, framing ethnicity as a matter of style.

Merton argued that the highly abstract and impersonal nature of money that Georg Simmel had identified, as well as the anonymity of metropolitan living, rendered wealth an apt symbol of prestige divorced from institutional controls. In *The Philosophy of Money* (1900/1990), Simmel argued that when monetary transactions replaced earlier forms of barter, profound changes in social interaction occurred.[4] When money became the prevalent link between people, bonds based in the ties of blood, kinship or loyalty, dissolved. Simmel's social philosophy demonstrated considerable ambivalence, however. According to his argument, when money displaced natural groupings by voluntary associations, it increased personal freedom and fostered social differentiation. Beyond its economic functions, for Simmel money symbolised the modern spirit of rationality, calculability and impersonality. On his part, Merton simply commented that the sources of wealth might be unknown to the community in which the plutocrat resided; whether acquired through fraud or institutionally, wealth could serve as a symbol of elevated status. His comment that through illegitimate means gangsters could achieve 'at least the simulacrum of culturally defined success', suggested a passing recognition of the instability of style as an indicator of social status (Merton, 1938: 678). The representation of the gangster both proclaimed the joys of self-gratification and suggested that the indulgent risked great danger.

Ruth commented that Capone deliberately exploited the contradictory moral status that he was perceived to occupy, as can be seen from the gangster's statements:

> I make my money by supplying a public demand. If I break the law, my customers, who number hundreds of the best people in Chicago, are as guilty as I am. The only difference between us is that I sell and they buy.

Everybody calls me a racketeer. I call myself a businessman. When I sell
liquour, it's bootlegging. When my patrons serve it on silver trays on Lake
Shore Drive, it's hospitality.

> (Capone, cited in Burns, 1931: 33)

This explains why Capone was the subject of a tale of success both horat-
ory and cautionary. Ruth described how the figure of Capone bore an
uncanny resemblance to ordinary Americans. Capone was an icon of
aggressive masculinity and raw virility as well as the ruthless efficiency of
modern business organisation:

> Capone's organization showed a disturbing proximity between ordinary,
> amoral business objectives – the pursuit of corporate profits – and those that
> generated terribly immoral and destructive acts.
>
> (Ruth, 1996: 129)

At this time, Americans struggled to come to terms with the power of the
corporation, and the Capone legend offered ambiguous messages about
the path to success in a business society.

Merton gave little thought to the plight of the faceless cog in the machine, and also neglected the significance of the constitution of masculinity. However, others did address these questions. Franz Alexander and
William Healy (1935/1969) recounted the case of Richard Vorland, a thief
who suffered blows to his 'masculine vanity'. In their introduction to
this text, the authors held that character was in part the product of
the ideological trends in a society. They emphasised the significance of
the levelling tendencies of 'machine civilisation' to contemporary ills. The
expansion of Fordist mass production and Taylorist scientific management, as well as the flourishing of corporate bureaucracy, was alienating,
and posed problems for independent masculinity:

> [M]achine civilization with its mechanizing and leveling tendencies
> strangulates individuality and compels the individual to become a part of the
> collective unit. Criminality remains one of those few outlets left through
> which the individual can express his spite against this pressure and
> emphasize his masculine sovereignty. It is a pathological attempt to regain a
> lost freedom.
>
> (Alexander and Healy, 1935/1969: 283)

Criminality was seen by Alexander and Healy as a compensatory reaction
to a deep sense of inferiority, and they described it as 'an attempt to
regain the lost self-esteem by a kind of pseudo-masculinity' (Alexander
and Healy, 1935/1969: 287). Merton addressed status and social ascent
rather than identity. After the revolution in morals and manners of the
1920s, this was a time when the American value system might have been
transformed. However, Merton did not take up any searching questions
about social change, social relations or individual identity.

Despite raising the spectre of the most notorious Prohibition Era gangster, Merton did not ponder the significance of the criminalisation of leisure and its blurring of boundaries. He (1936: 897) had earlier argued that purposive action could have important and unanticipated consequences, and mentioned a possible link between Prohibition and organised crime in this respect. However, he preferred to focus on the unanticipated consequences of the American Dream rather than repressive and unenforceable legislation. He had little to say about the widespread disdain for the liquor laws, and the manner in which the law created a vacuum of rules and gave rise to new social spaces. Mabel Elliott (1944) related criminal acts to the tradition of the American frontier, with its reckless lawlessness. She argued that the restive spirit of the pioneer created much of the pattern of freedom and liberty characteristic of the American way of life. On the frontier, she explained, social controls were at a minimum. This lawless heritage was the origin of contemporary criminal behaviour according to Elliott, 'the inevitable by-product of the customs and habits of a people impatient of restraints and controls' (Elliott, 1944: 192). Frontier culture's wildness, she contended, explained the American disrespect for formal legislative controls. Nowhere in Merton's essay were the thrills and pleasures of the modern consumer society or the freedoms noted by Simmel discussed. Merton only depicted the perils of disorder. Yet, quite ironically, Merton's mention of Capone's 'triumph' as amoral innovator reflects the fascination and repulsion described by Ruth.

Strain theory, functionalism and crime

The functionalism of Merton's strain theory made it a fitting complement to the New Deal's project to stabilise corporate capitalism. Merton contended that the persistent open-class ideology of the American society of his day, with its 'office-boy-to-president' stereotype, had once accorded approximately with the possibilities of vertical social mobility. He asserted that in his time the class structure had become more rigid. Merton claimed that although it was no longer empirically valid, the open-class ideology persisted because it continued to be functional to the maintenance of the status quo, offering a consoling hope to those who would otherwise rebel. He referred the reader to Karl Mannheim's (1929) concept of ideology to support this idea of a discrepancy between belief and reality. Mannheim (1893–1947) was concerned with the effects of social structure upon belief systems. Within his theory, ideologies were systems of ideas which gave a positive affirmation to the existing social order and the interests of the dominant groups within it:

> Ideologies are seen by Mannheim to be distorted world views, because they
> fail to take into account new realities which challenge the situation of the

dominant group. Ideological beliefs inevitably attempt to place a brake or restriction upon social change.

(Turner, 1995: 719)

This was the point at which his essay was most critical, yet at the same time most blind. The distinctive mark of functionalism was evident in Merton's insistence on the necessity of widespread conformity to the very existence of a society. He saw goals as a genuine consensus of values, despite his passing recognition that they also served those in power. The Chicagoan onus on respecting variation and faithfully depicting the multi-faceted character of urban existence, however incomplete and viewed through a Progressive lens, was abandoned in favour of general theory.

Merton also presented no analysis of race prejudice, although by the late 1930s, a new distrust of foreigners was evident. This 'anti-alien feeling' reached new heights in 1935 with the trial of Bruno Hauptmann, a German immigrant and 'illegal alien', for the kidnapping and murder of the infant son of the transatlantic aviator-hero Charles Lindbergh. In assuming the ubiquity of a singular American Dream, Merton's essay seems (albeit inadvertently) to collude with what Cooke (1950/1968: 29) described as the renewed affirmation of 'the American way' as 'a tribal chant, uttered most fearsomely by the fearful'.

By the postwar period, functionalist sociology was dominating the theoretical horizon. Two principal tendencies may be discerned, as follows:

1. The assumption of a monolithic culture.
2. The 'description' of rigid social roles that constrained behaviour, associated with specific class and gender positions.

Functionalist sociology propounded theories of social roles, which were prescriptive despite their claim to have arisen from objective value-free social science. In *Delinquent Boys*, Albert Cohen (1955) drew on Merton's strain theory, as well as the notion of cultural transmission employed by social disorganisation theory, to explain why delinquent subcultures were formed. This text was written in the context of a postwar alarm about urban youth gangs stealing for kicks and reveling in negativistic violence. Cohen made clear his debt to Merton, writing that:

> [T]hose values which are at the core of the 'American way of life', which help to motivate the behavior which we most esteem as 'typically American', are among the major determinants of that which we stigmatize as 'pathological' ... the problems of adjustment to which the delinquent subculture is a response are determined, in part, by those very values which respectable society holds most sacred.
>
> (Cohen, 1955: 137)

Cohen argued that lower class youth strove to emulate middle-class norms and values, but lacked the means to attain success, suffering consequently from 'status frustration'.

For Cohen, delinquent subcultures provided alternative means of achieving recognition and respect among the youth's peer group. Incorporating some insights from the work of Sutherland, he depicted delinquency as in part a collective response. He held that the incompatibility of social structure and culture produced points of pressure at which subcultures evolved. The gang, he explained, inverted the rules of middle-class society. Its subculture was characterised by negativism, malice, hedonism and instant gratification, seen for instance in vandalism and fighting. Criticising Merton's instrumentalism (his understanding of behaviour as goal-directed), Cohen claimed that not all crime and deviance was conducted in pursuit of wealth. He preferred to see delinquent behaviour as primarily expressive. He described three distinctive responses among groups of boys, calling them 'college boys' (conformists who aspired to improve through educational success), 'corner boys' (retreatists who accepted their inferior position) and 'delinquent boys' (innovators). Cohen drew on the psychological concept of 'reaction formation', which referred to the situation in which a person denied something reacts by disparaging it to excess. This enabled him to assert that delinquent boys developed an exaggerated hostility towards middle-class values.

Cohen's work was criticised by Sykes and Matza (1961) in their essay on 'subterranean values'. This opposed studies that theorised a definitive set of middle-class values against which delinquent values might be judged. Sykes and Matza argued that delinquent values permeated all social classes and should not be assumed to be limited to the lower working class. An equally pressing problem with strain theory is its combination of gender-blindness and sex-stereotypes. Like most other classic theories of criminality, strain theory was formulated from the study of males, for instance Cohen (1955: 44) stated that 'delinquency in general is mostly male delinquency'. This combined a set of unexamined assumptions about both sexes. Cohen excluded girls from his theory. He asserted that they were primarily interested in boys, dating and marriage, so gang delinquency was irrelevant to them when they suffered any status frustration. Their goals, he claimed, lay within personal relationships. The norms of educational and occupational success were assumed by him to be male concerns. Actually, over the twentieth century women have increasingly entered the education system and labour market, so Cohen's arguments merit considerable challenge. Furthermore, the manner in which advertising was directed at women, constructing them as the prime targets of consumer capitalism, questions the gendered assumptions of strain theory. Dorothy Parker presented us with a gendered image of strain in her story 'The Standard of Living' (1936). In this tale, two young urban stenographers who styled themselves as flappers go window-shopping. Annabel and Midge do their best to look 'conspicuous, cheap and charming' in their attempt to project a glamorous and hedonistic image (Parker, 1936/1974: 30). Confronted with the cost of an expensive string of pearls, wholly unobtainable to them, their reverie is threatened.

Yet they soon compulsively retreat into their make-believe fantasy as millionaire consumers.

Postwar reconstruction and the American way of life

By the postwar period, functionalist sociology began to trumpet the stable harmony of American society, hailing the successes of America, land of democracy and prosperity. Talcott Parsons, doyen of functionalism, insisted on the indispensable role, in every stable social system, of attachment to commonly held values. By the 1960s, functionalist sociologies had developed reifying conceptions of social role. Merton and Parsons depicted a restrictive and deterministic role structure, in which people occupied rigid positions. Comment focused less on the possibilities of achieving the American Dream than on the 'American way of life' as the defence of democracy and freedom. Parsonian theory fitted well with the postwar socio-political reconstruction, hailing the advent of a fully modern pattern of values and organisational structure:

> The leading postwar sociologist, Talcott Parsons, expressed the period's highly optimistic beliefs about 'modernization', and his theories bore the imprint of the Pax Americana. He saw the United States as the 'lead society' or model for global development; backwardness would be overcome by convergence of communist regimes with the U.S.-led West and the universalization of the West's 'evolutionary breakthroughs'.
>
> (Antonio, 2000: 46)

A sense of uniformity pervaded US society, a homogenizing trend. The status quo was depicted as a virtue, and dissensus figured as wholly 'anti-American'. The Beat Generation, an anti-establishment nonconformist literary movement centred on Allen Ginsberg, Jack Kerouac and William S. Burroughs, rebelled against the alienating complacency of postwar America. The Beats celebrated underworld and Bohemian lifestyles, defiant of accepted moral codes, and proclaimed their disappointment with America's false hopes. Allen Ginsberg's raw angry verse in *Howl* (1955) expressed vividly the despair and anger of those unable or unwilling to fit into the world of straight jobs and traditional family values: 'I saw the best minds of my generation destroyed by madness, starving hysterical naked, dragging themselves through the negro streets at dawn looking for an angry fix'.

From the early 1960s, theorists like Erving Goffman and Howard Becker launched a critique of the power of state institutions and social control agents to make unnecessary intrusions into people's lives. Hostile social reactions and official interventions were thought to warp people's sense of self-identity and induce in them feelings of painful differentness.

Notes

1. For studies of Merton's work, see Mongardini and Tabboni (1998), Sztompka (1986), Gieryn (1980), Clark et al. (1990) and Crothers (1987).
2. For analyses of the anomie tradition in the understanding of crime, see Clinard (1964) and Messner and Rosenfeld (1997). For some contemporary developments in this perspective, see Agnew (1992), Passas and Agnew (1995) and Adler and Laufer (1995).
3. For further studies of gangsters and their representation in popular culture, see Yablonsky (1997), Murphy (1994), Shadoian (1977), and Bergreen (1995).
4. On Simmel's analysis of money and modern culture and personality, see Poggi (1993).

Chapter 5

Social reaction, the deviant other and the stigmatised self

There is only one complete unblushing male in America: a young, married, white, urban, northern, heterosexual Protestant father of college education, fully employed, of good complexion, weight and height and a recent record in sports.

(Goffman, 1963/1990: 153)

The labelling perspective, first developed in America during the 1960s, examined the role of societal reaction in the development of criminal and deviant behaviour. The criminalisation of behaviours that offended the tastes of others, and the attribution of stigmatising features to minority groups, were held to have a potent effect upon the self-definition and subsequent conduct of deviants. The negative societal reaction to certain kinds of behaviours and lifestyles was hence viewed as a process of victimisation. The proliferation of forms of cultural and social difference on the one hand threatened an established vision of social order that resided in a static notion of a unified culture, and on the other hand offered new opportunities for self-expression. Labelling theory was premised on the hope of a more tolerant and open liberal pluralist society. While the moralistic agendas of those who had the power to define were challenged, as Sumner (1994) explains, the tendency was not to subvert established structures of power but to modernise and rationalise them. The principal competing framework at the time was functionalist sociology. This advised the readjustment of deviants to ensure maintenance of the established equilibrium of the social system. Labelling theorists, however, saw the proliferation of forms of deviance as an index of healthy diversity, for instance as seen in David Matza's (1969: 17) comment that: 'we do not for a moment wish that we could rid ourselves of deviant phenomena. We are intrigued by them. They are an intrinsic, ineradicable, and vital part of human society.'

In 1938, the House Un-American Activities Committee was set up by the US Congress, continuing to operate for twenty years. After the Second World War, this body began to focus specifically on the exposure of alleged communists. By then, the Soviet Union was emerging as a threatening world power rather than just the origin of a competing ideology. Before the war, the activities of the committee were widely seen as absurd. However, in the climate of the Cold War, Americans wanted somebody to blame for the Soviet Union's rise to power. Republicans in particular had much to gain from depicting the New Deal as a dangerous flirtation with Communism, with its rediscovery of the American poor and socially conscious idealism. Former state officials were accused of engaging in espionage and other subversive acts decades previously, and 'made to justify their past life in the present hysteria' (Cooke, 1950/1968: vi). The USSR came to be perceived as a menacing enemy to American democratic traditions, and public opinion turned from 'mild suspicion, to alarm, then to implacable and feverish distrust' (Cooke, 1950/1968: 36). The Truman administration began to investigate the 'loyalty' of all Government employees, and the House Committee was given huge funding to pursue the 'un-American'. Media attention directed at the activities of the Committee was considerable. By the late 1940s, the USA was convulsed with fear and hatred of the Soviet Union. The conviction of Alger Hiss for perjury (and espionage by implication) in the late 1940s, as one observer put it:

> brought back into favor the odious trade of the public informer. It gave the F.B.I. an unparalleled power of inquiry into private lives. . . . It tended to make conformity sheepish and to limit by intimidation what no Western society worth the name can safely limit: the curiosity and idealism of its young.
>
> (Cooke, 1950/1968: 340)

From 1950, Senator Frank McCarthy commenced his paranoid anti-communist campaign, arousing suspicion and anxious silence. The climate of the time is exemplified by 'private eye' movies like those starring Humphrey Bogart, 'a disguised form of playing safe and the easiest parody of serenity available to the bewildered and the thoroughly scared' (Cooke, 1950/1968: 11). Erving Goffman's (1963/1990: 97) reference to 'the profusion of skeletons in people's closets' can be seen in this light. He discussed the difficulties of leading a double life, 'a life that can be collapsed at any moment' (Goffman, 1963/1990: 109).

This repressive climate was the polar opposite of the 1960s counterculture, which particularly developed among middle-class youth, who saw consumerism and conventional mores as stultifying and sought a non-materialistic, expressive and meaningful alternative. Rejecting the 'emotional containment of affluence' (Pearson, 1975a: 83), increasing numbers of young people celebrated cultural diversity and personal liberation, experimenting with alternative lifestyles. Responses of 'the mainstream' to alternative cultural styles ranged from incomprehension to outright hostility. With the lifting of the malign shadow of McCarthyism, it was now possible to engage in open criticism of official institutions and their agents. As the decade played out, people began to lose confidence in the ability and/or willingness of the government to address serious problems of poverty, class inequality and racism (Lilly, Cullen and Ball, 1995).

Explanations based in notions of socially disorganised neighbourhoods or blocked opportunities were not commensurate with these social and cultural changes. The time was ripe for the emergence of a new paradigm for understanding the unconventional. Stan Cohen (1973/1976: 12) described the new approach as a 'skeptical revolution', in opposition to a canonical tradition which had taken its concepts to be accepted and unquestionable. This older orthodoxy had assumed that crime was by definition bad because it was against the law, and that deviance was bad because it breached the norms. In the new approach, no behaviour was seen as inherently bad, because deviant status was construed as the product of the power to label. As John Kitsuse (1962: 248) explained, this approach 'requires that the sociologist view as problematic what he generally assumes as given – namely, that certain forms of behavior are per se deviant'. The self-evident and commonsensical notion that certain forms of behaviour were deviant in themselves prior to their ascription with a social meaning was now to be suspended.

A neo-Chicagoan appreciative stance

Labelling theorists can be located in the Meadian tradition of studying people from the standpoint of their own conception of reality. David Matza (1969: 17) called for an appreciative rather than a correctional stance, based on understanding the truth of the act for the actor himself. His perspective of 'naturalism' involved a commitment to phenomena themselves and not to science. It was premised on the idea that man is a subject and not an object. Matza described labelling theory as 'neo-Chicagoan' in respect of the commitment to participant-observer research.

The arguments put forward by labelling scholars reveal why it was imperative to get at people's own understandings of their worlds. Within labelling theory, the idea of a 'deviant career' was a processual notion, suggesting that the process of becoming deviant was a gradual one of the construction of a role and identity outside of conventional norms and expectations. The attribution of deviance was also understood to be interactional, with the application of a deviant label in interaction between rule-maker and rule-breaker. Scholars who wrote from the perspective of symbolic interactionism argued that through their participation in an encounter, people constructed meanings about both themselves and the others involved. Through this process, people constructed a symbolic world out of their own subjective version of social reality. Sometimes these interactions led to the application of a deviant label to some of the participants in the encounter. Those so labelled may come to see themselves in terms of this label, and labelling may also effect the way in which those labelled are treated by others in the future.

Labelling is a feature of everyday life. We label things in order to comprehend our social world. While labelling may be a customary facet of the ordering of social life, a number of theorists claimed that the processes of labelling were selective and biased. They pointed out that behaviour that breaches rules and norms occurs all the time, but only some of it comes to be officially designated as deviant. John Kitsuse (1962: 256) wrote that the differentiation of deviant from non-deviant was increasingly the product of contingencies of 'situation, place, social and personal biography, and the bureaucratically organised activities of agencies of control'.

A further claim was that processes of labelling often had detrimental effects. Agencies of social control were depicted as counterproductive, in the sense that they created more deviancy than they prevented. It was argued that institutions and agents whose purpose was the exercise of social control had a vested interest in identifying targets for their intervention. Furthermore, the concept of 'deviancy amplification' highlighted the paradoxically magnifying potential of the exercise of social control (Wilkins, 1964). The very operation of processes of social control might make people who engaged in unconventional acts more deviant. This amplificatory effect, as Lilly, Cullen and Ball (1995) pointed out, might well be unintentional; in any case, it was ironic.

In *Crimes Without Victims* (1965), Edwin Schur posited a reciprocal relationship between policy and problem. He argued that a policy might cause new problems, or exacerbate old ones. Schur paid particular attention to the criminalization of deviance. He wrote that the definition of behaviour as criminal was an extreme form of stigmatisation, and pointed up its deleterious effects, arguing that, 'criminal conviction – perhaps even prosecution – may automatically and retrospectively effect crucial modifications in a person's identity' (Schur, 1965: 5). Schur noted Harold Garfinkel's essay on status-degradation ceremonies, which had argued that these had profound effects on self-identity, as well as the perception of the deviant other:

> [T]he work of the denunciation effects the recasting of the objective
> character of the perceived other: the other person becomes in the eyes of
> his condemners literally a different and new person . . . the former identity
> stands as accidental; the new identity is the 'basic reality.' What he is now is
> what, 'after all' he was all along.
>
> (Garfinkel, 1956: 421–2)

Schur pointed out that just because a law does not prevent certain acts from occurring, it does not follow that it is without any effect or impact whatsoever. His work addressed the ways in which legal definitions and law enforcement policies influenced the development of certain problems.

Some work within the labelling perspective seems almost fatalistic, whereas other scholars emphasised the choice exerted by the individual deviant. Interactionist explanations, such as those produced by Erving Goffman, rejected the determination of external structures and celebrated the individual's capacity to choose actions and to organise social settings. They focused on people's abilities to manage deviant labels and on the forms and consequences of public labelling and exclusion. However, other scholarship almost seemed to render the deviant passive, leading Nanette Davis (1975) to comment that, 'The conception of stigma as the crucial process in creating and perpetuating deviant careers suggests Leviathan qualities of social control. Typifying deviants as passive receptors in an all-powerful social mechanism, labelling theory views actors as more acted upon than acting.'

A further difficulty concerned the kinds of crime and deviance that labelling scholars tended to discuss. The labelling perspective focused on behaviours and actions where sympathy was more readily evoked for the deviant than for the victim. Often these were crimes without victims, for instance marihuana use and homosexuality. In *Crimes Without Victims* (1965), Schur pointed out that these offences had no apparent harm to others, and were also marked by a lack of public consensus over their illegal character. This came to be recognised as a serious limitation. Could the same arguments and concepts be employed in the analysis of, for instance, the crime of rape? Siding with the deviant might mean accepting as more authentic the deviant's version of his reality, in opposition to the version promulgated by the official line. It might also mean revalidating as either progressive or innocuous some actions conventionally defined as unacceptable or even pathological.

Theorising tagging, secondary deviance and stigma

The three principal scholars upon whose work labelling theorists explicitly drew were Frank Tannenbaum, Edwin Lemert and Erving Goffman. In *Crime and the Community*, Tannenbaum (1938: 19–20) had stated that the process of defining a youth as deviant began in a conflict between the youth and his community over the definition of a situation. He explained that some activities that the youth saw as adventure and fun were defined by the community as delinquent or evil. Over time, and with the continuing conflict over the definition of activities, the attitude of the community towards the youth hardened, and the youth as well as his acts began to be seen as evil. Tannenbaum argued that this process produced changes in the manner in which people interacted with the youth, who began to feel isolated and conscious of community views about him. He explained that people tended to view youths who broke the law as evil, abnormal and clearly differentiated from the law-abiding person. This argument led him to make the following assertion:

> [T]he process of making the criminal is a process of tagging, defining, identifying, segregating, describing, making conscious and self-conscious; it becomes a way of stimulating, suggesting, emphasising, and evoking the very traits that are complained of. . . . The person becomes the thing he is described as being . . . The way out is through a refusal to dramatise the evil. The less said about it the better.
>
> (Tannenbaum, 1938: 20)

This non-interventionist proposal was echoed in some of the policy implications that emerged from the labelling perspective, for instance as seen in Edwin Schur's (1973) slogan 'leave the kids alone whenever possible'.

Edwin Lemert told his readers in *Social Pathology* (1951) that he viewed deviance as but one aspect of social differentiation. He famously reversed the older conception that deviance leads to social control, writing that:

> Older sociology . . . tended to rest heavily upon the idea that deviance leads to social control. I have come to believe that the reverse idea, i.e., social control leads to deviance, is equally tenable and the potentially richer premise for studying deviance in modern society.
>
> (Lemert, 1967: v)

Lemert made an important distinction between primary and secondary deviance. Primary deviance, Lemert argued, designated the committing of a prohibited act. He held that this was ubiquitous, with most people's deviance remaining unlabelled, so they did not develop a deviant self-image. Secondary deviance, he contended, was behaviour produced by being placed in a deviant role. The concept of 'secondary deviance' hence described the effect of other people's reactions upon a person's self-image. For Lemert, social reaction turned situational deviance into systematic deviance, in the form of a process of the symbolic reorganisation of the self. He therefore described secondary deviance as follows:

> deviant behavior or social roles based upon it, which becomes a means of defense, attack, or adaptation to the overt and covert problems created by the societal reaction to primary deviation.
>
> (Lemert, 1967: 17)

This definition pointed up the importance of social reaction not only in defining deviance initially, but also in structuring its further development. Furthermore, Lemert held that social reaction bore little necessary relation some arguments about the 'social information' that individuals directly conveyed about themselves to others. He argued that the routines of social interaction established a framework of anticipations upon which the social identity of strangers was made meaningful, these anticipations becoming normative expectations. For Goffman, these expectations took the form of righteously presented demands, of which people were not usually aware because they operated in a tacit way. He explained that our assumptions about how people would, and should, conduct themselves, produced a virtual social identity that we imputed to the newcomer: 'norms regarding social identity . . . pertain to the kinds of role repertoires or profiles we feel it permissible for any given individual to sustain' (Goffman, 1963/1990: 82). Goffman explained that signs of the stranger possessing a negative attribute which differentiated him from others in the category to which we had assigned him reduced him in our minds from a whole and normal person to a tainted one. He clarified his idea by stating that he was concerned with undesirable attributes that were incongruous with the accepted stereotype of what an individual should be.

Goffman (1963/1990: 17) wrote it was possible for an individual to be protected by identity beliefs of their own, but commented that it was a pivotal fact that 'the stigmatised individual tends to hold the same beliefs about identity that we do'. This awareness of what others saw as a failing gave rise to pain and shame. Goffman wrote that persons with a stigma were considered less than fully human, and subjected to all manner of forms of discrimination which reduced their life chances. The stigmatised individuals that he discussed included homosexuals, the disabled and former mental patients. The book was concerned with 'mixed contacts', by which Goffman designated those moments when the stigmatised and the normals occupied co-presence. Goffman differentiated between the situation of the discreditable, whose stigma was not known to others, and the discredited, whose stigma had been revealed to or discovered by others. He argued that the discredited had to manage tension during social contacts, whereas the discreditable had to manage information about their failing. Goffman presented a convincing picture of the price of tolerance, of 'phantom acceptance'. He explained that what was seen as the 'good adjustment' of the stigmatised individual was of importance to normals because 'it means that the unfairness and pain of having to carry a stigma will never be presented to them; it means that normals will not have to admit to themselves how limited their tactfulness and tolerance is; and it means that normals can remain relatively uncontaminated by intimate contact with the stigmatised, relatively unthreatened in their identity beliefs' (Goffman, 1963/1990: 146–7).

Goffman explained that persons with a particular stigma tended to share similar learning experiences and changes in conception of self, which he termed the 'moral career'. This moral career was also powerfully influenced by institutional contexts as well as the accidents of life. In *Asylums*, he emphasised how the organisational structure of the total institution to the primary deviant act committed, often being either spur disproportionate.

Erving Goffman, in a number of beautifully crafted and sensitive showed his readers how perceptions and projections of social wc erated as a mode of social control. Goffman's work was directec level of what he termed the interaction order (that is, the level tions between the acts of persons in face-to-face co-presence). His provided detailed accounts of the dynamics of interpersonal ence and revealed in the form of general principles and illustrative v the kinds of norms regulating co-presence. These norms took tl of tacit ground rules establishing the grounds upon which acto municated. His approach drew upon the symbolic interactio George Herbert Mead, who had depicted the self as situation: socially anchored. This perspective can be seen in Goffman's de of the self as not a property of the person to whom it is attribu rather dwelling in the patterns of social control exerted in cor with the person by himself and those around him.

Goffman's kind of symbolic interaction developed a notion of vidual as a dramaturgical actor, performing and displaying aspect as well as providing the audience to the acts of others. This per suggested that persons spent much of their time framing their from the view of other people. The ideas of 'frontstage' and 'bạ developed by him conveyed an image of how selves were pai in terms of self-presentations before various audiences. Tony argued that this was not a view of people as cynical manipulato cooperating to protect both interaction and others' displaye Goffman argued for the prominent role of embarrassment, or cipation of it, in every social encounter. He discussed the probl occurred when the normal spatio-temporal segregation of audienc down and previously undisclosed aspects of a person's identity haviour were glimpsed by others. Furthermore, he described ho tially discrediting information was controlled and managed by tl an interest in preserving the smoothness of interaction.

Merton and Parsons had depicted a restrictive role structu employing notions of strain and conflict to indicate stresses and ties in a limited number of situations, which they theorised as dist to normal functioning (Chriss, 1999). Goffman however empl idea of 'role distance' to designate the quite frequent instances people placed a distance between their actual self and their cur in-role. In his approach, although social roles were confining, role distance people exercised a relative freedom. For Goffn dilemmas arose more frequently for more people than fun sociology seemed to suggest. He depicted the difficulties encoui people with the masks that they were required to wear.

In *Stigma*, Goffman (1963/1990) looked into the situation of vidual who was disqualified from full social acceptance, and d and the dominant ideologies of the mental hospital shaped the self of the mental patient as a process of mortification. Famously, he argued that mental patients suffered not from mental illness, but from 'contingencies', by which term he meant the actions of others (Goffman, 1961: 135).

Goffman argued that it was not appropriate to restrict the analysis to those persons who manifested Lemert's 'secondary deviance', writing that 'the most fortunate of normals is likely to have his half-hidden failing, and for every little failing there is a social occasion when it will loom large' (Goffman, 1963/1990: 152). This led him to assert that there was a continuum of the occasionally and the constantly precarious. He explained that most people fell short at some time of the common value-system in America, writing that 'there is only one complete unblushing male in America: a young, married, white, urban, northern, heterosexual Protestant father of college education, fully employed, of good complexion, weight and height and a recent record in sports' (Goffman, 1963/1990: 153). Following this line of thinking, stigma management was a general feature of society. The analysis therefore departed considerably from Merton's linking of social stratification, the American Dream, strain and 'innovation'. For Goffman, everybody felt the pressure of social expectations, although some people did more often than others.

Labelling others as outsiders

The name most associated with the labelling perspective is that of the Californian sociologist Howard Becker. In *Outsiders* (1963), Becker asserted that the question of who could impose their rules on others was one of political and economic power. He was overtly critical of crushing conformity, commenting that people were always forcing their rules on others. The opening statements of the book acknowledged the cultural relativism of moral indignation. Becker explained that when a rule was enforced, the person who had breached it might be regarded as an outsider, a special kind of person who could not be relied upon to live according to the rules agreed upon by the group. He pointed out that the person labelled an outsider might have a different perception of what was going on and hence look upon those who judged him as outsiders. He stated that some rule-breakers subscribed to the very rules they had broken and did not feel that their judgement was unjust, whereas others developed elaborate ideologies to validate their activities and depict their disapproval and punishment as wrong. He offered traffic violators as an example of the first kind of rule-breaker, and homosexuals as the second.

This recognition of diverse values, beliefs and behavioural codes, is evident in Becker's chapter on jazz musicians. This was based on his participant-observer research as a musician in Chicago. Becker explained the musicians' use of the derogatory term 'square' to denote outsiders to their world. He wrote that the square was perceived as an ignorant and intolerant person, to which jazz musicians opposed a view of themselves as 'hip'. Jazz musicians, Becker contended, thought that they were both different from and better than other people. This led them to believe that they should not have to be bound by conventional controls. Behaviour flouting conventional norms was hence greatly admired in jazz circles.

Becker stated that in failing to question the label of 'deviant', social scientists accepted common-sense assumptions that deviant behaviour resulted from some characteristic of the individual which made it inevitable, as well as accepting the values of the group making the judgement. He argued that this took for granted the situations and processes of judgement. Becker described as simplistic the statistical view of deviance as a quantifiable departure from what is most common, because it ignored questions of value. He criticised the conception of deviance as pathological and indicative of a diseased state, noting the lack of agreement on what constituted healthy behaviour. In support of these points, Becker referred to C. Wright Mills' paper 'The Professional Ideology of Social Pathologists' (1943). In this essay, Mills had related the concepts used in the study of social disorganisation to the social background of its scholars. Whether this was the essence of the work of Park and Burgess or not (and Mills did not indict them by name), the field of social pathology had taken a conservative turn. He commented that social pathologists tended to originate from small towns or farms. The influence of Charles Cooley on their work, Mills claimed, further entrenched the desire to preserve rurally oriented values, as for Cooley: 'all the world should be an enlarged, Christian-democratic version of a rural village. He practically assimilated "society" to this primary group community, and he blessed it emotionally and conceptually' (Mills, 1943: 175). This perspective, Mills wrote, enshrined an ideal of intimacy, and elevated middle-class morality in its implicit conception of the adjusted person living out Protestant ideals in small town America. As a 'hip' musician, Becker evidently did not associate his worldview with this narrowmindedness.

Becker commented that the use of medical metaphors as analogies by which to depict behaviours such as homosexuality and mental illness also obscured the significance of the processes of judgement, referring to Szasz's *The Myth of Mental Illness* (1961) and Goffman's *Asylums*. Furthermore, he criticised functionalist sociology's concern with stability and its disruption, for employing notions of health and disease. The goals of a group, Becker insisted, were decided in political conflict between factions with opposing definitions of the group's function. Purposes and aims were not given in the nature of organisation.

Writing that deviance is created by society, Becker gave what has emerged as one of the classic statements of the labelling perspective:

> [S]ocial groups create deviance by making the rules whose infractions constitute deviance, and by applying those rules to particular people and

labelling them as outsiders. From this point of view, deviance is *not* a quality of the act a person commits, but rather a consequence of the application by others of rules and sanctions to an 'offender.' The deviant is one to whom the label has successfully been applied; deviant behavior is behavior that people so label.

(Becker, 1973: 9)

This viewpoint emphasises that it is not the distinctive quality of the behaviour itself that is the decisive factor; a response to the rule-breaking is what is of significance.

Becker noted that the degree of social response to a given act varied considerably. He mentioned the phenomenon of 'drives' or what we might call crackdowns or clampdowns, in which officials decide to enforce a rule more concertedly for some time. Becker pointed out that modern societies did not demonstrate a simple organisation in which there was a consensus on what rules should exist and how they should be applied. He stated that rules were differentiated in terms of social class, ethnicity, occupation and culture. Unlike Goffman, Becker believed that 'the perspectives of the people who engage in the [deviant] behaviour are likely to be quite different from those of the people who condemn it' (Becker, 1973: 16). Deviants might feel that they were having rules forced upon them which they did not accept. Becker argued that rules for youth were made by adults, those for women by men, those for blacks by whites, those for foreigners and ethnic minorities by WASPs, and those for the lower class by the middle class. This led him to state that rules created and maintained by labelling were 'the object of conflict and disagreement, part of the political process of society' (Becker, 1973: 18).

Becker introduced the concept of the moral entrepeneur, a person who engaged in organised activity to enforce a rule or alter the moral constitution of society. He cited the role of the Federal Bureau of Narcotics in producing public awareness that marihuana was a problem as an instance of moral enterprise. Rules, Becker argued, rarely applied themselves; rather, they had to be continually reinforced. He explained that the moral entrepeneur might well have humanitarian motives, and stated that the crusading reformer was the prototype.

Becker believed that labels such as 'deviant' and 'criminal' were so stigmatising that they came to constitute what he called the 'master status' of the deviant, overriding any other role, position or self-conception that the individual might exercise or hold. The fact of the assigned label, once it is known, becomes much more important to people than any other known characteristics or activities of the individual. The master status of deviant becomes a defining one both for self-identity and social identity. The labelled individual begins to be excluded from conventional interactions, and is engulfed by the criminal role. The labelled person, Becker held, moves into a deviant group, which provides him with rationalisations, motives and attitudes that support deviant behaviour. Becker's relativistic view is summed up in his advice that we see deviance as 'simply a kind of behavior some disapprove of and others value' (Becker, 1963: 176).

Marihuana, policing and the fantasy crime wave

Jock Young's *The Drugtakers* (1971) demonstrates how labelling theory arguments and concepts were taken up and employed to critical effect in Britain. Young advanced an argument about how the societal reaction to marihuana smoking had a deviancy amplification effect, summed up by the idea that adverse reaction 'welds marihuana into the backbone of the subculture'. Young contended that certain fantasy stereotypes of the drug-taker were reinforced by police and judicial action, as well as proliferated by the mass media. His description of the production and maintenance of this stereotyped view of the marihuana smoker also involved a criticism of how some extant criminological theories colluded with this process. Young argued that the social world was segregated less in terms of distance than in terms of meaningful contact. He stated that the stereotypical drugtaker–drugseller relationship depicted in the mass media was based in absolutist notions of society, which assumed that most individuals share common values and agree on what is conformist and what is deviant. This could only cast the deviant as a fringe phenomenon consisting of psychologically inadequate individuals who live in socially disorganised or anomic areas. Following this line of reasoning, the majority societal response served to deny the legitimacy of alternative norms and the reality of conflicts of interest.

Young argued that the cumulative effect of intensive police action impacted on the social world of the marihuana user in such a way that some aspects of the stereotype began to become reality. The drugtaking community, according to Young, united in a common sense of injustice at harsh sentences and media distortions, producing theories to explain their social position. In this process of increasing cohesion and the development of explanatory ideas, the sense of being a group with definite interests outside those of mainstream society was heightened. Young wrote that at some point there began an 'ossification' of deviancy and explained that the further the drugtaker evolved deviant norms, the less the chance there was of him re-entering the wider society. With increasing police concern and action, marihuana smoking became more secretive and of greater importance to the group 'as a symbol of their difference and of their defiance against perceived social injustices . . . marihuana comes to be consumed not only for its euphoric effects and as a sign of membership of an exclusive bohemian elite, but as a symbol of rebellion against an unjust system.'

Young described how a particular 'fantasy crime wave' was built up. According to his account, the mass media fanned up public indignation over marihuana use, pressure to take action increased on the police, and the police acted more vigilantly, making more arrests. With this intensified police action, the statistics for marihuana offences soared. The public, press and magistracy, were alarmed by the new figures and called for even more action on the part of the police . . . and so the spiral went on. Young held that police action not only produced the exclusion of the marihuana smoker from mainstream society, but also caused changes in the content of bohemian culture. He identified a likely 'spiral of theoretical misperceptions and empirical confirmations' resulting from the tendency of policy makers to mistake the changes caused by societal reaction for verification of their presumptions about the essential nature of the drugtaker.

Whose Side Are We On?: the political commitments of partisan sociology

One effective way of enquiring into the political commitments of the labelling perspective is to re-stage what is known as the Becker–Gouldner controversy. In 1967, Howard Becker made an address with the title, 'Whose Side Are We On ?' The following year, Gouldner focused on this essay as part of his critique of the labelling theorists.

Becker opened his essay by noting the considerable disagreement between those sociologists advocating neutral, technically correct and value-free research, and those who argued that scholarship was shallow and pointless if it did not express a deep commitment to a value position. Becker claimed that this was a false dilemma, for the reason that all research was contaminated by personal and political sympathies. This led him to state that, 'the question is not whether we should take sides, since we inevitably will, but rather whose side we are on' (Becker, 1967: 239). Becker explained that partisan sociologists were accused of showing too great a sympathy with the subjects of their studies, and indicated the divergence of perspective as follows:

> [W]hile the rest of society views them as unfit in one or another respect for the deference ordinarily accorded a fellow citizen, we believe that they are at least as good as anyone else, more sinned against than sinning.
>
> (Becker, 1967: 240)

He described the existence of a 'hierarchy of credibility', by which he meant the assumption that members of the highest group had the right to define the way that things really were. Refusing to accept the view promulgated by these 'superordinates', Becker explained, expressed disrespect for the entire established order. According to him, most sociologists were politically liberal. As he put it, 'we usually take the side of the underdog' (Becker, 1967: 244). Becker went on to ask whether the inevitability of taking sides meant that such distortion was introduced as to render scholarship useless. His answer was that this could be avoided by marking clearly the limits of what had been studied. This, he explained, involved a clear statement of one's vantage point.

In 1968, Alvin Gouldner published an essay criticising partisan sociology, and especially what he saw as the Becker school's glib rejection of the myth of neutrality. Gouldner's argument was essentially that Becker might ostensibly side with the underdog, but his views were really those of the liberal Establishment of America. Gouldner wrote that the Becker school found itself at home in the 'cool world' of hip, drug addicts, jazz musicians and drifters. Their orientation to the underworld, he explained, not only involved studying it but also speaking on its behalf. Gouldner wrote that while Becker might side with the underdog, he also had an attachment to his own self-interest. Put differently, Becker was also on his own side, for instance, he had the provenance of research funding to consider. Furthermore, Gouldner stated that Becker's bland prose style ironically conveyed detachment. He claimed that while Becker invited partisanship, he also rejected it, creating a myth of the purely cerebral social scientist who was devoid of emotional commitment. As Gouldner pointed out, this assumed that passion only produced costs, and overlooked the possibility that it could serve to enlighten and sensitise.

Gouldner wrote that Becker's approach assumed that good liberals would instinctively recognise the true underdogs. He wished to clarify the grounds of Becker's commitment to the underdog, writing that: 'A commitment made on the basis of an unexamined ideology may allow us to feel a manly righteousness, but it leaves us blind' (Gouldner, 1968/ 1973: 34). Gouldner pointed out that an underdog standpoint contributed to better sociology because it brought to public view various underprivileged aspects of social reality. He explained that these aspects were unknown or neglected because they departed from the conceptions of reality of the powerful and respectable.

Gouldner wrote that there was no special virtue in being powerless, because neither weakness nor power were values to be prized in themselves. For him, the suffering of the underdog was what should make a compelling demand upon the sociologist. Sociologists, he suggested, bore a responsibility to understand and to communicate the suffering of the underdog, especially given that much of their plight might be avoidable. Instead of either bias or complacency, Gouldner seemed to suggest that the researcher could take a kind of middle position. Gouldner complained that the suffering of the deviant was not what involved the Becker school with the underdog. While he found their rejection of the smug narrowness, bigotry and ethnocentrism of the small-town middle-classes valuable, he accused the partisan sociologists of being guilty of romanticising and exoticising their subjects:

> [T]heir pull to the underdog is sometimes part of a titillated attraction to the underdog's exotic difference . . . equivalent to the anthropologist's

(one-time) romantic appreciation of the noble savage . . . Becker's school of deviance is redolent of romanticism. It expresses the satisfaction of the Great White Hunter who has bravely risked the perils of the urban jungle to bring back an exotic specimen. It expresses the romanticism of the zoo curator who preeningly displays his rare specimens. And like the zookeeper, he wishes to protect his collection; he does not want spectators to throw rocks at the animals behind the bars. But neither is he eager to tear down the bars and let the animals go. The attitude of these zookeepers of deviance is to create a comfortable and humane Indian Reservation, a protected social space, within which these colourful specimens may be exhibited, unmolested and unchanged.

(Gouldner, 1968/1973: 37–8)

Gouldner strongly criticised the passivity of the deviant represented in Becker's theory. He wrote that while this might win them sympathy and tolerance, the deviant was viewed as 'not man-fighting-back . . . but rather, man-on-his-back' (Gouldner, 1968/1973: 39). In casting the deviant as a victim, a product of society rather than as a rebel against it, partisan sociology did not study political deviance, for instance the actions of protesters in the civil rights or peace movements. Gouldner commented that Becker's perspective produced a picture of the underdog as mal-treated by a bureaucratic establishment. Partisan sociology was essentially a critique of the low-level officialdom that managed the caretaking insti-tutions of society. The critique was not directed at the master institutions of society. As Gouldner pointed out, Becker might have acknowledged that most of his fellow sociologists were liberals, but he failed to address the consequences of their position. Gouldner commented that this un-examined and comfortable liberalism explained the complacency of the partisan sociologists. He argued that partisan sociology's discrediting of local officials was quite compatible with the new welfare state. Liberal-ism, Gouldner stated, was by this time 'the well-financed ideology of a loosely organized but coherent Establishment' (Gouldner, 1968/1973: 55). Partisan sociology was – despite its 'cool' image – embedded in the lib-eral Establishment.

Becker gave a response to a number of the criticisms made of partisan sociology in 'Labelling Theory Reconsidered' (1973). He wrote that criti-cisms of labelling theory had come from all political persuasions. Labelling theory, he reported, had been accused of espousing unconventional norms as well as refusing to support anti-establishment positions, or even appear-ing to support anti-establishment causes while subtly favouring the status quo. Interactionist theories had been seen as 'corrosive of conventional modes of thought and established institutions' (Becker, 1973: 197), and depicted as mischevious or subversive. This work had also been the ob-ject of attack from the Left. Against this, Becker set out to reassert that labelling theory had a critical thrust. He admitted that interactionist studies of deviance focused on lower-level officialdom, but argued that this im-plied the casting of doubt on higher authorities, who were responsible for their subordinates. Becker gave two principal reasons why the inter-actionist approach should be considered radical. Firstly, he asserted that by studying the actions of moral entrepreneurs, labelling theory violated society's hierarchy of credibility:

> They question the monopoly on the truth and the 'whole story' claimed by those in positions of power and authority. They suggest that we need to discover the truth about allegedly deviant phenomena for ourselves, instead of relying on the officially accepted accounts which ought to be enough for any good citizen.
>
> (Becker, 1973: 207)

Becker's other argument for interactionism's radicalism concerned how it worked to demystify the respects in which those in power ruled in part by obfuscation. Geoff Pearson (1975b) argued that Gouldner had not made the radicalising effect of partisan sociology intelligible, writing that:

> Misfit sociology enables the social scientist to do the impossible: remain a social scientist within a theoretical mood which is highly suspicious of academicism; engage in deviance-welfare concerns despite radical opposition to much welfare ideology; engage in action which appears 'relevant' whilst maintaining distance from traditional and 'discredited' political channels.
>
> (Pearson, 1975b: 163)

The labelling perspective brought a major challenge to the epistemo-logical assumptions of the theories of crime and punishment of its day. It also provoked complex questions about the political engagement of the intellectual. However, Gouldner's critique of its unexamined assumptions still stands. Three decades later, Ngaire Naffine (1997) expressed a num-ber of feminist criticisms of partisan sociology, writing that while their methods gave voice to male deviants, the women who featured in the work were not similarly enabled. She explained that if women appeared in la-belling perspective accounts, it was only as the objects, and never as the subjects, of knowledge. Naffine objected that Becker's concern with the offender's standpoint did not produce any re-evaluation of the feminine. She noted that while Becker himself was an unorthodox American male in a number of respects, he was highly orthodox in his views of women. Becker's project of rendering visible the worldview of the male offender, she argued, came at the cost of the continuing exclusion of woman, or the perpetuation of negative stereotypes of the feminine. In *Outsiders*, for instance, women were represented as symbolising the ties of conventional life, and were depicted as the unimaginative drudges of domesticity. They were the very epitome of 'square'. Noting Gouldner's critique of Becker, Naffine supplemented this with a gesture to the specifically gendered character of Becker's vision: 'we might add, in feminist vein, that Becker was the great white *male* hunter whose romantic flirtation with deviant culture had much to do with his own style of masculinity' (Naffine, 1997:

41). The Marxist perspectives that distanced themselves from labelling theory largely replicated this unwittingly gendered vision.

From stigmatisation to criminalisation

The decade of the 1960s was a tumultuous one, with major challenges to the basic assumptions of the postwar order, and numerous protests against the established institutions of Western democracy. The times occasioned a crisis in social thought, which seemed to call for a paradigm revolution, a wholly new way of looking at things (Gouldner, 1971). With the easing of the active repression of intellectuals, artists and leftists that had crippled critical scholarship during the 1950s, the climate was more favourable to subversive work. The emergence of mass insurrection and dissent gave rise to analysis of the processes by which political acts were redefined as unlawful. Furthermore, this iconoclastic challenge to the establishment took the form of a politicisation of the meaning of crime itself.

The labelling perspective had been concerned with human diversity, and developed an appreciative stance towards crime and deviance. In the 1970s, radical approaches were advanced, which claimed that the labelling perspective, with its liberal-pluralist model of society, could not accommodate questions of power. Radicals criticised its limitations and unspoken assumptions. However, radical criminology did retain the concern with societal reaction, incorporating this into an analysis of class conflict. The concern now was less with stigmatisation (the effect of discrimination and bias) than with criminalisation (the use of the criminal law by the ruling class to further its ends). It now became a mantra that the act of labelling was not just a matter of value judgements and contingencies, but an important strategy of capitalist rule.

Some of the points of departure can be seen in an influential critique of the labelling perspective published by Alexander Liazos (1972). This pointed out three major ideological biases in labelling theory, that according to Liazos obscured the unjust character of the system and the persistence of conditions of inequality:

1. The very focus on the identity and subculture of the deviant defeated the stated aim of demonstrating that the deviant was not different from us.
2. The crimes of the elite had been neglected.
3. Despite claims to the contrary, the sociology of deviance did not explore the role of power in the designation of 'deviance'.

Liazos opened his essay with a reminder of C. Wright Mills' critique of the field of social pathology (1943), which had argued that due to their social backgrounds and moralities, the scholars of 'social disorganization' had been blind to fundamental problems of social structure and power. This, he claimed, had led them to propose ameliorative, piecemeal reforms as the solution to various 'social problems'. Liazos held that despite the new perspective of labelling theory, questions of power remained absent. He felt that the small-town morality had ostensibly gone, with labelling theorists not considering the phenomena that they studied to be necessarily harmful. However, he contended that a moralistic tone still lurked beneath the disavowals. Furthermore, Liazos held that the focus remained on the individual deviant and the problems that he represented to himself and others, rather than on broader social, historical, political and economic contexts.

Liazos pointed out that the continuing use of the term 'deviant' with its many pejorative connotations, belied statements about the equality of deviants. He cited Thomas Szasz's comments about how the term 'deviant' was rarely used to designate somebody who departed from the norm in a way that was socially validated. For instance, a Nobel Prize winner was not usually censured as deviant on account of their unusual success. He pointed out the omission from critical scrutiny of the crimes of the corporate economy and the state's acts of violence, writing that:

> Reading these authors, one would not know that the most destructive use of violence in the last decade has been the war in Vietnam, in which the U.S. has heaped unprecedented suffering on the people and their land. . . . Moreover, the robbery of the corporate world – through tax breaks, fixed prices, low wages, pollution of the environment, shoddy goods, etc. – is passed over in our fascination with 'dramatic and predatory' actions.
>
> (Liazos, 1972: 107)

Liazos objected that the unethical, illegal and destructive acts of those who were often respected members of the community, and did not come to be labelled as deviant, were overlooked. He wrote that the political and economic system thrived on violence, employing an expanded meaning of the notion of violence:

> [A] person can be violated by a system that denies him a decent job, or consigns him to a slum . . . or manipulates him through the mass media . . . covert institutional violence is much more destructive than overt individual violence. We must recognize that people's lives are violated by the very normal and everyday workings of institutions. We do not see such events and situations as violent because they are not dramatic and predatory . . . but they kill, maim, and destroy many more lives than do violent individuals.
>
> (Liazos, 1972: 111–12)

Liazos criticised the concentration on the deviant at the expense of the agents of social control, commenting that studies of prison subcultures ignored the conditions that lead to imprisonment and writing that:

[O]nly now are we beginning to realize that most people are political prisoners – that their 'criminal' actions (whether against individuals, such as robbery, or conscious political acts against the state) result largely from current social and political conditions, and are not the work of 'disturbed' and 'psychopathic' personalities.

(Liazos, 1972: 109)

He explained that this new understanding of the term 'political prisoner' arose largely as a result of the writings of political prisoners like Malcolm X. Furthermore, Liazos noted that it was not just a few 'radicals', but actually a large number of prisoners, who had developed a consciousness of their imprisonment as political.

Occasional references to the larger social and political structure were seen in labelling theory analyses, but Liazos complained that there was no detailed or deep analysis of these issues. He stated that the focus instead fell on the deviant's problems, motives, acquaintances, and other personal factors. Liazos noted the labelling theorists' interest in the agents of social control and the power to impose labels. However, like Gouldner he criticised their concentration on lower and middle level agents like policemen instead of the ruling institutions and groups. He pointed out that the police were doing somebody else's work. Liazos closed his essay by advising that 'we should banish the concept of "deviance" and speak of oppression, conflict, persecution, and suffering' (Liazos, 1972: 119). This suggestion was taken up by radical criminologists from the 1970s.

Chapter 6

The state, the ruling class, and crime

The extension of law has created new criminals, criminals who are no longer so readily identifiable with the stereotypical 'criminals' or 'delinquents' of orthodox 1950s criminology – the disaffiliated or disorganized urban working-class adolescent. The population at risk of criminalization is much more ambiguous and extensive, including not only the criminologist himself, but also the spokesmen and membership of the oppositional social, political and economic movements at large.

(Taylor, Walton and Young, 1975: 2)

The year 1968 was a particularly momentous one, and is now widely taken as symbolic of the global political radicalism of the era:

Nineteen sixty-eight was an attempt to create a new world, a new starting point for politics, for culture, for personal relations . . . a time for asking questions of authority. A time to first challenge and then break all taboos: political, social and sexual. What was striking was the speed with which ideas of liberation spread throughout the world.

(Ali and Watkins, 1998: 7–8)

The events of May 1968 in Paris occupy an especially privileged place in the memory of this year. French students acted collectively against their perception of the university as a dehumanising and impersonal know-ledge factory. At a revolt by students in the Parisian suburb of Nanterre, repressive measures were taken against the protesters. A series of violent clashes between demonstrators and police culminated in the Night of Barricades. On the night of 10 May, after a peaceful demonstration, stu-dents and youths occupied an enclave in the Latin Quarter and built up barricades, the symbol of the insurrectionary power of the people. The police employed brutal methods to clear them out. Hundreds were injured and several died. A large part of the organised working class of France came out in solidarity with the students. Events snowballed into a general strike involving 10 million workers, that paralysed the country and threatened to topple de Gaulle's government. The memory of May '68 is one of a collective spirit of communication and action that bravely opposed the forces of conformism and attacked hierarchical structures.

In the USA, Columbia University students occupied a number of buildings on campus. The New York City police cleared them out violently, beginning a sustained period of national campus unrest. The University came to be seen as an agent of an oppressive state. Students opposed authoritarian and bureaucratic structures with a call for self-determination. Their protests were a highly visible indication of a rising tide of disenchantment and dissent among young people, increasingly hostile to conservative values and institutions. In London, Ronny Laing, Juliet Mitchell and others, opened the 'Anti-University', declaring their intention to oppose the intellectual bankruptcy and spiritual emptiness of contemporary state-sponsored education.

Martin Luther King, Jr's assassination in 1968 was marked by the most widespread racial violence in American history. Civil disorder erupted in over a hundred cities, expressing the rage and despair of blacks. At the Olympic Games in Munich, two sprinters raised a Black Power salute as the national anthem of the USA was played in honour of their victories. Black communities accused the FBI of encouraging hard drugs and armed gangsterism in an effort to depoliticise and split the ghettos. Violent racism was also seen in other countries. In Britain, Enoch Powell called non-white British citizens a 'national danger'. Over the Channel, a right-wing demonstration in support of de Gaulle directed anti-Semitic feeling against the student leader, Daniel Cohn-Bendit, with chants of 'France for the French' and 'Cohn-Bendit to Dachau'.

Mass-based activism and dissent was also seen in the emergence of the anti-nuclear movement and anti-Vietnam protest. For the young, thermonuclear weapons were not only perceived as a 'specific threat to the future', but were also 'symbols of the general truth of the present: their radical lack of control over the forces governing their lives' (Anderson, 1965: 10). Televised images of counter-attacks following the Têt Offensive in Vietnam in 1968 brought graphic evidence of the savagery of the conflict into people's homes. Massive destruction was wrought with carpet bombing, napalm, mortars, rockets and nausea gas. Worse still perhaps, in the My Lai Massacre, an officer oversaw the events as his GIs shot women, children and old men, raped women and mutilated corpses. The involvement of university research with the military provided one focus for student protest against the Vietnam war in the USA. An interesting depiction of student protests against Vietnam, as well as the repressive policing of them, can be seen in *Born On The Fourth Of July* (Stone, 1989, Universal). This film narrated the painful disillusionment of a wounded GI, played by the actor Tom Cruise. Yet the initial fury of the soldier against anti-Vietnam protestors as cowards and traitors to their country turns into an empowering indictment of the murderous nation that had found him so expendable. The USA increasingly came to be seen by its own citizens as well as other commentators as an imperialist bully, fast losing any legitimacy as a defender of democracy. Students burnt their draft cards and chanted 'Hey, hey, LBJ, how many kids did you kill today?' For a vocal and expanding sector of the population, slaughtering people whose views differed from one's own, and the massive expenditure on the development of Doomsday weapons, occasioned a sickening insight into the brute aggression of advanced capitalism:

> The intimate relationships between military expenditure, the great corporations and 'big government', within what President Eisenhower called 'the military–industrial complex', became the object of political agitation. C. Wright Mills (1956, 1969) argued that these echelons of power formed a 'power elite', which had become an 'irresponsible history-making institution' in the dangerous conditions of nuclear stalemate. The policies of this 'power elite' – in welfare, law-making, foreign investment and military policy, power relations pursued on a global scale – ceased to be viewed as naturally benign. America, the paradigm case of 'pluralistic affluence' in the 1950s, had become, by the end of the 1960s, a society which some commentators described as verging towards social disintegration.
>
> (Hall and Scraton, 1981: 464)

A profusion of forms of dissent challenged the complacently hierarchical social order of Western states, with their valuing of deference and conformity, and hostility to difference and criticism. All over the world, protest movements struggling to radically change societies engaged in a creative explosion of activism.

Radical scholarship received a renewed impetus. Much of this identified itself as grounded in Marxism, Marx having written that 'to be radical is to grasp things at the root' (Marx, 1971: 137). Broadly, Marxist approaches were concerned with explaining the capitalist mode of production and social formation, and working towards its replacement by a society based in the redistribution of wealth (and hence power). Marxists revealed the ways in which the powerful used resources like the law to achieve and maintain their dominance. On this view, understanding crime and the societal reactions to it merited a sophisticated comprehension of the political economy of advanced capitalism. Radical criminologists had broader concerns than merely solving the 'crime problem', having a normative commitment to the abolition of inequalities of wealth and power. Thinking about crime was seen by them as vital to the quest for a more just and equitable society. The intelligentsia were conceived as the catalysts to revolutionary change. Intellectuals could expose the contradictions riven into the structure of capitalist society, which were necessary to its continued existence, but also rendered it potentially unstable. Education and scholarship were thus conceived as a political practice, and a vital site at which counter-discourses could be mobilised.

Three major claims emerged from radical theories of crime and punishment:

1. Criminalisation was central to the maintenance of the capitalist social order.
2. Criminals were political revolutionaries who had seen through the inequalities of their class position.
3. There had been an emphasis on working-class instead of ruling-class crime, which must be reversed.

Linked to these three claims was the indictment of previous criminological theories for colluding with the status quo, in effect for legitimating social engineering:

> Critical scholars refused to practice criminology as an auxiliary discipline to criminal law enforcement, and saw it as their task to examine the functioning of the criminal justice system as an instrument of the state to keep power relations as they are.
>
> (van Swaaningen, 1997: 79)

In a reaction against functionalist models of society, Marxists rejected theories that explained social phenomena and institutions in terms of their cohesive functions within an interconnected, socio-cultural system.

Radical criminologists published works that sought to take into account the significance of certain structural dimensions of social existence upon crime and criminalisation. This chapter looks into works that addressed the significance of class-based relations of power and inequality. Marxist criminology was both a materialist criminology and a working-class criminology. It was materialist in that it foregrounded the significance of the differential ownership of the means of production in industrial capitalism in its explanatory schema. It was a working-class criminology in the sense of what Bankowski, Mungham and Young (1977: 42) called 'a criminology *of* and *for* the working-class'.

The New Left and deviance-marginality

The intense political and cultural turbulence of the period between 1968 and 1975, with its new political sensitivity, brought a new range of theoretical tools and forms of action. Radical scholarship was very much part of what has been called the 'New Left'.[1] This was a movement which sought to regenerate Marxism as a revolutionary critical force, by means of a re-interpretation of Marxist theory. It took the form of a reaction against the determinism of orthodox Marxism and its resurgence. New Left scholars referred to the early writings of Marx in order to emphasise the aspect of alienation rather than that of exploitation. They also combined Marxism with some theoretical concepts and arguments from existentialism and psychoanalytic theory. For the New Left, socialism was not to be restricted to political and social revolution, but must also eliminate the alienation felt by the individual. Cultural transformation was as important as social and political change.

The approach of the New Left can be described as a humanistic Marxism, in that it was based on a recognition of the political disfigurement of the human subject under the alienating forces of advanced capitalism. Their ideology was based on freedom from repression, and was hence influenced by some neo-Freudian ideas as well as Marxist ones. An important source of ideas for the New Left was found in the work of the Frankfurt Institute of Social Research, or 'critical' school. This group, which included Theodor Adorno, Max Horkheimer and Herbert Marcuse, had originated in pre-war Germany and fled from Nazi persecution to the USA in 1934. Their work sought to elucidate the manipulation of consciousness. In his book *One Dimensional Man* (1972), Marcuse published a critique of alienated existence in the postwar world of affluence and conformity. According to him, the majority of people were not conscious of the need for revolution. As Marcuse (1968) stated plainly, what was sought at this time was liberation from an affluent society rather than from a society of scarcity. Postwar Western states went through a period of unparalleled economic prosperity and stability in the 1960s and 1970s. This was a time in which the material needs of more people could be met, more often, than had hitherto been the case. As Marcuse explained, in such conditions, the struggle for liberation did not have a mass basis. The majority of oppositional forces were integrated into the system through various mechanisms of manipulation, indoctrination and repression. Marcuse argued that the negation of conditions of servitude required as a prerequisite the abolition of the institutions and mechanisms of repression. Authentic liberation, he insisted, could only be achieved on this basis. He contended that repression had pervaded to the deepest roots of individual existence. In his socialist utopia, the liberation of human sensibility and sensitivity would induce a collective transformation of the human environment that would remove all that currently effected the mutilation of the human organism. Marcuse stated that the affluent late capitalist state spread aggression and suppression throughout the globe. He wrote that the new possibilities of freedom were met by an unparalleled aggression, which he saw as a violent defence of comfortable servitude. This aggression of the affluent society, he suggested, was seen in its inflation of the image and power of the enemy. The Ku-Klux-Klan issued a death threat against Marcuse, whose work was widely seen as one of the principal inspirations behind the student revolts of the 1960s.

The New Left also drew upon continental European philosophy, and in particular the existentialist theses of the French philosopher Jean-Paul Sartre. Sartre's work seemed important to some scholars because it foregrounded questions of freedom, action and responsibility. Although he was later to retract or qualify some of the ideas that he propounded in it, Sartre's lecture of 1945 'Existentialism and Humanism' is a lucid exegesis of key dimensions of his thought. In this lecture given in Paris, Sartre explained the key proposition that 'existence precedes essence' to mean that man was nothing else but what he willed and what he made of himself. Man, Sartre mused, was a series of undertakings, whose life was to be understood within a philosophical viewpoint that produced an ethics of action. This ethics was needed because 'we cannot decide a priori what it is that should be done' (Sartre, 1945/1980: 49). For Sartre, man was his own judge, and must always seek to surpass himself if he was to realise his full humanity.

Marcusan and Sartrean concepts and arguments provided a set of tools for critically engaging with the notion that the social order, as currently constituted, was the negation of human freedom. For those wanting to develop critical theories of crime and punishment, these ideas gave their work a political validity, as well as supplying to them a number of key explanatory concepts and arguments. The humanistic aspect of radical criminology can be seen in its recognition of human diversity, and its understanding of deviance as an expression of individual uniqueness. A vision of a healthily pluralist society in which self-expression would be fostered was advanced. Deviance was hence understood as a mode of emancipation from a warping, conformist, culture. Crime and deviance were reframed as political practices of refusal or dissent to repression. This approach sometimes seemed to suggest an anarchistic celebration of disorder, with rules and consensus viewed as crushing the creativity of the human soul. Radical criminology had both a resonance, and in some cases direct links, with the liberation movements of this period, for instance the gay liberation movement, the women's liberation movement and the anti-psychiatry movement. These new social movements aimed for a free human existence, seeking to revalidate what had been stigmatised, criminalised, and medicalised. They also signalled a reassessment of who the revolutionary agents were, beyond the industrial proletariat, and how they could be mobilised.

Irving Horowitz and Martin Liebowitz (1968) published an essay, 'Social Deviance and Political Marginality', that received considerable interest from critical scholars. These two American sociologists noted that the times brought a blurring of the customary distinction between personal deviance and political marginality. Their classic essay described how New Left politics merged with social deviance. This process was occurring because political marginals were adopting deviant lifestyles, at the same time as social deviants were becoming more politically aware. Horowitz and Liebowitz saw the rise of guerrilla style tactics, and the civil disobedience of race riots, as key instances of the merging of deviance and politics, as 'deviance-marginality'. They explained that the Old Left had disapproved of deviance, having had a Puritan ethos concerning sexual mores, and prioritising politics over personal life. The New Left, however, held to an ideology of freedom from repression and demonstrated positive affect towards a libertarian ethos. This, Horowitz and Liebowitz claimed, involved a positive response to deviant and marginal groups. The hero for the New Left was thus not the working class man, but the alienated man who sought his emancipation from external constraints.

Horowitz and Liebowitz noted that the boundary between political behaviour and personal deviance was obliterated in the student protest movement, with its celebration of deviance in the face of a system which had robbed the young of their right of self-expression. The strategy, they wrote, was one of disrupting the workings of the machine rather than taking control of it, through non-participation and non-acceptance. All of these actions demonstrated a rejection of conventional political styles. Horowitz and Liebowitz (1968) argued that the convergence of social deviance and political marginality gave rise to a new politics in which the use of violence became a legitimate strategy. Stan Cohen (1973/1976) wrote that distinctions between protest, unrest, dissent, and delinquency, had in the past seemed a common-sense way of understanding the world. These had also been employed by criminologists to describe different forms of violence. However, as Cohen explained, the emergence of new forms of unrest and massive civil disobedience in the USA showed that these distinctions were based on ideological positions. This led Cohen to posit that 'the distinction between the criminal and ideological cannot be taken for granted' (Cohen, 1973/1976: 108). Tony Platt (1975: 98) wrote that 'the most imaginative criminology has been written by criminals', and included in his list black militants like Eldridge Cleaver, Angela Davis and George Jackson.

The Black Power movement expressed a new kind of racial consciousness among blacks in the USA in the 1960s. It moved away from the goal of integration and away from the practice of non-violent methods of struggle towards armed resistance. The new black politics was conceived as a revolutionary struggle against racism and imperialism. The idea of Black Power originated in the SNCC (Student Nonviolent Coordinating Committee), which had been founded in 1960 by black college students aiming to overturn segregation. In 1966, Stokely Carmichael took over leadership of SNCC and made it a blacks-only group. In the same year, the Black Panther party was founded in California, a more self-consciously militant political organisation. In Carmichael's address of 1967, he identified the system to be overthrown as that of international white supremacy and international capitalism. For Carmichael, rejecting the definitions imposed by white Western society was the first step towards black liberation. He stated that the West used force to impose its culture on the colonised. Carmichael told his audience that non-whites came to imitate Western ways, and explained that in the present day there was a deadly fight for cultural integrity. The anger of Carmichael's position comes across clearly in his statement that whites were in no position to give independence, and could only learn to stop oppressing blacks. Carmichael depicted the ghettos of US cities as the result of identical patterns of white racism, calling these 'internal colonies' (Carmichael, 1968: 161). He linked capitalism with racism, stating that the struggle for Black Power did not seek to replace white rulers with black rulers, seeing capitalism as exploitative by nature. Carmichael described the 'young bloods' of the black proletariat as the true revolutionaries, who saw relentless hatred of the white enemy as the basis of fight by any means.

Black revolutionaries like Eldridge Cleaver (1967/1972) often cited the work of Frantz Fanon and Malcolm X in support of the idea that blacks could only achieve manhood through revolutionary political struggle. Malcolm X joined the Nation of Islam while serving ten years' imprisonment for burglary. A recent film about him opened with footage of the police beating blacks to the soundtrack of Malcolm X's highly-charged speech:

> I charge the white man with being the greatest murderer on earth. . . . There is no place in this world that that man can go and say he created peace and harmony. Everywhere he's gone he's created havoc. Everywhere he's gone he's created destruction. . . . He can't deny the charges. You can't deny the charges. We're the living proof of those charges. You're not an American; you are a victim of America. Being born here doesn't make you an American. . . . You and I, we've never seen democracy; all we've seen is hypocrisy. We've never seen the American dream. We've experienced only the American nightmare.[2]

Commenting on Fanon's *The Wretched of the Earth*, Cleaver (1967/1972: 45) stated that, 'what this book does is legitimise the revolutionary impulse to violence'. The Black Panthers spread the message that black people must 'arm themselves against a racist country that was becoming increasingly repressive' (Cleaver, 1967/1972: 33–4). They insisted that the oppressor had no rights which the oppressed were bound to respect. Black urban guerrillas dreamed of liberating black communities with the gun, abolishing police power over black people.

This incendiary climate forced many critical intellectuals to reconsider their positions. As Stuart Hall (1974) pointed out, the emergence of mass politics brought a vocal and visible challenge to Parsonian sociology. Scholarly journals saw heated polemics, meetings were disrupted by protests, and presidential addresses were interrupted. Yet radical scholarship was not simply equivalent to radical politics. The relations between the two were far from obvious, and hence deeply controversial (Becker and Horowitz, 1972).

Normal alienation, war, and the violence of modern society

The anti-psychiatry movement sought to bring radical innovation to the conventional practice of psychiatry. A New Left approach can be seen in the claim that psychiatry functioned to exclude and repress those elements society wanted excluded and repressed. The arguments advanced produced a convincing illustration of the processual character of the attribution of deviance. Furthermore, sometimes the claim was made that madness was a breakthrough that was a form of political protest. Simply put, the anti-psychiatry movement, which involved psychiatrists, patients and activists, saw the practice of psychiatry as a damaging process of labelling. They argued that psychiatric diagnosis was scientifically meaningless, a way of labelling socially undesirable behaviour. The attribution of mental illness, and the 'treatment' of those called insane, were seen as invidious political acts. In anti-psychiatry and the criticisms directed at it, we see prefigured problems that were to emerge in some radical criminology.

The New Left understanding of alienation was developed to great effect by both Ronny Laing and David Cooper. They saw alienation as endemic to modern society, and as arising from the violence done by people to others. For Cooper, the most immediate forms of alienation arose from the class division of a society in which murder could be seen as an act of compliance with a murderous system. He used the example of the murder of the Manson family at the height of the Vietnam War to assert that crime was a form of obedience to capitalist social organisation. For Cooper, what conventional psychiatrists and popular opinion called 'madness' was a move towards disalienation.

In the preface to the 1965 edition of *The Divided Self*, Laing argued that alienation was the normal condition, because the so-called normality in which people lived was schizoid. Dishonest interaction between people meant that the way of interacting was itself a disease. Drawing on existentialist ideas, Laing contended that people were pushed towards schizophrenia when their relationships with others forced them to live more according to their false than their true selves. Laing referred to the Cold War, racism and the arms race as examples of the madness of so-called normal life, writing that:

> A man who prefers to be dead than Red is normal. . . . A man who says that Negroes are an inferior race may be highly respected. . . . A little girl of seventeen in a mental hospital told me she was terrified because the Bomb was inside her. That is a delusion. The statesmen of the world who boast and threaten that they have Doomsday weapons are more dangerous, and far more estranged from 'reality' than many of the people on whom the label 'psychotic' is affixed.
>
> (Laing, 1965/1975: 11–12)

Laing (1968) maintained that the apparent irrationality of the individual labelled as psychotic became intelligible once seen within the context of the irrationality of the family, and that this in its turn should be placed within the context of larger organisations and institutions. He stated that the complete enclosure of the subject of madness within a medical metaphor was depersonalising, removing the patient from the social context without which his behaviour could only be seen as mad. Laing saw psychiatric practice as institutionalised violence. He described the horrifying brutality of the Vietnam War as a normal manifestation of the normal state of affairs, an instance of collective paranoid projective systems that were a manifestation of the spiral of alienation in which everyone was trapped.

The *Report From Iron Mountain* was published in 1966, accompanied by claims that it was a leaked secret report of a group asked by the US government to determine the nature of the problems that would confront the US in the eventuality of world peace. Whether it was indeed the report of a state-appointed study group or a clever hoax, it is a telling and chilling sign of the times. The anonymous writers of the report stated that its war-making potential was the principal structuring and stabilising force in US society, hence a transition to world peace threatened unparalleled changes. This led them to question whether the abolition of war was desirable in terms of social stability. They described the war system as crucial to people's allegiance to a society through their acceptance of an external menace. The authors of the report also claimed that war legitimised the institution of the police, which it described as 'armed organizations charged expressly with dealing with "internal enemies" in a military manner' (Report from Iron Mountain, 1966/1968: 72). The bland amorality of the report seems to offer much support for Laing's and Cooper's linkage of alienation, paranoia and violence. Regardless of its true authorship, it is revelatory of the brutal, complacent and bureaucratic mindset opposed by the New Left. The normal insanity of brutal capitalist imperialism was represented in the film *Apocalypse Now* (Ford Coppola, 1979), with its enduring image of helicopters flying through the dawn to the tune of Wagner's 'The Ride of the Valkyrie', armed with napalm bombs. As Colonel Kurtz, memorably played by Marlon Brando, put it, 'we train young men to drop fire on people. But their commanders won't allow them to write fuck on their airplanes because its obscene.'

Some participants in the anti-psychiatry movement presented mental illness as a creative form of deviance, a bold yet painful choice. Laing, for instance, made a case for psychotic experience as a reflection of another actuality concealed by the mystifications of modern civilisation; as a form of breakthrough from normalised repression rather than a 'breakdown'. In *The Death of the Family*, Cooper (1971/1973) criticised the bourgeois nuclear family as an ideological conditioning device, performing a crucial social mediating function by which it reinforced the power of the ruling class in an exploitative society. He (1971/1973: 12) described normality as 'the sorry fate of most of us', and described the role of the family in inducing conformity. Cooper argued that the 'normal', obedient citizen was so estranged from their spontaneous impulse to action that one might as well regard them as out of their mind. He (1971/1973) stated that most people made little effort to resist repression, submitting with little dissent to 'this chronic murder of their selves'. Cooper's understanding of normal alienation led him to suggest that the understanding of 'madness' should be transformed into 'an extension of awareness rather than being a source of frightened victimization of a minority' (Cooper, 1971/1973: 58). Cooper explained that for him revolutionary acts were those by which the individual transcended his conditioning, in the direction of the spontaneous self-assertion of full personal autonomy. He insisted that personal liberation was a prerequisite to macro-political action, by which he meant actions that rendered the bourgeois power structures impotent. Without this necessary movement towards freedom, alienation produced terrible effects. This led him to comment that, 'the bourgeois state is a tranquillizer pill with lethal side-effects' (Cooper, 1971/1973: 35).

Critics of anti-psychiatry retorted that mental illness was a devastating experience for both the sufferer and their relatives and friends. They complained that the anti-psychiatry writers were romanticising and glorifying pain. Commenting on Laing's approach to schizophrenia, one critic took an admonitory tone:

> Some people do learn valuable things from abnormal experiences; some even escape from the coils of the system but many, probably most, are wretched. . . . I regard this kind of weird, surrogate vampirism of another's terrible experience as being gravely immoral.
>
> (Warrington, 1973: 15)[3]

However, the assertion that mental illness was meaningful action helped to bring important changes in the practices of psychiatry.

The National Deviancy Conference

The National Deviancy Conference (NDC) was a group of sociologists and criminologists who challenged the aims and theories of British criminology, criminal law and penal policy, and existed between 1968 and 1979.[4] The aim was to establish an umbrella organisation which might include activists in radical social work, the anti-psychiatry movement, and the radical penal lobby. The NDC held a series of symposia, from which five volumes of papers were published (Cohen, 1971; Taylor and Taylor, 1973; Bailey and Young, 1973; National Deviancy Conference, 1980; Fine et al., 1979). A recent retrospective from one of the key members of the NDC describes the general approach taken:

> Positivism was perhaps the main enemy: its ontology was seen to take human creativity out of deviant action, its sociology erected a consensual edifice from which deviants were bereft of culture and meaning, its methodology elevated experts to the role of fake scientists discovering the 'laws' of social action and its policy, whether in mental hospitals, social work agencies or drug clinics, was self-fulfilling and mystifying.
>
> (Young, 1998: 17).

An important strategy was the criticism of the fundamental concepts and perspectives of earlier theories of crime and deviance. As Taylor and Taylor (1968) argued in their essay 'We Are All Deviants Now', much deviancy theory was based in a conservative theory of values. They objected that strain theory took the existing society for granted and that labelling theory left aside questions of whose interests the definers represented, as well as the ways in which their actions reinforced the nature of capitalist society.

Probably the best-known product of the NDC was the controversial book *The New Criminology*. Published in 1973, this book has often been described as a 'watershed' in critical thinking about crime. Its authors, Ian Taylor, Paul Walton and Jock Young, stated that a major reappraisal was forced by the conditions of the time. Among these, they drew attention to the criminalisation of vast numbers of middle-class youth for hedonistic and/ or oppositional offences, and the failure of the institutions of the state to disguise their inability to adhere to their own rules and regulations. This state of affairs, they argued, called for a political economy of criminal action, as well as of the social reaction to it. Taylor, Walton and Young made overt their intention to politicise what were generally being taken as technical issues. Against the predominantly pragmatic, atheoretical and correctional orientation of mainstream criminology, the authors announced their commitment to a 'normative criminology'. This would assume the form of a socialist criminology insistent on the need to eradicate social and economic inequalities. *The New Criminology* radicalised labelling theory by going beyond the identification of stereotypes, and the development of purportedly truer descriptions of the social worlds of deviants, to demand a profound transformation of existing social arrangements:

> The task is to create a society in which the facts of human diversity, whether personal, organic or social, are not subject to the power to criminalize.
> (Taylor, Walton and Young, 1973: 281–2)

From this normative stance, the authors criticised earlier criminological theories, making the bold claim that, 'any criminology which was not normatively committed to the abolition of the inequalities of wealth and power was inevitably bound to fall into correctionalism' (Taylor et al., 1973: 281). The critique of social reaction developed in labelling theory became a strategic anti-correctionalism. The authors believed that the advent of a socialist society would bring a celebration of diversity without the need for criminalisation, hence raising the utopian figure of a future crime-free society. John Muncie (1998) explained that *The New Criminology*'s oppositional stance signalled the transformation of criminology from a science of social control into a struggle for social justice. As Paul Walton (1998) put it, the radical textual strategy of *The New Criminology* 'seeks to produce a community of readers who are wedded to social change' (Walton, 1998: 4).

The New Criminology advanced a voluntaristic argument as to how deviance was chosen, writing that not only was deviance a conscious choice, it was also a political one. The central tenet of labelling theory, that 'deviance is not a quality of the act the person commits' (Becker, 1963: 9), was opposed by radical theorists. They objected that action took place in a world that was not free of social meanings that actors were aware of. The focus of labelling theorists on the definitions arising in the minds of others, they suggested, had overlooked the significance of the choices made by individuals to engage in deviant acts. As Paul Walton noted, the radical approach involved a considerable shift in focus 'away from the view of the deviant as a passive, ineffectual, stigmatised individual (what Gouldner has called 'man on his back') towards that of a decision-maker who actively violates the moral and legal codes of society' (Walton, in Taylor et al., 1973: 163). The deviant actor of radical theories was hence 'a creative, but purposeful, deviant who consciously decides to transgress law and order' (Walton, in Taylor et al., 1973: 163). In this new view, deviance was construed as a challenge to authority and as predetermined by structural inequalities. These structural inequalities were held to prevent actors from pursuing their interests except by deviant means. This led Walton to claim that, 'much deviancy – both "political" and "non-political" – must be viewed as a struggle or reaction to normalized repression' (Walton, in Taylor et al., 1973: 163).

A critique was made of the Marx and Engels relegation of crime to the 'dangerous classes' or *lumpenproletariat*, as a falsely conscious, demoralised response of defeated people to oppressive economic conditions. The term *lumpen* means 'rags and tatters', and *lumpig* can be translated as 'shabby'. Marx and Engels tended to characterise the *lumpenproletariat* as a rabble who were immune to historical transformation. They insisted that this bunch of scoundrels were not the active agents of political struggle, sharply differentiating them from the true proletariat, or working class. The *lumpenproletariat* were depraved, passive individuals with a propensity to crime and no trade, who were parasitical upon society. The Russian anarchist Mikhail Bakunin believed that the *lumpen* were the vanguard of revolutionary action. However, he later castigated himself for his romanticisation of the outcast. Franz Fanon, however, insisted upon a transvaluation of the *lumpenproletariat*, writing that they threw themselves into the struggle against colonialism. Radical criminologists preferred this view, depicting deviance as a struggle against normalised repression, a breaking through from accepted and taken for granted rules that distorted the positive potential of the human species.

Radical criminology and the romanticisation of crime

The very idea of a radical criminology was subjected to vociferous criticism in a number of respects. The criticisms already made of anti-psychiatry were levelled at radical criminology. Taking up an oppositional stance to institutions and structures that were believed to exploit and harm people did not provide an automatic guarantee that one was acting in the best interests of the oppressed. Furthermore, the iconoclastic utopianism of radical politics did not follow the established canons of sober academic practice. The explosively creative atmosphere of May '68 had produced slogans like 'Be realistic – demand the impossible'. To the extent to which it breathed of this heady air, radical criminology left itself open to the charge of failing to produce reasoned argument. As might be expected, advocates of objective, 'scientific' approaches found radical criminology particularly anathematic, responding with hostility to its indictment of correctionalism.

Criticism came from all corners. Socialists themselves were not convinced about the possibility and desirability of a radical criminology. Could radical criminology claim any authority from the Marxist tradition? For Karl Marx and Friedrich Engels, crime might be an inevitable effect of capitalist economic conditions, but criminal behaviour was not associated by them with class consciousness. This led Paul Hirst to deny any possibility of a Marxist criminology. He decried the attempt made by Taylor, Walton and Young to identify criminals as political heroes, writing that:

> The romanticisation of crime, the recognition in the criminal of a rebel 'alienated' from society, is, for Marxism, a dangerous political ideology. It leads inevitably . . . to the estimation of the lumpenproletariat as a revolutionary force.
>
> (Hirst, 1975a: 218)

Hirst (1975b) reasserted Marx's identification of crime with a non-productive *lumpenproletariat* or 'social scum' of no interest with regard to the revolutionary socialist struggle.

Paul Rock (1973: 103) criticised what he saw as the 'romanticism which views all criminals as primitive innocents who are engaged in inarticulate political conflict with institutional authority'. He insisted that the political status of an activity was derived from the meaning that it had for the participants. Elliott Currie asserted that *The New Criminology* offered little guidance as to how one might identify progressive forms of deviance, objecting that: 'an approach that can't distinguish between politically progressive and politically retrogressive forms of deviance doesn't provide much of a basis for real understanding or political action' (Currie, 1974: 139).

Bankowski, Mungham and Young (1977) saw Taylor, Walton and Young's vision of radical criminology as unconvincing, arguing that they had not demonstrated its superiority over other genres of criminology. Furthermore, they suggested that the approach was limited to 'a reification of personal moral outrage at the manifest inequalities of capitalist societies' (Bankowski et al., 1977: 38). Bankowski and associates wrote that for

Taylor, Walton and Young, the role of criminology lay in mapping the contours of repression in capitalist society, and that the working class emerged in this approach as the primary repressed group. This had led Taylor, Walton and Young to formulate an express politico-practical purpose for their critical criminology in helping to transform society. This notion of critical criminology, Bankowski and co-authors suggested, seemed to endorse its belief in the superiority of Marxism over other social philosophies by reference to its concern with practical activity. However, they pointed out, positivism also evinced this concern, although for different reasons. Bankowski, Mungham and Young proceeded to state that Taylor, Walton and Young had assumed their own radicalism rather than demonstrating it, ultimately failing to produce a convincing set of arguments as to how their critical criminology was subversive. In summary, Bankowski and co-authors (1977: 49) felt that Taylor, Walton and Young had only achieved a 'privatised and limited conception of what socialist diversity can mean'. The libertarian utopianism of radical criminology was perhaps of greatest benefit to radical scholars themselves:

> [T]he criminology of liberation aims at freeing criminology from its
> dependence on the powers that be so as to make it available for the
> purposes of revolution. But then who does the criminology of liberation
> *actually* liberate? Only, I suspect, the conscience of the critical criminologist.
>
> (Pavarini, 1994: 45–6)

Radical criminologists and legal scholars had seen the law as in essence 'bourgeois law'. A number of complex debates ensued, concerning the precise relationship between the state, the ruling class and the legal order. Just how did law protect the interests of the ruling class? Some accounts almost seemed to suggest a conspiracy theory explanation. Against this view, the historian and activist E.P. Thompson, best known for his book *The Making of the English Working Class*, presented a number of publications that mounted a defence of the institutions of British liberalism from a number of dangerous encroachments (see Thompson, 1980):

> On the left, he observed a tendency to dismiss 'bourgeois legality' as a mere
> façade behind which the manipulative rule of power and money went on
> unabated. On the right, he discerned a growing authoritarianism in British
> society, in the 'Official Secrets Act', the political screening of juries, the
> spread of wiretapping, and the manufacture of consensus by 'a compliant
> press [and] a managed television'. Both these tendencies, left and right,
> contributed to an erosion of precious civil liberties – liberties rooted in
> historic struggles for democratic self-rule and without which his own vision
> of a new democratic spirit would become meaningless.
>
> (Bess, 1993: 26)

In *Whigs and Hunters* (1975) Thompson presented a detailed study of the 'Black Act' (9 George 1 c.22). This statute, enacted in 1723, created at a blow fifty new capital offences. It specified the death penalty for various offences of hunting, poaching and damaging or destroying property, while armed and with a 'blacked' face, and especially on royal land. Thompson commented that before the eighteenth century, a comprehensive armoury of death had not been employed to defend property. He argued that the displacement of authority was the real emergency that had occasioned the framing of this bloody statute. However, his study led him to challenge the Marxist-structural critique of law as reductionist. Thompson rejected its simple formulation of law = class power, arguing that his historical study produced a more complex and contradictory picture. He indicated his agreement with some elements of the Marxist-structural critique, for instance that law was the site of conflict, and that in some respects it served the interests of the ruling class. However, he pointed out that the ruled employed law to fight for their rights. The ruled, Thompson insisted, also took up the rhetoric of the '"free-born" Englishman" with his inviolable privacy, his habeas corpus, his equality before the law' (Thompson, 1975: 264). Thompson also stated that while the powerful might make the rules, they were also bound by them, and hence law functioned as a curb to absolute power. Put simply, saying that class relations were mediated by the law was not the same thing as saying that the law was no more than that. Thompson insisted that the law had its own characteristics, its own history and its own logic of evolution. He argued that while law was central to the purchase on power of the eighteenth-century gentry, it was inherent in the nature of law that it could not be reserved for their exclusive use. He noted the interesting paradox that law brought power within constitutional controls at the same time that it enhanced its legitimacy and also inhibited revolutionary movements, and advised readers that:

> I am insisting only upon the obvious point, which some modern Marxists have overlooked, that there is a difference between arbitrary power and the rule of law. We ought to expose the shams and inequities which may be concealed beneath this law. But the rule of law itself, the imposing of effective inhibitions upon power and the defence of the citizen from power's all-intrusive claims, seems to me to be an unqualified human good.
>
> (Thompson, 1975: 266)

In summary, Thompson's arguments sought to demonstrate that it could not be assumed that the law benefited only the powerful.

Mainstream criminology dismissed radical criminology as 'ideological', in the process of doing so disavowing its own ideological nature. Leon Radzinowicz depicted radical criminology as blinkered, writing of Marxist theorists of crime and punishment:

> They have distorted and diminished the impact of their message by their vivid exaggerations. In their anxiety to interpret crime simply as part of the whole spectrum of deviance they have blurred important distinctions,

resorted to misleading analogies. The radicals have felt bound not merely to question but to contradict all that has gone before. . . . They have overstated the heterogeneity of social values, ignoring the large measure of consensus, even amongst the oppressed, in condemning the theft and violence that makes up the bulk of traditional crime. They have postulated an irreconcilable opposition between 'law and order' on one hand, and 'human rights' on the other, blinding themselves to the genuine functions of law, police and courts in safeguarding people's rights. And they have indulged in exaggerated hopes of human nature, been over-optimistic about what society will tolerate, either now or in the future.

(Radzinowicz and King, 1977/1979: 87)

A stern reprimand indeed. Radzinowicz characterised radical criminology as extreme. Perhaps radical criminologists would mischeviously retort that conventional criminology was extremely dull! Radzinowicz suggested that radical criminology was an attitude towards crime and not an explanation of it. He hinted that radical criminology's 'extremism' arose from its iconoclastic wish to achieve maximum impact. He did not pause to consider the processes through which conventional criminologies constructed their own credibility. His comment that Marxist criminologists had not taken the extent of consensus about crime among the poor seriously enough did hit a more important note. Two different responses to this question can be seen among left-wing scholars, as will now be discussed.

Left intellectuals, crime and policy research

From the late 1970s, an acrimonious dispute between self-styled 'left realists' and a number of other critical criminologists emerged. Far from being simply an internecine dispute, this debate raised important questions about the role of the intellectual. These questions were not new, but became more pressing as crime and punishment emerged as increasingly politicised issues. The 1970s saw increasing unemployment, labour unrest, falling standards of living, and the emergence of law and order campaigns as a response to a sense of crisis. Crime became swiftly a major focus of right-wing rhetoric and policy-making. Among left-wing scholars, two divergent ways of engaging with these circumstances may be discerned. These were left realism, and the critical analysis of modes of rule.

Left realism was particularly developed by Jock Young, Roger Matthews, and John Lea.[5] Its advocates explained that it was principally inspired by three problems, which can be summarised as follows:

1. Feminist criticisms about how radical criminologists had been disinterested in the victims of crime.
2. Local criminal victimization surveys which suggested that crime among the lower classes was a considerable problem. This suggested a movement away from the focus on ruling-class crime seen in radical criminology.

3. Frustration at the continuing inability of the left to influence crime and penal policy as well as a concern that the law and order agenda was being hijacked by the new right in the late 1970s.

Some radicals felt that certain aspects of their critical enterprise required re-examination. This is the sense in which the self-styled 'left realists' gave radical criminology (including their own previous work of this kind) the denigratory epithet of 'left idealism', a retrospective portrayal that van Swaaningen (1997: 201) pointed out was 'crude and simplistic'. Substantively, the argument was that crime and its effects must be taken seriously. They produced a particular picture of the 'reality of crime', for instance writing that crime is:

> [T]he run-down council estate where music blares out of windows early in the morning; it is the graffiti on the walls; it is aggression in the shops; it is bins that are never emptied; oil stains across the streets; it is kids that show no respect; it is large trucks racing through your roads; it is always being careful; it is a symbol of a world falling apart.
>
> (Lea and Young, 1984: 55)

In their earlier revolt against correctionalism, Taylor, Walton and Young had condemned the unquestioning relationship of orthodox criminology with the extant social order, which according to them: 'could see part of its task as the effective management of intervention and reform in the penal system on behalf of existing social arrangements' (Taylor et al., 1975: 7). They insisted that the knowledge produced by radical theory was intended for the use of those involved in struggles for change. Scholarship, they wrote, must go beyond mere description to find ways of 'changing the world whilst investigating it' (Taylor et al., 1975: 24). Radical criminology, Taylor and co-authors had assured their readers, would not be an adjunct of the forces of social control, instead feeding back research into political practice. Their attempts to resist collusion with an exploitative status quo left them open to the charge of having done little to engage with and change it.

Geoff Mungham wrote that the shortcomings of radical criminology were part of a broader inability of the Left to produce any persuasive solutions to the nation's problems:

> [T]he radical criminology of Taylor et al. seems to have almost nothing of policy or prescriptive value to contribute toward the more immediate and urgent debates about the nature of criminal justice policy in Britain and, more generally, about the possibility of developing, as Cohen (1979: 49) puts it, 'middle-range policy alternatives which do not compromise any overall design for fundamental social change.' Their silence on these issues is more than deafening, it is also dangerous. To do nothing, or merely to brush off these concerns as 'reformist' or as dragging us into yet more correctionalist traps, is only to give over the field to the Right and to general reaction.
>
> (Mungham, 1980: 29)

Taking on board some of these criticisms, left realists embarked upon a dual strategy of on the one hand attacking right-wing criminologies, and on the other advancing an alternative view of the nature and causes of crime. Unfortunately, the particular ways in which they did so meant that left realists engaged less with social movements than with electoral achievements (van Swaaningen, 1997: 197). They persistently challenged the reactionary works of right-wing theorists such as Wilson (1975) and Murray (1990).[6]

Left realism resurrected elements of social democratic theory, in a 'return to a Mertonian analytical and political perspective' (Pitch, 1995: 42). The central concept of left realism was that of 'relative deprivation' (Lea and Young, 1984), which related discontent to the perception that one was deprived in comparison to comparable others, engendering a sense of unnecessary injustice. According to Lea and Young, the mass media disseminated a standardised lifestyle, and mass state secondary education had raised the minimum expectation, producing an 'excess of expectations over opportunities'.

In left realism, there was the claim that surveys were social democratic instruments that should guide policy-making. Two of the principal of these were the Islington Crime Surveys (Jones et al., 1986; Crawford et al., 1990). However, as Stan Cohen suggested, left realism did not iron out the difficulties in relating politics, theory and policy, writing that, 'I am uneasy about the triumphalist narrative of realism – with its impatient dismissal of sceptical questions as a romantic hangover from the past, a distinction from the demands of "confronting crime"' (Cohen, 1998: 11). On her part, Pat Carlen (1998: 66) criticised the populism of left realism and its appeal to global and moralistic notions of individual responsibility. As she pointed out, the assumption that common sense understandings of crime were non-problematic implied that an 'easily recognisable reality' exists that was accessible through empirical research (Carlen, 1992: 59).

One of the claimed stimuli of the left realist approach was the feminist insistence that the victims of crime must not continue to be overlooked. However, Alison Young and Peter Rush (1994) criticised the left realist invocation of the concept of the universal victim to establish a common concern about crime. They wrote that the claim that we are all victims now was dependent upon a unitary category of victim. As Young and Rush explained, in the process of elaborating this universalising claim, the features of the victim blur and she loses her specificity. They stated that within a left realist approach, the victim of crime was unmarked, neutral; the victim could be anyone. Young and Rush criticised the incipient masculinity in the construction of street assault as the exemplary event. They objected that the left realist focus on street crime obscured the significance of crimes against women. The rhetorical structures of left realism, Young and Rush argued, excluded conjugal violence, as well as discounting the position of the feminist critic by claiming that criminologists were distant from those that they studied. The doctrine of separate spheres of criminal and criminologist was blind to the position of women in society, as extensively described in a decade of feminist scholarship:

> The feminist critic never has been and never could be an armchair theorist. As feminist analyses of victimisation, risk and fear have demonstrated all too often, women are assailed and assaulted in their everyday lives: by the images on advertising hoardings that line the streets on their way to work, by the images on noticeboards at work, by the fear of walking home at night and by watching sexual violence on television when they get home. There is therefore no 'outside' for women. Further, the doctrine of separate spheres can say nothing about conjugal violence and child abuse. To focus on conjugal violence: the woman criminologist may well be living with an abusive partner. She is then not at all 'divorced' from the object of study; rather, she may well be married to it.
>
> (Young and Rush, 1994: 162)

Similarly, Ngaire Naffine pointed out that there was little sustained engagement with feminist writings in left realism, leading her to observe that: 'The realists' gaze never shifts from the "unmarked" man of the streets' (Naffine, 1997: 66).

A number of critical criminologists objected that left realism made unwarranted claims elevating its progressive status above other forms of critical work. Sim, Scraton and Gordon (1987: 40) objected that Jock Young had caricatured the complexities of the left interventionism of the 1970s and 1980s, setting up an 'idealist straw man'. They described a variety of ways in which individuals had worked to exploit contradictions within the system, seeking reforms which might not be simply turned to the advantage of the powerful. Furthermore, they (1987: 45) argued that John Lea and Jock Young had contributed through their work to the racist identification of black communities as 'dangerous classes'. Left realists had tied their contribution to the Labour Party, Sim, Scraton and Gordon write, leading one to question the extent to which such an allegiance could effect social change. Critical criminologists objected that the policies emanating from a left realist position 'accept rather than challenge the terrain of the powerful' (Sim et al., 1987: 59). It is to the theories advanced by these critical criminologists that the discussion now turns.

Ideology, hegemony and law and order

A number of critical scholars set out to analyse the massive reformulation of the political Right that took place from the 1970s (Hall and Jacques, 1983; Campbell, 1984). This period saw economic decline and the fragmentation of order become dominant concerns. Scholars began to focus on analysing the changing mode of class rule employed at this social conjuncture, and emphasised the significance of crime and punishment to the maintenance of order. The Right was reframing political discourse. Critical theorists showed that a number of 'folk devils' were being constructed as explanations for economic and social decline, including trade unionists, welfare scroungers, race rioters, Irish terrorists, black muggers and Greenham women. Left-wing theorists began to rethink the notion of the political, coming to see it as a field in which social groups were shaped. They advanced original analyses of the political fashioning of classes, and of the ways in which the political worked to constitute interests. The central task of critical theorists was to elucidate just how the state was able to generate and maintain the support of a diverse constituency. Law and order rhetoric and practices were understood by critical criminologists to be a crucial part of the construction of popular consent. Images of crime and law were seen as powerful ideological devices by which a broad range of people identified themselves with the ideas and interests of the powerful. Just what ideologies are, and how they work, have been matters of considerable debate. However, a basic definition might be as follows:

> Ideology is the set of ideas and representations in which people collectively make sense of the world and the society in which they live. . . . Ideology is a characteristic of all human societies, but a given ideology is specific to a particular culture at a particular moment in its history. All ideologies are developed in relation to the concrete, material circumstances of human life – they are the means by which knowledge is made out of those circumstances.
>
> (Dyer, 1998: 2)

Critical scholars set out to unpack the precise ideological character of images of crime and deviance, as well as calls for more police and harsher punishment.

Two theorists particularly drawn upon by those interested in this approach were Antonio Gramsci and Louis Althusser. Their theories provided important explanation of why the working class was not necessarily revolutionary. Gramsci (1891–1937) was a member of the central committee of the Italian Communist Party. In 1926, he was arrested due to his opposition to the fascist dictatorship of Benito Mussolini, and condemned to twenty years' imprisonment. In 1929, Gramsci was given permission to write, and began the documents that were to be published under the title of *Prison Notebooks*. He died in prison in 1937. The principal Gramscian concept employed by critical criminologists was that of 'hegemony', which theorised the notion of the leadership of the people of all classes in a given nation-state through the universalisation of ruling class interests.[7] Hegemony concerned a dominant class giving its ideas an image of universality. It was conceptualised by Gramsci as a kind of intellectual, moral and philosophical leadership, attained through the active consent of major groups in society. Power is maintained through securing the consent of subordinate groups. This is achieved through the negotiated construction of a political and ideological consensus which incorporates both ruling and subordinate groups. According to Gramsci, this consent must be constantly reproduced and renegotiated. It can never be taken for granted. Furthermore, Gramsci saw that there was a battle for hegemony between opposing groups.

Gramsci held that the state operated most efficiently when it functioned through consent rather than force, through direction rather than domination. For him, the state was the key instrument through which the narrow rule of a particular class was enlarged into a universal class leadership exercising authority over the whole social formation. Gramsci saw consent as the key legitimating support of the capitalist state. An important characteristic of the consensus, he argued, was is its commonsensical appearance, a feature crucial to understanding how individuals voluntarily assimilated the worldview of the dominant group. Gramsci explained that physical force and coercion were also sometimes resorted to by the state, but rule was principally maintained through intellectual, moral and cultural inducement. He argued that coercive control was employed by a state when its degree of consensual control was low or fractured. A crisis of hegemony of this kind was thought by him to occur when incurable structural contradictions revealed themselves.

The French philosopher Louis Althusser (1918–90) advanced a theory of how individuals are subjected by a dominant ideology. In his essay 'Ideology and Ideological State Apparatuses' (1968), Althusser started from the proposition that the reproduction of labour power required more than merely the material conditions of its reproduction. This was because labour power must be competent; it must be diversely skilled according to the requirements of the socio-technical division of labour. He hence asserted that the reproduction of labour not only required the reproduction of skills, but also of a submission to the rules of the established order. How did this come about? Why are people obedient? Broadly, Althusser believed that people's subjectivity, their sense of self-identity, was constituted by external structures like language and political institutions. He maintained that ideology worked by transforming individuals into subjects through processes of interpellation and recognition. His famous example of processes of interpellation involved a policeman hailing a person with the cry of 'hey you'. In turning around, one recognised oneself as the subject of this act of hailing. Interpellation, according to Althusser, operated by imposing obviousnesses that people could not fail to recognise. This process had the effect of making an unequal order appear natural and inevitable. It also explained how ideology leads people to see themselves as self-determining agents when they are actually shaped by ideological processes.

By the late 1970s, the mass media were taken to be one of the most important instruments in the maintenance of hegemonic rule and the ideological inculcation of class positions. From the early twentieth century, scholars had noted the power of the mass media. They now took up the detailed study of practices of signification and their relationship to the reproduction of the status quo. The remainder of this chapter will discuss how certain radical criminologists took up the concepts of hegemonic crisis and ideological interpellation, and applied them to the elucidation of the relationships between crime, punishment and modes of rule.

The enemy within: law, order and authoritarian rule

Policing the Crisis (Hall et al., 1978) was the product of the Centre for Contemporary Cultural Studies at the University of Birmingham, directed at that time by Stuart Hall. The work of the CCCS in the 1970s saw the convergence of deviancy theory with cultural studies.[8] The work of writers like Paul Willis, John Clarke and Dick Hebdidge was based around the connections of youth culture and the sociology of deviance. Paul Gilroy worked on black cultural politics. *Policing the Crisis* is known to criminologists as a study of the societal reaction to black muggers in 1970s Britain. It advanced a series of arguments about how crime provided a symbolic source of unity in an increasingly divided class society at a time when traditional modes of producing consensus were diminishing. Its title comes from the idea that policing the blacks amounted to coercively policing a crisis in the authority of the state.

Hall and co-authors relocated the concept of moral panic as it had been developed by Stan Cohen (1973/1976) onto a deeper level of analysis, seeing it as a surface manifestation of a hegemonic crisis. They pointed up the historical specificity of the 'black muggers' moral panic, demonstrating that moral panics were political phenomena. They contended that the mass media did not so much create news as reproduce and sustain dominant interpretations of it, and therefore could be said to function as an instrument of state control. As Hall and Scraton (1981) pointed out, there had been a simplistic and generalised conception of the state in the work of Becker, Matza (who called it 'Leviathan') and Lemert (who had referred vaguely to 'the societal control culture'). Critical criminologists worked with the latest theories of state and class rule.

Policing the Crisis substantiated its theoretical innovations through a detailed and eloquent interpretation of how certain representations organised consensus. The book demonstrated that the moral panic, which was ostensibly about the incidence of black mugging, was really about something other than street crime. Hall and colleagues described how mugging became an index of the disintegration of social order. The authors explained that in the 1960s and 1970s there was a strong upsurge of conservative moral indignation about crime, and linked this to the manufacture and management of consensus. They read prevalent English ideologies of crime from the character of public reaction to the Handsworth case. This was a case which led to two youths from Handsworth in

Birmingham receiving sentences of ten and twenty years' imprisonment for their mugging of an elderly man. The attack had been a brutal one, especially as the youths had returned to inflict further injuries on the man two hours after the original attack.

In analysing the discourses surrounding this crime, Hall and co-authors identified a traditionalist view of crime, which had recurrent themes around questions of family, discipline and morality, and looked into how this traditionalist perspective came to dominate. The images deployed, they argued, produced and sustained a powerfully conservative sense of Englishness. The task of these critical scholars was to understand its power to generalise itself across social and class divisions. Their research found that the images might be imprecise, ambiguous and elusive, but they were still powerful. One of the main images identified by Hall and colleagues was the notion of respectability, which they described as follows:

> Respectability is the collective internalisation, by the lower orders, of an image of the 'ideal life' held out for them by those who stand higher in the scheme of things; it disciplines society from end to end, rank by rank.
>
> (Hall et al., 1978: 141)

In addition to respectability, there was the repeated theme of a need for social discipline, as well as the idea of England as a disciplined society. Furthermore, Hall and co-authors described a series of notions about hierarchy and authority, for instance the idea that society was hierarchical by its very nature. The image of England, they explained, consisted of various purportedly self-evident national qualities as well as the assumed superiority of the English. These themes, Hall and co-authors argued, connected with and identified crime, inserting it into a discourse about normality, rightness and their inverse. The images cohered in a picture of stability, leading Hall and colleagues to reflect that crime figured within this ideology as an 'evil' which was the reverse of the 'normality' of 'Englishness', an evil which if left unchecked might destroy the stability of social order. It was in this way, Hall and his associates argued, that ruling-class ideas came to be associated with common sense.

Policing the Crisis looked into what occurred when social changes undermined some of the supports to this set of images of social order, producing anxiety. One consequence was a predisposition to the use of scapegoats into which experiences felt to be disturbing could be condensed and symbolically rejected. Hall and co-workers explained that in the postwar period, there were important breaks in the traditional ideologies. Firstly, affluence was seen as hedonistic, permissive, and as producing a loosening of controls. This perception especially produced anxiety among the lower middle classes who had invested much in the Protestant virtues of thrift, respectability and moral discipline. Secondly, there was an erosion of traditional working-class community, in which the interconnections between family and neighbourhood were loosened, and communal spaces and informal controls were weakened. Hall and colleagues stated that there was a strong tendency to reduce this change to a problem of 'generation gap'. It is in this context, they argued, that the mugger's form came to reflect the content of the fears and anxieties of those who imagined and then 'discovered' him:

> In the vocabulary of social anxiety blacks and Asians were ready-made symbols for, and symptoms of, a succession of dislocations: in housing, neighbourhood, family, sex, recreation, law and order. To communities beset by a 'sense of loss', their race and colour may well have mattered less than their simply otherness – their alienness.
>
> (Hall et al., 1978: 160)

On this view, the public definition of crime by the media mobilised a deep structure of anxiety, supported by traditionalism.

Hall and co-authors stated that this crisis of authority precipitated a crisis of hegemonic rule. They contended that a crisis of consensus management was produced by changes in the scale, position and character of the postwar British state. They indicated that they were employing Gramsci's notion of hegemony, and explained their understanding of this as follows:

> A crisis of hegemony marks a moment of profound rupture in the political and economic life of a society, an accumulation of contradictions. If in moments of 'hegemony' everything works spontaneously so as to sustain and enforce a particular form of class domination while rendering the basis of that social authority invisible through the mechanisms of the production of consent, then moments when the equilibrium of consent is disturbed, or where the contending class forces are so nearly balanced that neither can achieve that sway from which a resolution to the crisis can be promulgated, are moments when the whole basis of political leadership and cultural authority becomes exposed and contested.
>
> (Hall et al., 1978: 217)

Hall and his fellow authors argued that the response to this situation of hegemonic crisis was a tilt in the operation of the state away from consent towards coercion, and a powerful orchestration to support this shift. They held that the forms of state intervention became more overt and more direct. The reaction to mugging, they claimed, was one of the forms in which this crisis of hegemony manifested itself. They contended that the mass media were crucial in shaping public consciousness, with the signification of events in the mass media being one crucial terrain where consent was won or lost.

The Conservative electoral victory of 1979 that brought Margaret Thatcher's first term of office as Prime Minister saw the accelerated emergence of an authoritarian state which relied heavily upon regulation via the rule of law. As Hall (1980) put it, we were 'drifting into a law and order society'. His book described the construction of a law and order consensus that he termed 'authoritarian populism'. As well as constructing welfare recipients as scrounger folk-devil figures, Hall wrote, the police operated as the shock troops of the law and order society. Critical criminologists analysed the ways in which political opposition was depicted as part of a rising tide of crime and lawlessness and subjected to criminalisation. A number of academics published alternative information to challenge official accounts and media reportage of the policing of protests including the coal dispute of 1984/5 (Fine and Millar, 1985; Scraton and Thomas, 1985), and the Northern Ireland 'troubles' (Boyle, Hadden and Hillyard, 1975).

Further work built on *Policing the Crisis* to expose and challenge the coupling of popular racism with notions of black criminality. Paul Gilroy (1982) pointed out that E.P. Thompson's notion of the 'freeborn Englishman', discussed above, involved the exclusion of blacks, and described the racist ideologies of black criminality employed by the police. As Gilroy (1987: 90) later put it, Thompson had a 'tendency to idealize legality and become mesmerized by constitutional archaisms'. He explained that these intersected with racist common sense and were an important part of the construction of an authoritarian state in Britain in the 1970s. In this way, Gilroy argued, commonsense knowledge of alienness was grounded in authoritarian legality. In 'The Myth of Black Criminality', Gilroy described how the rule of law and the maintenance of public order mobilised popular racism to maintain support for a state in crisis. He presented a number of trenchant criticisms of left realism, denouncing its 'capitulation to the weight of racist logic' despite its 'polite social democratic rhetoric' (Gilroy, 1987: 113). He wrote that realist analyses ignored the history of police–community relations, and especially that within black communities.

Critical theories of crime, punishment and power

Albert Cardarelli and Stephen Hicks (1993) described the hostile counter-reaction to radical criminology, as well as its later accommodation (albeit in somewhat diluted form) within mainstream American criminology. They also discussed the changed role that universities occupied within culture, with the shift towards an understanding of students as vocationally-orientated consumers. This, they explained, made for conservatism in the academy: 'Today, the role of the academic in society is largely informative rather than transformative' (Cardarelli and Hicks, 1993: 552). These political and cultural shifts explained in some respects the waning of Marxist theories of crime and punishment. Fortunately, there is more to the story than this pessimistic ending. New critical theories have been developed for understanding relationships between crime, punishment and power in the changing conditions of the later twentieth century, and it is to these that we now begin to turn. Feminist and Foucauldian scholars also set out to question assumptions and commonplace obviousnesses, and to reveal these as political. In important respects, these approaches further radicalised the meaning of crime and punishment, by raising a number of profound epistemological questions about the conditions of knowledge production.

In the next chapter we turn to feminist theories of crime and punishment. These both drew on the burgeoning left-wing scholarship and activism described in this chapter, and found it necessary to embark upon a separate enterprise. Juliet Mitchell (1971) wrote that Women's Liberationists drew on 'the politics of experience' employed by the New Left to develop a revolutionary consciousness of their oppression. As with the 'deviance-marginality' theorised by Horowitz and Liebowitz, women's liberation fused the personal and the political. Many of the originators of the Women's Liberation Movement had been active in the student movement, civil rights struggle, draft resistance, or other Left movements. They broke with these groups on account of the continuing disinterest in women's issues and rife sexism that they encountered. Women's Liberationists decided to stop tolerating the macho sexism of some radical men. Two women circulated a paper at the SNCC conference in 1966 which asked 'why is it in SNCC that women who are competent, qualified, and experienced are automatically assigned to the "female" kinds of jobs such as typing . . . but rarely the "executive"?' Their answer to their own question was 'the assumption of male superiority'. This was certainly reflected in Stokely Carmichael's infamous response, 'The position of women in SNCC is prone' (cited in Isserman and Kazin, 2000: 179). Some radical women found that their discussions revealed broader, and shared, dissatisfactions. They began meeting to articulate their own needs and chose to organise around the specific oppression of women. The position and experience of women was placed within a critical analysis of patriarchy, the rule of men. These feminists asserted that women's oppression was primary, and went deeper than economics. For them, the enemy was first and foremost men rather than capitalism. This principle had great ramifications for theories of crime and punishment.

Notes

1. On the New Left and the libidinal politics of the counter-culture, see Pearson (1975a, Ch. 4).
2. *Malcolm X*, dir. Spike Lee, Largo International.
3. See also Sedgwick (1982), Clare (1976) and Kotowicz (1997) on anti-psychiatry.
4. On the NDC, see Cohen (1981). Critical criminologists also set up international links during this period. See van Swaaningen (1997: 82–4) on the

European Group for the Study of Deviance and Social Control, set up in 1973. This book also discussed a variety of European critical criminologies, covering some approaches not described in this book, for instance abolitionism. Van Swaaningen made the important point that it is not the same thing to be radical in different countries, for instance in a military regime instead of a social democracy. For a selection of papers from European critical criminologists of this period, see Bianchi, Simondi and Taylor (1975).

5. For key texts within a left realist approach, see Lea and Young (1984), Kinsey et al. (1986), Young (1987) and Young and Matthews (1992). For discussions of the left realist approach, in addition to those described in this chapter, see Walklate (1998, Ch. 4), Lowman and MacLean (1992) and Stenson and Brearley (1991).

6. On New Right criminologies, see Tame (1991).

7. On Gramsci and his writings, see Ransome (1992) and Simon (1991).

8. On the CCCS at this time, see Redhead (1995: Ch. 3).

Chapter 7

Women's oppression, crime and society

> The costs to criminology of its failure to deal with feminist scholarship are perhaps more severe than they would be in any other discipline. The reason is that the most consistent and prominent fact about crime is the sex of the offender.
>
> (Naffine, 1997: 5)

Modern feminism is generally taken to have fallen into two relatively distinct phases. First-wave feminism sought the equality of the sexes, for instance campaigning for suffrage and equal access to the world of work. From the mid-1960s, a second wave of feminists began to ask new kinds of questions and develop new concepts. Second-wave feminism took the form of a Women's Liberation movement. Women's Liberationists claimed that women were the most fundamentally oppressed people. They set out to change the whole structure of society at every level. These feminists sited the fundamental basis of women's oppression in the development of the feminine psyche, as well as women's ideological and socio-economic role as mother and housewife (Mitchell, 1971). Within the analysis of patriarchy (the rule of men), woman's body and her sexuality were key sites of the coercive and violent power of men. This meant that instead of focusing on the public realm of society, second-wave feminism addressed the domestic sphere. Women's liberationists took the issues of abortion, rape, wife-battering and pornography as important feminist issues. Furthermore, they engaged in a sustained indictment of sexism, the widespread assumption that women were inferior to men. This chapter discusses feminist criminologies, published from the time of Heidensohn's (1968) essay, drawing out their relationship to second-wave feminism.[1]

In this chapter, three distinctive feminist perspectives are delineated, namely, liberal feminism, radical feminism, and the sociology of masculinity. Before embarking upon this discussion, a few qualifications and clarifications are warranted. Firstly, this chapter does not exhaustively cover the full range of academic feminisms that have emerged. That much would be beyond its scope. I have concentrated on those feminist approaches which have been most influential within feminist criminology. Secondly, the various feminisms are not always rigorously discrete. For instance, a scholar might draw upon arguments and concepts from both liberal and radical feminisms at different points in her work. Finally, when compared with other non-feminist approaches, for instance strain theory, the feminist perspectives discussed in this chapter have as much in common as there is dividing them. What the diverse feminisms share is a number of guiding assumptions about the purpose and basic tenets of scholarship. It may be generally stated that what is at issue for feminists is woman's place, her condition or 'estate' (Mitchell, 1971), and how this might be improved or transformed. Feminists have a normative commitment to revealing, and attempting to eliminate, the subordination of women by men. This overall rationale has been taken to require the following:

1. Within feminist theory, gender is a complex socio-cultural and historical product rather than a natural fact.
2. For feminists, the production of knowledge in non-feminist scholarship reflects a male view of the world that is oppressive to women.
3. Feminist scholars maintain that women should not be rendered invisible by research or marginal to it, but affirmed as central within intellectual inquiry.

Liberal feminism, discrimination and reform

The main problematic of liberal feminism was women's unequal access to the public sphere. Liberal feminism saw women's subordination as based in a number of customary and legal constraints that blocked their entrance to, or success in, the public realm. They noted that the belief that women were naturally less intellectually or physically capable than men was used to exclude them from academia, the market and government. Liberal feminists believed that the existing discriminatory conditions could be reformed to make possible the equal presence and representation of women within the public sphere. A classic text of modern liberal feminism is Betty Friedan's *The Feminine Mystique* (1963), which contended that the idea that women could find satisfaction exclusively in the traditional role of wife and mother left housewives feeling empty and miserable. Friedan's cure for woman's plight was work outside the home, through which she believed that women could achieve full development as human beings. However, liberal feminism was criticised for its tendency to accept male values as human values. In *Feminist Politics and Human Nature* (1983), Alison Jagger criticised liberal feminism for adopting male values. Critics contended that liberal feminism can do little to really change society.

Correcting mainstream theories: liberal feminist criminology

How was the liberal feminist perspective taken up by feminist criminologists? Liberal feminism in criminology took the form of a methodological approach that can be termed 'feminist empiricism':

> This term denoted feminists who question the objectivity of so-called scientific work on women, while generally accepting that it is possible to be objective and neutral. . . . Feminist empiricism endeavours to develop a scientific understanding of women as the missing subjects of criminology, to document their lives both as offenders and as victims. It also points out the crude stereotyping of women.
>
> (Naffine, 1997: 30)

This approach proceeded from the acknowledgement of sexist bias and discrimination, to seek to put right these shortcomings by producing a fairer understanding. Feminist empiricism viewed traditional criminology as distorted, and disputed the claims that had been made about women on the basis of meagre evidence.

Feminist criminologists launched a critique of mainstream, traditional criminology. Whereas for Marxist criminologists the criminological tradition was judged by its ability to account for the fact of social class, feminist criminology saw this tradition as 'malestream'. In *Women, Crime and Criminology*, Carol Smart (1976) stated that a feminist critique of existing studies of female criminality was needed as a precursor to substantive empirical study of women criminals. Undertaking this task, she wrote that the small amount of work on female criminality shared a wholly uncritical attitude towards sexual stereotypes of women and girls, and had the effect of confirming the presupposition of their biologically determined inferior status.

Smart noted that there was a paucity of studies on female criminality, indeed a considerable silence surrounded the subject. This, she contended, reflected a pervasive belief in the relative insignificance of women's crime, which was in turn part of a broader belief in the general insignificance of women's actions. Huge numbers of studies simply ignored the existence of female offenders, assuming that the male included the female. Equally deplorable was the fact that those studies that did exist evinced a clearly male-orientated bias. Simply put, studies on women criminals were full of sexist stereotypes and anti-feminist ideology. Smart claimed that most studies referred to women in terms of their biologically determined domesticity and passivity. Furthermore, she believed that unreconstructed notions about women's nature led to a focus on 'sexual deviance' (prostitution) as the centre of enquiry on female criminality, institutionalising the double standard.

Smart noted the durability of the Lombrosian legacy in relation to female criminality. She pointed out that despite theoretical advances in the study of male criminality, the study of female criminality remained arrested at the positivist stage. This meant that women's deviance was understood as based in biological or psychological drives and urges considered peculiar to the nature of women. This arrested theoretical development, she argued, was reflected in policy. The new Holloway Prison regime, with its 'sick role' model, was particularly symbolic of the tendency to perceive female criminality as 'irrational, irresponsible and largely unintentional behaviour, as an individual maladjustment to a well-ordered and consensual society' (Smart, 1976: 145).

Smart drew upon the critique of positivism in *The New Criminology* (Taylor et al., 1973), pointing out how the positivist model allowed the world 'as it is' to remain unchallenged. Furthermore, the determinist vision of human nature in positivism legitimated interventionism. For Smart, this determinist position on human nature was: 'the complete antithesis of an emancipatory project, a project oriented towards self-consciousness and a realization of the possibilities for radically changing material conditions' (Smart, 1976: 29). Simply put, positivism was anti-feminist. The determinist view, Smart argued, was oriented towards control over behaviour that deviated from norms. It hence diagnosed those whose acts departed from predefined normative standards as pathological, and in need of 'treatment' to produce conformity. As Smart explained, this paradigm dismissed the political significance of deviance:

> deviant individuals are not considered to be social critics, rebels or even members of a counter culture, rather they are treated as biological anomalies or as psychologically 'sick' individuals. Their actions are not interpreted as having particular social significance, as being possibly rational responses.
>
> (Smart, 1976: 29)

Feminist empiricism called for more criminological research on women offenders. It embarked on a project of delineating how women could be added in to the existing non-feminist theories. Improvements in knowledge could be achieved by removing sexist and androcentric biases. Feminist empiricism hence aimed to correct, but not to transform, the methodological norms of empiricism. The strategy was to remedy deficiencies by inserting women. Feminist scholars like Shacklady Smith (1978) set out upon reworking past theories so that they took account of females.

An important concern for feminists was that of women's lack of equality before the law. What happened when women came before the courts, accused of a criminal offence? Feminists engaged themselves upon debunking what came to be known as the 'chivalry thesis'. This notion conveyed the view that women were treated more leniently within the criminal justice system due to male chivalry. However, an alternative 'doubly deviant' thesis was advanced, which held that women were doubly punished if their rule-breaking was compounded by perceived role-breaking. Those perceived to have failed as women, for instance divorcees, were treated more harshly. Studies demonstrated that women in court had a stronger defence if they presented an image of conventional femininity and conformity. They were more likely to be incarcerated when they were seen as beyond social control. Following this line of thinking, Myra Hindley has received an exceptionally punitive sentence because she transgressed accepted notions of conventional femininity by participating in the murder of children (real women are maternal).

Could women be added in to extant theories as liberal feminists had hoped? Eileen Leonard (1982) thought not, writing that theoretical criminology was biased to the core, replete with assumptions reflecting a male and not a female reality. This, she argued, meant that it was wholly unable to explain female patterns of crime:

> Initially I thought it might be possible simply to add what had been overlooked, and to elaborate an analysis of women in terms of existing theory. I quickly discovered that this is impossible. Theoretical criminology was constructed by men, about men. It is simply not up to the analytical task of explaining female patterns of crime. Although some theories work better than others, they all illustrate what social scientists are slowly recognizing within criminology and outside the field: that our theories are not the general explanations of human behaviour they claim to be, but rather particular understandings of male behaviour. A single theoretical canopy has been assumed for men and women, although their social realities are extremely diverse.
>
> (Leonard, 1982: xi–xii)

Leonard called for the construction of new methods and theories, for non-sexist ways of describing social reality.

Its critics objected that feminist empiricism tended to accept men as the norm, unwittingly setting them up as the human standard. For instance, engagements with the chivalry thesis questioned whether women were treated the same as, or different from, men. Men hence represented that to which women might be compared. This approach hardly challenged the validity of the norm itself:

> [P]erhaps the principal shortcoming of feminist empiricism is its tendency to leave the rest of the discipline in place, unanalysed and unchallenged. It tends not to comment on the project and methods of the mainstream, that is the way in which men's lives are documented and interpreted.
>
> (Naffine, 1997: 36)

These particular limitations are not ones that radical feminism could be accused of.

Radical feminism and the analysis of patriarchy

Radical feminism worked from the basis of a structural analysis of male domination. Kate Millett (1970) used the term 'patriarchy' to capture the fundamental fact of male domination and the universal oppression of women by men. Radical feminists argued strongly that it was the patriarchal system that oppressed women, a system characterised by power, dominance, hierarchy and competition. Instead of the liberal feminist claim that women could make it in the system, radical feminists argued that patriarchy could not be reformed; it must be broken down. As well as the removal of patriarchy's legal and political institutions, radical feminists contended that its social and cultural institutions, for instance the family and the church, must be eradicated:

> Radical feminism recognizes the oppression of women as a fundamental
> political oppression wherein women are categorized as an inferior class
> based upon their sex. It is the aim of radical feminism to organize politically
> to destroy this power struggle with men, and that the agent of oppression is
> man in so far as he identifies with and carries out the supremacy privileges
> of the male role.
>
> (New York Radical Feminist Manifesto, cited in Ware, 1970: 58)

An important practice of the Women's Liberation Movement was 'consciousness-raising'. Consciousness-raising was a practice of speaking out about one's experiences and feelings in small women-only groups with no leader. The aim of the activity was to affirm the validity of women's experiences, and to connect their understanding of these with a feminist view of the subordinate position of women in society. Consciousness-raising brought to light the previously hidden and personalised, politicising situations and experiences that had hitherto been accepted by women as natural or unavoidable:

> Women came into the movement from the unspecified frustration of their
> own private lives, find that what they thought was an individual dilemma
> is a social predicament and hence a political problem. The process of
> transforming the hidden, individual fears of women into a shared awareness
> of the meaning of them as social problems, the release of anger, anxiety, the
> struggle of proclaiming the painful and transforming it into the political –
> this process is consciousness-raising.
>
> (Mitchell, 1971: 61)

The practice of consciousness-raising hence brought to awareness the previously invisible facets of patriarchy. It was also a fount of collective knowledge upon which social action could be based.

If feminist empiricism may be described as the methodological approach associated with liberal feminism, the advocacy of 'women's standpoint' can be identified with radical feminism. Feminist standpointism emerged from the practice of consciousness-raising, given that this was a 'a group exercise designed to unlock the door to collective truths unmediated by the opinions of men' (Brownmiller, 2000: 5). The insistence on women's standpoint also came out of a critique of liberal feminism. Dorothy Smith (1973) argued that researching women without revising traditional assumptions about epistemology and methods made women a mere addendum to the principal project of studying men, as well as leaving unchallenged the way that men themselves were studied. Feminist standpointism hence emphasised the need to place women's experience at the centre of knowledge.[2] Some standpoint feminism followed Nancy Hartsock (1983), who contended that women's oppressed position provided the possibility of a more complete and accurate understanding than those that could be produced by men. According to this view, by virtue of their social positioning, women could produce a less distorted view of their situation. Others went less far, and only proposed that a social science of use to women must proceed from a sound grasp of the forms of oppression that women actually experienced. But how did one arrive at a true (radical feminist) understanding of this kind? Hartsock explained that a feminist standpoint was not simply given by the women's experience, but emerged through their reflexive engagement in the struggle against oppression. The authentic view was attained through a political process of feminist consciousness-raising.

In *Sexual Politics* (1970), Kate Millett wrote that patriarchy was maintained through the manipulation of consciousness, and was not simply a form of power rooted in institutions like the economy. In this classic text, Millett contended that patriarchy was universal, all-pervasive, and so well-entrenched a power system that it hardly needed to be visible. She explained that patriarchy was achieved through socialisation, and maintained through ideologies and institutions. Patriarchal ideology, Millett explained, exaggerated biological differences between men and women, allotting dominant characteristics to men and subordinate ones to women. Institutions like academia, the church and the family, conditioned women so that they internalised a sense of their inferiority to men. Millett wrote that if a woman refused to accept patriarchy, and rejected conventional femininity, men used coercion to accomplish what conditioning had not. She asserted that despite intimidation, women had never been wholly under male control. Periods of advance for the women's movement were followed by misogynistic countercultures. Millett depicted neo-Freudians and Parsonian functionalists as reactionaries. She berated Freud's ratification of traditional roles and Parsons' rigid gender dimorphism, which posited that women's subordination to men was natural. Feminist criminologists drew on radical feminism's indictment of patriarchal ideology to challenge popular and academic explanations of women's crime, and to develop original analyses of rape and domestic violence as central to the oppression of women.

Critics of radical feminism objected that its focus on the body produced a somewhat deterministic picture of human nature, for instance in the notion that women's biology produces a distinctively female psychology. Jean Elshtain (1981) criticised radical feminism, and especially Susan Brownmiller's *Against Our Will* (1975). She claimed that it was a mistake to argue that men and women were ontologically different. Elshtain contended that the depiction of men as corrupt, and women as innocent, denied individuality and history. She noted that the term 'patriarchy' had a powerful emotional force, but argued that as a concept it was a blunt instrument. She also challenged the advocacy of women's standpoint. Elshtain advised a reconsideration of the concept of 'pure voice' seen in the idea that the victim, in her status as victim, speaks in a pure voice; 'I suffer, therefore I have moral purity' (Elshtain, 1981: 225). Radical feminist theory has also been taken to task for failing to differentiate between women. Radical feminism advanced a series of claims about the universality and identical characteristics of the oppression of women at all times and in all places. Later, there was a retreat from universalism and an acknowledgement of the diverse range of women's experiences.[3] Something of this debate is pointed up in Marcia Rice's (1990) work on black female offenders as 'the other dark figure in crime'. She wrote that feminist criminology had failed to see that traditional criminology had constructed racist as well as sexist ideologies of femininity. Furthermore, Rice criticised the ethnocentrism of feminist orthodoxies, and called for a black feminist perspective on crime.

'She Did It All For Love': radical feminism and the criminal woman

The ambivalence towards the *lumpenproletariat* in Marxist thought discussed in Chapter 6, was echoed in feminist theory's limited interest in criminal women. A small number of women who committed certain kinds of crimes became heroines for the Women's Movement. The most famous of these is probably Valerie Solanas, who shot the artist Andy Warhol in 1968. Solanas had founded a one-woman organisation called SCUM, or Society for Cutting Up Men. This advocated murder, asserting that women should retake their rightful position by force. Vivian Gornick's (1971) comments on Solanas explain some aspects of the heroisation that she received:

> Solanas understands full well that the enemy is not really men, but women against themselves; she understands that the revolution will not occur until women simply refuse to play their customary roles, and against this understanding she constructs a revolutionary female whom she calls the SCUM female, the female who will lead the struggle.
>
> (Gornick, 1971: 141)[4]

Other feminist heroines included Joan Little and Inez Garcia, who shot men they claimed had raped them. Feminist lawyers defended their cases, and women campaigned on their behalf. These feminist heroines tended to be women whose crimes could easily be seen as enraged forms of fighting back against a specific male oppressor. The assumptions behind feminist support for their cases ran close to the romanticisation of crime that Marxist criminologists were accused of. Indeed, in a comment that foreshadowed criticisms to be made of Marxist criminology, Juliet Mitchell wrote that women's pain must not be glamorised:

> [M]any feminists claim that as society oppresses women, all women 'criminals' are political prisoners. It is not belittling the plight of prisoners if one points out that they certainly don't see themselves as such. After all, politics is, in part, a question of political consciousness. The reasons why women are in prison, and their conditions there, are clearly matters for Women's Liberation to concern itself with; the maximalist analysis of their so-called political status does not follow from this.
>
> (Mitchell, 1971: 70)

The general run of female offenders, whose crimes were not direct reactions against male oppressors, remained of marginal concern to feminist theory and the Women's Movement.

From around 1968, feminist criminologists began to advance non-sexist theories of women's crime. This body of scholarship was especially important for feminism given the controversial link drawn between the Women's Liberation Movement and women's criminality. The anti-feminist argument was advanced that a new violent female offender was the product of women's liberation. Scholars like Adler (1975) and Simon (1975) claimed that female emancipation would necessarily cause an increase in female deviance. This conservative backlash thesis of the criminal woman as the 'dark side of liberation' was easily debunked by empirical research, which showed that there was no appreciable link between women's emancipation and either rising rates, or more serious forms, of women's offending (Chesney-Lind, 1980: 16–17). This response to feminism indicates the provocative character of activities undertaken as a challenge to women's oppression.

Marcia Millman's essay 'She Did It All For Love' (1975) demonstrated vividly how conceptions of deviance and control were limited by a systematically male-biased perspective of the world and its activities. Millman wrote that the mass media constantly exposed viewers to speculation about deviance, promulgating stereotypes of both deviant and conventional behaviour. Academic understandings were just as bad. Sociological stereotypes of deviance closely resembled those of popular culture. Millman explained that women tended to be portrayed as the natural enemies of exciting men in both fictional and academic works. Women were equated with the 'stupid relentless bourgeois society that ultimately crushes whatever is original and spirited about these modern heroes' (Millman, 1975: 251). Women were basically portrayed as 'dumbly law-abiding', and associated with stupid conventionality.

Exceptions to the assumption of stupid conventionality called for the production of a new stereotypical explanation. To illustrate her argument, Millman discussed the press coverage of the 'conversion' of Patty Hearst to revolutionary sister and terrorist action. Hearst, heiress to a vast fortune, was the grand-daughter of the corrupt media magnate depicted by Orson Welles in *Citizen Kane* (1941, RKO). In 1974, when she was a nineteen-year-old student, she was kidnapped from her flat on the Berkeley campus in Los Angeles by the Symbionese Liberation Army (SLA). The left-wing urban terrorist group released a statement describing Hearst as a prisoner of war, the target being her father, 'corporate enemy of the people', and proclaiming 'death to the fascist insect that preys upon the life of the people'. Patty converted to become an active member of the SLA. A photograph of her standing in front of their cobra emblem, which expressed the revolutionary unity of all people against the common oppressor, was released. She was holding a machine gun and dressed in revolutionary garb. The photograph was accompanied by a statement, which explained that she had chosen to fight for the freedom of all oppressed people:

> To those who would bear the hopes of the future of our people, let the voice of their guns express the words of freedom. . . . I've become conscious and can never go back to the life we led before. . . . One thing which I learned is that the corporate ruling class will do anything in their power in order to maintain their position of control over the masses . . . the law and order programs are just a means to remove so-called violent (meaning aware) individuals from the community in order to facilitate the controlled removal of unneeded labour force from this country. . . . How long will it take before we all understand that we must fight for our freedom?

Marxist criminology, as shown in Chapter 6, drew considerable inspiration from the words of revolutionary men, as well as from dissident acts of various kinds. However, Marxist criminologists did not see women's deviance in the same light, and tended to ignore or trivialise it. Millman explained that the coverage of Hearst's conversion involved plenty of speculation about the motives for her actions. While the men of the SLA were seen to have sincere political motives, Hearst was portrayed as driven by sexual desire and the pleasures of romance. The press initially drew on a homophobic narrative that replaced political conversion with the notion of being converted to lesbianism. It was reported that Hearst had been lured by the 'sexual thralldom' exercised by a captivating SLA lesbian. Although Millman did not comment on the content of this image, it worked to suggest a passive Hearst driven by uncontrollable lust towards the enticingly alien. This seduction tale made both becoming a lesbian and becoming a terrorist irrational, involuntary and extremist. Later, readers of this cautionary yet threatening tale could sigh with relief after the news that Hearst was in love with a male SLA activist. This was taken to confirm the speculation that she did it all for love.[5]

Hearst had initially been seen as a victim by the police and media. This assumption was shattered when security cameras captured images of her brandishing a machine gun during a bank heist and shouting 'Get down or I'll blow your motherfucking heads off'. Hearst was convicted of grand larceny for her part in this crime. She served two years of a seven year sentence, after convincing President Jimmy Carter that she had been brainwashed into terrorism. Carter commuted her sentence, stating that Hearst would not have become a participant in her criminal acts had she not been subjected to the degrading experiences that she had suffered as a victim of the SLA. In 2000, Hearst's appeal for a pardon was being considered by Bill Clinton. However, her activities with the SLA were about to receive massive media coverage. Sara Olsen, a middle-aged doctor's wife and mother of three living in suburban Minnesota, was charged with conspiring to kill police officers in 1975 by planting pipe bombs under squad cars. It was ruled that all the alleged crimes and activities of the SLA, including those connected with Patty Hearst, would be admissible as evidence. A deathbed confession made to the FBI by a man who had harboured fugitive SLA members, stated that Hearst had been an eager SLA member, had staged her own kidnapping and refused his offer to help her to escape.

Each of these images of Patty Hearst as seduced against her will or better judgement, love-struck or brainwashed victim, all illustrate Millman's argument that sociological and popular depictions of women's deviance reflected and reproduced the belief that only men took a serious stand against society:

> [T]heir deviance is understood as only secondary and politically uninspired. It is derivative of their acting like women: falling in love (with a deviant man), being a little too out of control of their emotions (becoming mentally ill), using their sexuality exploitatively but not that differently from other women (becoming a prostitute), or exhibiting some other neurotic weakness or impulsiveness common to women (as becoming a shoplifter).
>
> (Millman, 1975: 253)

Simply put, women's deviance was not seen as creative. Millman complained that women had become associated with the dullest, most oppressive aspects of society. This was, as Juliet Mitchell had put it, 'a society which sees women as always unserious' (Mitchell, 1971: 13). Women's actions were taken to be unimportant and of no interest. Women's deviance, Millman explained, was viewed in narrowly sex-stereotyped and unappealing terms, while male deviance was seen as 'the expression of creativity and a courage to stand up to society's hypocrises'. Millman gave several examples of how (male) sociologists had identified with their male deviant subjects and emphasised their attractive features, for example in Becker's partisan sociology. She pointed out that only male deviants were studied with such empathy and appreciation.

Dorie Klein (1973) drew on radical feminist writing to critique the continuing presence of stereotypical ideas about women's nature in work on women's criminality:

> The writers see criminality as the result of *individual* characteristics that are only peripherally affected by economic, social and political forces. These characteristics are of a *physiological* or *psychological* nature and are uniformly based on implicit or explicit assumptions about the *inherent nature of women.* This nature is *universal,* rather than existing within a specific historical framework.
>
> (Klein, 1973, cited in Muncie et al., 1996: 160)

She pointed out that none of the theorists of women's crime wrote from a feminist or a radical perspective. This, she claimed, led them to focus in their work on how social integration could be achieved:

> Most of the writers are concerned with social harmony and the welfare of the existing social structure rather than with the women involved or with women's position in general.
>
> (Klein, 1973, cited in Muncie et al., 1996: 161)

She explained that the point of theorising about women's crime and delinquency in this work was always to return them to purportedly natural feminine roles. Klein described that within an ideology of absolute difference between the sexes, women were depicted as by nature sexual beings. This reflected the location of women as domestic workers in a rigid sexual division of labour:

> The specific character ascribed to women's nature and those critical to theories of female criminality are uniformly sexual in their nature. Sexuality is seen as the root of female behaviour and the problem of crime. Women are defined as sexual beings, as sexual capital in many cases, physiologically and socially. This definition reflects and reinforces the economic position of women as reproductive and domestic workers.
>
> (Klein, 1973, cited in Muncie et al., 1996: 161)

Klein argued that the definition of ideal femininity was a ruling class one, and was classist, racist and sexist. The valorised conventional form of femininity operated as a defense of the status quo, directed at the adjustment of women to the existing social order rather than stimulating social change. The polarised opposites of the bad lusty woman and the good chaste woman acted as conservative forces in the continuation of the oppressive nuclear family.

Like Marcia Millman, Klein noted the recurrent notion of women's mediocrity, or limited range of mental possibilities, writing that women were depicted as conformist and dull due to purportedly innate physiological limitations. To substantiate this argument, she discussed Freud's conception of women as masochistic and men as aggressive, citing in support Millett's critique of Freud as a demon patriarch in *Sexual Politics* (1970). Klein explained that the Freudian framework depicted deviant women as aggressive individuals who were trying to be men, and noted with disdain Freud's ideal of women as sheltered darlings. She referred to Millett's analysis of how Freudianism had functioned to stem the tide of feminist revolution, writing that:

> Freudianism has had an unparalleled influence in the United States (and came at a key point to help swing the tide against the women's movement) to facilitate the return of women during the depression and postwar years to the home, out of an economy which had no room for them. . . . Healthy women would now be seen as masochistic, passive and sexually indifferent. Criminal women would be seen as sexual misfits.
>
> (Klein, 1973, cited in Muncie et al., 1996: 162)

Klein argued that academic understandings of women's crime and deviance did not link woman's condition to the sources of her oppression. Feminists transformed functionalism's purportedly descriptive sex role theory into a critique of how rigid and prescriptive sex roles were actually a mode of social control. What functionalist theory had claimed were natural sex roles beneficial to society were seen by feminists as ideological tools for keeping women in a subservient position. For instance, Albert Cohen, as seen in Chapter 4, had claimed that girls did not form delinquent subcultures because their goals lay within personal relationships. Klein gave the example of *The Adolescent Girl in Conflict* (1966), in which Konopka employed strain theory to state that boys were instrumental but girls were expressive and interpersonal. 'Unadjusted' girls were hence to be readjusted by being given opportunities to be pretty, sociable women. Konopka had seen female dependence and sociability as physiological characteristics of all women. Against this kind of view, Klein insisted upon the sex/gender distinction (sex is biological, gender is cultural).

Theories of women's crime produced by men had been sexist. Feminist criminologists set out to produce more authentic accounts. The focus on 'experience' from standpoint feminism can be seen in their exploration of the potential of allowing women to speak for themselves. Research committed to this precept exposed women's experience of the enforcement of a domestic role in penal regimes, of a petty and coercive system of control and a medicalised approach to their crimes. For instance, Pat Carlen's *Criminal Women* (1985) opposed a male-centred view of female offenders by turning to the women themselves and seeking their stories. In allowing the female offender to speak for herself, this approach insisted that women become the knowing subjects of their own histories. Carlen explained that this approach would invest the female offender with a rationality and purpose that had previously only been attributed to male offenders.

Radical feminism and violence against women

In addition to drawing on radical feminism's indictment of patriarchal ideology to challenge explanations of women's crime, feminist criminologists participated in the politicisation of rape and domestic violence. Anti-violence campaigns were a highly visible activity of the Women's Liberation movement, and feminist criminologists wrote about violence against women from the outset. Before the advent of second-wave feminism, people had generally assumed that violence against women was a rare occurrence. The women's movement revealed that it was actually quite common, as well as exercising a fear in women's lives that contributed to their oppression. Expanding the definition of violence beyond that of extant legal categories, and challenging strongly the image of law as a protector, they linked violence against women centrally to women's oppression. Radical feminists advanced the claim that force and its threat were the ultimate foundation of male supremacy. The interest in violence against women was not a purely scholarly enterprise, but arose from a grassroots concern to protect women more adequately. Rape Crisis Centres and shelters for battered women were both political educators and providers of practical services. For instance, they combined phone lines, counselling and a supportive environment, with the study and dissemination of information about the reality of violence against women.

The methodological approach of feminist standpointism was central to the study of rape, sexual assault and wife abuse. Feminists felt that doing something about misogynistic practices required the development of more authentic knowledge about women's experiences of them and of the criminal justice system. The feminist anti-rape movement was founded on the testimony of raped women. Texts were based on a strategy of letting women tell their experiences. The existing literature on rape was all victim-blaming, which seemed emblematic of the patriarchal worldview. Put simply, for feminists, women were the true authorities on things that had happened to them. The approach of feminist scholars who wrote about rape was far from that of Becker's partisan sociology. As Smart (1990) explained, because researchers, as feminists, also occupied the world of the socially subjugated, this comprised not empathy but shared knowledge.

Rather than simply seeing rape as an act carried out for the purpose of sexual gratification, feminists emphasised that it was a violent act of aggression done to humiliate and terrify women. They wrote that the threat of rape served to preserve the male control of women in all societies. In the minds of women, knowledge of the possibility of rape acted as a powerful form of social control. Rape functioned as a control by means of the fear that it induced, ensuring women's acceptance of the inevitability of male domination. As Jalna Hanmer (1979/1981: 190) explained, the effect of rape upon women's consciousnesses was often unbeknown to them: 'The importance of fear and its threat may be so highly masked that control appears effortless. . . . In a woman's life fear of violence from men is subtle and pervasive.' This was one reason why consciousness-raising was such an important practice.

Radical feminists argued that rape was surrounded by a series of myths which covered up its general social acceptance in all except the most extreme cases. They advanced the controversial argument that rape was not actually aberrational, given the construction of male and female sexuality in patriarchal society:

> In a society where men and women are seen as divided as initiator and consenter, aggressive and passive, predator and prey, wolf and chick, then rape is not abnormal. Obviously some rapists are very disturbed but they make up only two and a half per cent of the spectrum of male/female relationships.
>
> (London Rape Crisis Centre, 1977/1981: 210–11)

Radical feminists held that men had controlled women's sexuality for the purposes of male pleasure. They particularly directed their attention to ways in which men attempted to control women's bodies, arguing that men had constructed what was taken to be normal female sexuality to serve male interests. It was hence a central task of radical feminism to free women from male-defined and male-controlled sexuality. Menachem Amir's *Patterns in Forcible Rape* (1971) had shown that rapists had no emotional characteristics distinguishing them from men who had not committed this offence. Given this finding, the New York Radical Feminists asked, 'it it possible that the average male is programmed to be a rapist?' (Connell and Wilson, 1974: 1). Following this line of thinking, rape was the logical conclusion of the essential relationship pertaining between men and women.

Carol Smart drew upon this feminist work in *Women, Crime and Criminology* to address the limited study of rape within criminology as well as the presence of invidious myths about male and female sexuality in what work did exist. She insisted that: 'neither rape nor prostitution can be understood in isolation from an analysis of the position of women and the attendant sexual mores operating within a given culture' (Smart, 1976: 102). This entailed understanding the existing power structure between men and women, leading to the realisation that: 'Rapists may then be said to be "normal" given a social context in which male sexuality and aggression are equated and female sexuality is repressed and rendered passive' (Smart, 1976: 102).

Susan Brownmiller's *Against Our Will* (1975) is perhaps the most well-known of the many radical feminist books on rape. Brownmiller closed the Introduction to her book with a comment which has since become famous:

> From prehistoric times to the present, I believe, rape has played a critical function. It is nothing more or less than a conscious process of intimidation by which *all* men keep *all* women in a state of fear.
>
> (Brownmiller, 1975: 15)

According to this argument, all men in some sense benefit from the actions of the few that commit the act of rape. Brownmiller described men as natural predators, and linked women's fear of rape to her domestication by protective mating as well as her estrangement from other women. At base, her account rested on a view of rape as neither cultural, nor historical, but physiological in origin. For her, the anatomical possibility of forcible intercourse itself produced the male ideology of rape.

Brownmiller pointed out that men controlled the definitions of sex, hence an attack on the cultural values that upheld the ideology of rape was as crucial as the quest for better laws and an improved criminal justice system. Her argument wasn't simply that all men were potential rapists, but that rapists were the shock troops of the patriarchy:

> A world without rapists would be a world in which women moved freely without fear of men. That some men rape provides a sufficient threat to keep all women in a constant state of intimidation. . . . Rather than society's aberrants or 'spoilers of purity', men who commit rape have served in effect as front-line masculine shock troops, terrorist guerrillas in the longest sustained battle the world has ever known.
>
> (Brownmiller, 1975: 209)

The point is that, as Susan Griffin put it, 'rape and the fear of rape are a daily part of every woman's consciousness' (Griffin, 1979: 4). She described how she had been told as a girl that strange men wanted to harm little girls, that she must avoid dark streets, must not talk to strangers, lock doors and be modest. Brownmiller also wrote that women receive quite a training in victimhood, describing how girls heard from an early age that it was females and not males that were raped.

Brownmiller advised that women needed systematic training in self-defense from childhood, but in principle opposed private solutions to rape, writing that: 'to accept a special burden of self-protection is to reinforce the concept that women must live and move about in fear and can never expect to achieve the personal freedom, independence and self-assurance of men' (Brownmiller, 1975: 400). The intimidatory force of the threat of rape functioned as a form of constraint upon women's independence:

> Women are given sets of rules and regulations designed to keep them penned in. Women are warned to hide themselves from male eyes as much as possible. The message is clear: if a woman does not live a life of fear and does not follow the rules then she is responsible for her violation.
>
> (Dublin Rape Crisis Centre, 1979/1981: 204)

This perspective can be seen in feminist responses to police advice issued during the killing campaign waged against women in the north of England by Peter Sutcliffe. Feminists took to the streets to 'reclaim the night', criticising police warnings that women should stay indoors at night, and stating that instead there should be a curfew on men (Bland, 1984/ 1992).

Radical feminists also unveiled the extensive patriarchal ideologies surrounding the occurrence and function of domestic violence. Tackling spouse abuse challenged male supremacy and patriarchal rule within the family. As Hague and Wilson (2000) explain, women subjected to domestic violence in the postwar period, and before the rise of Women's Liberation, had nobody to turn to. They write that there was a resurgence of the traditional family ideal in postwar Britain, which was presented as natural. Additionally, the therapeutic society of the 1950s promulgated individual approaches to many kinds of 'problems'. All of this amounted to the blaming of battered women, and left them few avenues of escape. The campaign against domestic violence began with the first shelter for battered women, set up in Chiswick in 1971. Rebecca and Russell Dobash pioneered the refuge idea in Scotland and also researched on domestic violence. In *Violence Against Wives* (1979), they wrote that despite the fact that for women and children the family was the most violent of places, the myth of family bliss and security persisted. They stated that the belief in the sanctity of the family made it analogous to a fortress. Dobash and Dobash argued that domestic violence must be seen for what it was, one of the most explicit expressions of patriarchal domination. They insisted that to understand domestic violence, it must be placed in its social and cultural context:

> [W]e propose that the correct interpretation of violence between husbands and wives conceptualises such violence as the extension of the domination and control of husbands over their wives. This control is historically and socially constructed.
>
> (Dobash and Dobash, 1979: 15)

Distinguishing liberal feminism and radical feminism

At this point it may be useful to briefly review some important differences between liberal feminism and radical feminism. They are summarised schematically in the table below:

Perspective	Liberal feminism	Radical feminism
Problem	Discrimination	Patriarchy
Goal	Reform	Revolution
Methodological approach	Feminist empiricism	Feminist standpointism

Ideal-typical examples of these perspectives as seen in feminist criminologies might be modifying strain theory to admit a statistically-based analysis of women's offending (liberal feminist) and interviewing female rape victims to ascertain and sensitively diffuse their self-blaming (radical feminist).

Men as men: the sociology of masculinities and men's crime

Over the last decade, the character and reproduction of different kinds of masculinities has received critical scrutiny. The sociology of masculinity emerged from men's involvement in feminism, as well as the growing field of gay and lesbian studies. Both of these produced a range of theories of sexual identity and sexual relations. Feminist criminologists were interested in this work from the outset. Cain (1990) commented that feminist criminology must consider what it was in the social construction of maleness that was so criminogenic. Until quite recently, gender was largely excluded from the understanding of men's crimes. Criminology sexualised women criminals, but failed to address the maleness of men's crime. When the disproportionate gender ratio of crime was discussed, criminology tended to address the reasons why women were more conformist rather than why so many more men than women committed crimes. General theories of crime were still advanced which were based in the study of criminal men. These were basically theories of the offending behaviour of young, urban males. They may have been about men, but no critical analysis was made of the significance of their subjects' masculinity. The significance of crime for the constitution of masculinity was largely overlooked. What significance did men's understandings of themselves as men, and their lived experiences as men, have to their crimes? Furthermore, in what respects might connections between masculinities and crime be related to men's subordination of women? A number of competing frameworks for understanding links between masculinities and crime have emerged, the principal of which are discussed below.[6]

Judith Allen (1989) blamed the neglect of masculinity on the sex/gender distinction posited by feminist theory (sex is biological, gender is cultural). She explained that feminist criminologists had taken up the sex/gender distinction to enable them to deny that there was any necessary link between biological sex and gender attributes, capacities and behaviours. This is how she explained the consequences for the study of men's criminality:

> [T]he body is denied any place in the formation of subjectivity, consciousness, or personhood. . . . Behaviours and practices such as criminalities are thus investigated as solely matters of mind, attitude, influences, identities, cultural patterns. In an area of behaviour as sexed as criminalities, the fact that mainly persons with the sexed bodies of men predominate is accorded no significance.
>
> (Allen, 1989: 31)

Allen hence argued that feminist criminologists must discard the sex/gender distinction, along with other dichotomies such as the mind/body split. We must, Allen asserted, theorise the male body, understood in cultural and psychical terms.

As described above, radical feminism theorised the maleness of rape as a problem of power. It dispatched the notion that rape was an activity only conducted by abnormal males, and connected rape to the organisation of society as a whole. Rape was construed as a foundation of patriarchy in which all men were implicated. However, this theory of rape as a key tactic in the social control of women obscured the significance of differences among men. A sociology of masculinity emerged in earnest from 1977 with Andrew Tolson's book *The Limits of Masculinity*, which described diverse masculinities rather than one unitary form, and saw masculinity as a product of gender relations rather than sex roles. Bob Connell's (1987) social constructionist theory viewed men's gender not as an individual possession, but in terms of institutional practices located in structures of power. He explained that sex role theory connected unproblematically a biological term (sex) with a dramaturgical one (role), having the result of negating the question of power relationships. Connell stated that there was a plurality of masculinities, moving away from a fixed model of a unitary masculinity towards an understanding of the differences which existed. Furthermore, Connell argued that masculinities were hierarchically ordered. He described a hegemonic masculinity of normative heterosexuality which was the culturally exalted form. This hegemonic masculinity, he explained, must be constantly produced and reproduced.

James Messerschmidt (1993) advanced a 'doing gender' perspective to explain men's crime. This viewed criminal activities as ways of constituting diverse and differentially empowered masculinities. Messerschmidt sought to explicate how structures were constituted and reconstituted through the everyday actions of social actors. He argued that masculinity was enacted by practices within different social situations that maintained certain kinds of relationships, both between men and women, and among men. For Messerschmidt, crime was one way in which masculinity could be expressed, a form of social practice invoked as a resource, when other resources are unavailable, for the accomplishment of masculinity.

Tony Jefferson (1994, 1996, 1997b) advanced a psycho-social theory of subjectivity, which drew out the fragile, contingent and contradictory character of masculinity. He argued that Connell's idea of hegemonic masculinity did not recognise a psychologically complex subject for whom the meanings of 'masculinity' were not confined to a largely negative list of traits. In his reading of the case of the boxer Mike Tyson, who was convicted of the crime of rape by an Indiana court in 1992, Jefferson emphasised the connections between masculine desires and crime, as well as the unconscious motivations of Tyson's aggressive conduct. Tyson emerged from this account as an anxious subject engaging in a flamboyant hyper-masculine violence, plagued by defensive splittings and projections.

His ever-escalating acts of aggression and contempt for women were ambivalent. Jefferson's approach enables us to understand the fusion of the pleasures of crime with the pleasures of the masculine. He pointed out that we need to understand the pleasures of crime as well as the opportunities for criminal behaviour.

Feminist criminologies and questions of gender and crime today

Like the radical criminologies discussed in Chapter 6, feminist criminologies have been subject to both rejection and limited accommodation within academia. In response to the emergence of feminist criminologies, a number of scholars engaged in attempts to show that there was actually no appreciable gender difference in criminal and delinquent behaviour. They demonstrated considerable hostility to feminist work on women criminals, and claimed that by doing more empirical work, general, universal criminological theories might be maintained (Jensen and Raymond, 1976; Silverman and Sinitz, 1974). Feminist criminology has also been incorporated into the regular field of criminological enquiry, but this has often been in ways that have circumscribed the not inconsiderable challenges that it makes to the conventional practices of criminology. Those who study any aspect of gender and crime write into an evidently politicised field. It seems important that feminists resist the tendency for gender to become simply one more factor included in objectivist multi-factorial general theories of crime. The study of gender and crime must retain its original commitment to working towards the abolition of women's oppression. Furthermore, the important epistemological contributions made by feminist criminologies, concerning authentic and emancipatory modes of knowledge-production, must not be forgotten.

Feminist criminologists continue to report that their approach remains outside of the mainstream of criminology. According to Ngaire Naffine (1997), criminology remains a male-dominated discipline principally about academic men studying criminal men. She described the ghettoisation of questions of gender, commenting that, 'the standard case is the study of men as non-gendered subjects and the speciality is the study of women as gendered beings' (Naffine, 1997: 2). Naffine complained that male criminologists overwhelmingly remained insensitive to the significance of their own cultural constitution as men, reflecting a blindness of men to their own maleness which is a problem pervasive in Western culture. She pointed out that claims of neutrality and universality convey the message that their speaker can speak on behalf of everyone. Naffine argued strongly against this assumption, writing that: 'This is an imperialist gesture that silences the others who fail to agree, but who lack the authority, or the opportunity, to express a different point of view' (Naffine, 1997: 12). This exclusionary gesture, she contended, can be traced to the originary out-look of criminology, which believed that a rigorous scientific approach could guarantee impartiality.

Over the last decade, there has been a considerable decline in the mass base of feminist activism, as well as a popular backlash against femin-ism. However, there is a continuing complexity and vitality of academic feminisms, to which theorists of crime and punishment can turn. The divergent feminist criminologies that have emerged over the last three decades have reflected the multiplication of approaches within the broader area of feminist theory. A founding claim of feminism was that women have common interests arising from a common experience, of which they should become aware. This recognition provided the basis for collective action aimed at changing the position of women in society. However, over the last two decades the self-evidence of this set of propositions has been challenged by the recognition of important differences among women. The notion of a shared universal category of woman was held by some to perpetuate the silencing of certain groups of women, for instance black and lesbian women. The project of discovering and acting upon what united women was depicted as an imposition of white Western notions that denied diversity. Like the Left approaches described in the preceding chapter, feminism has seen contentious debates, bitter divisions and the consolidation of factions. However, rather than representing a breakdown in feminist thought, the multiplicity of voices evidences fem-inism's continuing vitality as a mode of critique that changes with the times. A range of postmodern feminist criminologies have emerged, some of which are discussed in Chapter 9. These continue to challenge and to transgress the boundaries and assumptions of criminological practice.

Notes

1. For useful overviews of feminist criminologies, see Carrington (1998), Daly (1997), Daly and Chesney-Lind (1988), Gelsthorpe (1997), Valverde (1991) and Simpson (1989). Similar developments can be discerned in the field of feminist legal studies (see Minda, 1995: 116–48 and Lacey, 1998).
2. For overviews of standpoint feminism, see Longino (1993) and Hekman (1997).
3. For an analysis of the problems associated with the notion of a single 'women's standpoint', see Spelman (1990).
4. The story of Solanas is depicted in the film *I Shot Andy Warhol* (Harron, 1996, Orion Pictures). See Harron and Minahan (1995) for the SCUM Manifesto.
5. The film *Patty Hearst* (1988, Atlantic, dir. Scrader), starring Natasha Richardson as the heiress turned guerrilla, was based on Hearst's account.
6. See Jefferson (1997a) for a more detailed overview.

Chapter 8

Foucault, penality and social regulation

Visibility is a trap.

(Foucault, 1975/1991: 200)

From the mid-1970s, the French philosopher Michel Foucault (1926–1984) published a number of works that advanced arguments about how modern forms of knowledge and power produced distinctive forms of subjectivity.[1] The Foucauldian corpus included works on the asylum, the hospital and the regulation of sexualities, as well as on changing forms of punishment. What these seemingly diverse topics have in common is study of the emergence and operation of modern forms of power, and their connections with disciplines like psychiatry, clinical medicine, sexology, psychoanalysis and criminology. Foucault drew out a number of important connections between the rise of the human sciences and the regulation of individuals and populations. His work has been taken to depict the condition of modernity itself as a 'prison house of technical knowledge' (Beck, 1998: 11).

By the time that he began to focus on the problem of punishment and power, Foucault was already a well-known intellectual. He had published on the birth of the asylum and the history of psychiatry in *Madness and Civilization,* and on the constitution of modern medical knowledge in *The Birth of The Clinic.* The work best known to criminologists is *Discipline and Punish,* first published in 1975. Foucault's detailed analysis of the mechanisms of power in the nineteenth-century prison offered a new way of thinking about imprisonment at a time when a vocal and increasingly politicised prisoners' movement was organising.[2] In the early part of *Discipline and Punish,* Foucault stated that he had come to see the prison as political in the light of the events of the late 1960s as much as from his research into its history.

Foucault was a key member of the Groupe d'Information sur les Prisons (GIP) during the 1970s. Other prominent intellectuals involved with the group's activities included Gilles Deleuze, Jacques Donzelot, Hélène Cixous and Jean-Paul Sartre. Membership of the organisation did extend far beyond left-wing circles though, and groups were set up all over France. Donzelot (1975) explained the purpose of the GIP as the aim of connecting prisoners' movements with other social groups in struggle, writing that imprisoned inmates were not integrated into the broader struggle of the workers that arose from the events of May 1968. He discussed a number of processes that, he believed, contributed to the isolation of the prisoners' struggle. In 1970–1, several ultra-leftist militants who had been sent to prison began protests that sought the granting to them of a special status as political prisoners. The publicity occasioned by the protest spread some news about the condition of French prisons. However, as Donzelot pointed out, by claiming a special status, these leftists cut both themselves, and politicised proletarians outside the prison walls, off from common-law inmates.

Donzelot explained that the GIP set out to make information a weapon by making visible the intolerable conditions of prison life, and by returning the right to speak to the prisoners. He asserted that the criminological perspective obtaining in France at the time had suppressed the radical nature of the inmates' grievances. The GIP circulated a questionnaire drawn up by some inmates around the prisons and launched a press campaign. Donzelot wrote that the left-wing press had largely scorned the '*question pénitentiaire*'. The GIP organised discussions in working-class districts on the meaning of the prisoners' revolts, finding that they met with hostility or incomprehension. As he explained, the workers could not see what their struggles could have in common with those of prisoners. As Foucault explained in one of his many interviews, the goal of the GIP was not to secure specific rights and improvements, but 'to question the social and moral distinction between the innocent and the guilty' (Foucault, 1971/1996: 227). The deeper point made by the GIP was that the dividing line separating those in the prison from those outside was not obvious.

It is in this context that *Discipline and Punish* should be understood. As Barry Smart put it, prison riots 'are considered by Foucault to have been not so much about the relative adequacy of prison conditions, as about the very materiality of the prison as an "instrument and vector of power" over the body' (Smart, 1983/1992: 68). Foucault (1972/1996: 211) stated that the antijudicial struggle against judges, courts and prisons was not a fight against injustice or an attempt to improve the efficiency of certain institutions, but a struggle against power. The GIP sought to attack an oppressive system 'in places where it is called something else – justice, technique, knowledge, objectivity' (GIP, 1971, cited in Eribon, 1991: 228). The group's pamphlets included one on the killing of the black inmate George Jackson in a California prison, and another on prisoner suicides, which it depicted as dramatic acts of individual insubordination. Foucault and the GIP opposed the repressive quelling of dissidence, claiming that 'police control is tightening on our everyday life. . . . We live in a state of custody' (cited in Eribon, 1991: 224). Indeed, the police used violent means to respond to GIP protests. Foucault stated that he saw the penal system as the form in which power was most obviously seen for what it was (Foucault, 1972/1996: 210).

Foucault's genealogical method

What can be said about Foucault's method? It was around this time that Foucault initiated a form of critical practice called 'genealogy', or 'the history of the present'.[3] Whereas reformist histories of the triumphs of new technologies and the good intentions and struggles of reformers sought to justify the present, Foucault's genealogy aimed to destabilise it. For instance, his work firmly rejected the narrative of humanitarian reform, indicting what could be called the dark side of the Enlightenment. Foucault described genealogy as 'the critical ontology of ourselves' (Foucault, 1984: 45), meaning that it exposed how what was taken for granted and given as necessary had once been otherwise. The genealogist hence investigated the historical events that had led people to understand themselves in particular ways. This intellectual practice was conceived by Foucault as a critical reflection on the limits of contemporary understandings, in order that they might be transgressed and transformed (Foucault, 1984: 50). The strategy of revealing as contingent some of society's most cherished beliefs and basic assumptions was an effective one, especially given that Foucault provided support for his ideas in the form of detailed historical studies.

As we can see from Foucault's involvement with the prisoners' movement, his understanding of the role of the intellectual was not one of standing outside a struggle and expressing its truths. Neither was his practice intended to be one of representing people. It was rather, he hoped, an activity conducted alongside those who struggled against power. This strategy differed from those of the Communst Party or the Union in that these bodies are representative agencies. Foucault saw in the prisoner's movement the emergence of a counter-discourse, commenting that:

> If the discourse of inmates or prison doctors constitutes a form of struggle, it is because they confiscate, at least temporarily, the power to speak on prison conditions – at present, the exclusive property of prison administrators and their cronies in reform groups.
>
> (Foucault, 1972/1996: 214)

Speaking on behalf of, or in the name of, the prisoners, was avoided by GIP, who instead wanted to publicise the inmates' own revelations. The intellectual's role was hence to bring to light subjugated knowledges. The GIP was disbanded in 1974, after the prisoners had set up their own action committee. The activities of the GIP had made this conflict visible, and squarely focused public opinion, if only for a time, on questions of punishment and power. Its activities accorded with Foucault's understanding of transformation, as brought about by rendering it impossible to carry on thinking about things in the same way:

> A critique is not a matter of saying that things are not right as they are. It is a matter of pointing out on what kinds of assumptions, what kinds of familiar, unchallenged, unconsidered modes of thought the practices that we accept rest. . . . Practicing criticism is a matter of making facile gestures difficult.
>
> (Foucault, 1981/1990: 154–5)

For instance, *Discipline and Punish* and the activities of the GIP suspended the notion that less physically painful punishment was necessarily more humane.

As with all thinkers of repute, Foucault's work has been the subject of intense criticism, which demonstrates its challenging character. Jürgen Habermas (1987) objected that Foucault ran the risk of assimilating questions of truth to questions of power by locating his project fully within struggles against power. Foucault's genealogy was openly partisan, denying that objective knowledge was a possibility. Nancy Fraser (1989) questioned the normative position from which Foucault wrote. Where indeed was Foucault's own gaze located? From what position did he write? On the question of subjugated knowledges, Gayatri Spivak (1988) questioned the assumption that the marginalised had privileged access to the structures of their own experiential contexts. She argued that we could not take for granted the idea that subjects had complete, or even adequate, understanding of their situations. Foucault responded to criticism, as well as to changing times, by modifying his theses. This critical reflection on his work was cut tragically short by his death in 1984.

The concept of disciplinary power

Foucault insisted upon the inseparability of knowledge and power. This rested on two related propositions that may be stated as follows:

1. There is no knowledge without the exercise of power.
2. There is no power without knowledge.

Foucault's work was directed at elucidating the changing forms of the relationship between knowledge and power, and their implications for the nature of modern subjectivity. His point was not that knowledge and power were identical, but that one must study the relation between the two.

In *Discipline and Punish*, Foucault employed the example of changes in the mode of punishment to illustrate a broader argument about a transformation in the relations between knowledge and power. He stated that in the old regime before the French Revolution, the dominant form of punishment had been the public spectacle of corporal and capital punishment. This reflected a particular relationship between power and knowledge, which Foucault termed monarchical power. In monarchical power, he argued, the exorbitant power of the sovereign was displayed in costly and magnificent rituals to the people. *Discipline and Punish* opened with an account of one of these spectacles of the crushing terror of sovereign power, in the horrendously botched execution of Robert-François Damiens in Paris. These displays were infrequent, and also unreliable because the crowd sometimes took the side of the criminal. Hence Foucault argued that they became ineffectual in maintaining ruling power. According to him, the power of the old regime was, while not chaotic in action, so intermittent in operation that it was highly inefficient. Monarchical power had a 'weak capacity for "resolution", as one might say in photographic terms' (Foucault, 1996: 230). Foucault argued that social and economic change rendered sovereign power obsolete, requiring power to circulate through progressively finer channels.

He argued that the reforms to the criminal law called for in the eighteenth century, and discussed earlier in Chapter 1, were not brought about due to changing sensibilities, but must be understood as part of an effort to reconfigure the mechanisms of power. Foucault claimed that the reformers were less concerned with the abuse of the power to punish than with its bad distribution, writing that:

> What was emerging no doubt was not so much a new respect for the humanity of the condemned. . . . as a tendency towards a more finely tuned justice, towards a closer penal mapping of the social body.
>
> (Foucault, 1975/1991: 78)

In sum, beneath the humanisation of penalties, Foucault discerned a strategy for the redistribution of the power to punish.

Monarchical power was superseded by a new modality of control which implied 'an uninterrupted, constant coercion' (Foucault, 1975/1991: 137). Foucault contended that a new form of power-knowledge emerged. This involved a reversal of the axis of visibility, from everyone seeing the display of the power of the monarch, to a micro-power in which each person could be seen in their individuality. According to Foucault, disciplinary power is dispersed throughout the micro-level relations that constitute society, and does not emanate 'from above' like monarchical power. How might this capillary power work? Foucault firstly advanced a number of important arguments about connections between space and power. In his earlier text *Madness and Civilisation*, the production of knowledge with the operation of dividing practices took the form of exclusion. The mad were exiled, or segregated into the space of the asylum. In *Discipline and Punish*, the production of knowledge and the exercise of power did not take the form of exclusion, but of spatial distribution:

> [E]ach individual has his own place; and each place his individual. . . .
> Disciplinary space tends to be divided into as many sections as there are
> bodies or elements to be distributed. One must eliminate the effects of
> imprecise distributions, the uncontrolled disappearance of individuals.
>
> (Foucault, 1975/1991: 143)

Foucault saw the organisation of the spatio-temporal as crucial to the operation of disciplinary power, establishing relations of proximity and succession. This strategy could be seen in the timetable, which lays out a programme of activities.

Discipline and Punish explored the relations of power, knowledge and the body. In this book, the body emerged as a vital component in the operation of power relations, being the site at which power and knowledge are localised. Foucault contended that subjectivity was the product of the exercise of disciplinary power upon the body (Foucault, 1975/1991: 29). He explained that disciplinary power shaped and trained the body, as seen for instance at Mettray Colony for juvenile delinquents, where the combination of observation and exercise made training 'an instrument of perpetual assessment' (Foucault, 1975/1991: 294). The corrective penality that he depicted operated through the repetition of exercises to restore obedience. The example of Mettray illustrated Foucault's argument that subjectivity is produced 'around, on, within the body' by the working of a correctional mode of power that could also be seen in factories, schools, barracks and hospitals.[4] This conception of the subject assumed a symbiotic relationship of power and knowledge which required a direct hold on the body. Foucault argued that in studying disciplinary power, there was no need to consider the question of its mediation through the subject's consciousness, because this form of power directly took hold of the body. This thesis contrasted markedly with Althusser's ideas about ideological interpellation.

The Foucauldian approach ushered in a reconceptualisation of power away from Marxist models of class rule, and towards a recognition of the power of the norm. Foucauldian studies also departed from the perspective of standpoint feminists, who held that power was wielded by a particular group. As Smart (1989) pointed out, Foucault demonstrated more interest in how the mechanisms of power worked than in the old questions of who had power. Indeed, Foucault contended that it did not matter who exercised power. He stated that the panopticon was a machine that any random individual could operate. Foucault stated quite explicitly in *Discipline and Punish* that power was not a possession, or a property, but should be understood to be a strategy. This is what might be called a shift from a substantive to a relational concept of power. Instead of focusing on the primary oppression of women or the working class, he thought that it was important to theorise the ways in which every inhabitant of modern societies was subjected to certain forms of subjection.

Marxist approaches favoured a historical materialist conception of history, summarised in Engels' classic definition as follows:

> [T]hat view of the course of history which seeks the ultimate cause and the great moving power of all important historical events in the economic development of society, in the changes in the mode of production and exchange, in the consequent division into distinct classes, and in the struggles of these classes against one another.
>
> (Marx and Engels, 1970: 383–4)

This understanding of history posited that the development of societies could be seen to fall into marked periods, these corresponding to stages in the mode of production (that is, the forces of production of, for instance, raw materials and tools, and the relations of production, i.e. the organisation of the production process).[5] Furthermore, while the New Left had believed that capitalist order worked through repression, Foucault insisted that disciplinary power was productive.[6]

A book which characterises the Marxist approach is Georg Rusche and Otto Kirkheimer's *Punishment and Social Structure* (1939). This book received little attention for over twenty years, and its revival in the late 1960s should be seen in the context of the emerging radical criminology. The starting principle of *Punishment and Social Structure* was that successive changes in the mode of production were correlative with changes in the punishments meted out by society. According to its authors, this meant that the origins and development of penal systems should be studied as determined by primarily economic forces. Rusche and Kirkheimer strongly denied that punishment should be understood as reducible to the end of crime control, advising their readers to suspend the notion that crime and punishment were linked. The kind of reasoning employed by them can be seen in the formula, 'the poorer the masses became, the harder the punishments in order to deter them from crime' (Rusche and Kirkheimer, 1939/1968: 18). In discussing the decline of bodily punishment, Rusche and Kirkheimer insisted that the changes were not the result of humanitarian concerns, but instead were related to the need of productive labour.[7] While approving of *Punishment and Social Structure*'s challenging of any self-evident link between crime and punishment, Foucault (1975/1991: 25) remarked that the strict correlations drawn in that text could be challenged. His departure was to site systems of punishment within a political economy not of capital but of the body.

This different conception of power was further elaborated in *The Will to Knowledge* (1976), in which Foucault stated that power was not just, or even primarily, negative, repressive and juridical. This led to a focus on the procedures of normalisation rather than those of law. As Charles

Taylor (1986: 75) put it, 'what is wielded through the modern technologies of control is something quite different, in that it is not concerned with law but with normalization'. Foucault argued that the law had a diminishing significance, and that the procedures of normalisation progressively colonised those of law. Putting the matter another way, the law increasingly operated like a norm. He hence decentred law from his analysis and focused on the new forms of regulation and surveillance. However, as Carol Smart (1989) argued, the power of law had not simply receded in modern societies. Indeed, law could be seen to have extended its terrain. Smart suggested that we instead think of two parallel mechanisms of power, law and normalisation. François Ewald (1990) argued that for Foucault, the norm was not opposed to the law but to the juridical (law as the expression of the sovereign's power).[8] He explained that normative laws were not established with reference to a set of universal principles, and did not emanate from the sovereign's will. They instead functioned to regulate conduct.

Critics of *Discipline and Punish* objected that in its focus on the workings of power there seemed to be no space left for resistance. Historical research has shown that from the beginnings of the prison system, inmates have employed a whole panoply of practices to test and to thwart the eye of power, such as tattooing and illicit communications systems (O'Brien, 1982). In *The Will To Knowledge*, Foucault clarified his position in stating that resistances were 'inscribed in the latter [power] as an irreducible opposite' (Foucault, 1976/1990: 96). Nevertheless, Lois McNay stated that Foucault's emphasis of a corporeally centred disciplinary power produced a conception of subjectivity that was 'impoverished' (McNay, 1994: 122). As Axel Honneth commented, the Foucauldian subject 'represents psychic processes as the result of constant conditioning' (Honneth, 1991: 189).[9] A different kind of criticism came from Cronin (1996), who complained that Foucault's understanding of subjectivity was so radical that it made it impossible to see any determinate social location of the exercise of power. He felt that Foucault's divorcing of the notion of strategy from that of the intentional subject was illuminating but ultimately obscured the question of purposefulness.

Criminology and the invention of *homo criminalis*

Foucault's work argued that power and knowledge were interdependent, and in doing so claimed that disciplines like criminology, psychiatry and psychology were part of the exercise of new forms of power. For Foucault, the procedures of individualisation and normalisation constituted the roots of the human sciences. He argued that outside the prison, the threshold of biography was lowered. In the older monarchical power, personal information about the character and lives of people had only been collected about the famous and the rich. In disciplinary power, however, the aim was to produce knowledge about every person, capturing their uniqueness by comparing them to the norm. Foucault claimed that criminology, psychiatry, psychology and sexology produced knowledge of this kind about individuals. He also held that this kind of knowledge was produced as integral to the operation of institutions such as families and schools.

Pasquale Pasquino presented a paper to Foucault's seminar at the Collège de France in 1979, with the title 'Criminology: The Birth of a Special Savoir'. This sited the intelligibility of criminology within a history of the transformations of punitive rationalities, making visible the surface of emergence of criminology in the movement away from classical jurisprudence. Pasquino wrote that the classical theory of penal law assumed what he called the figure of *homo penalis,* who was 'nothing more or less than the citizen, the man of the Contract' (Pasquino, 1979/1980: 20). Classical penal theory established free will as the basis of the power to punish, seeing this as common to all and hence understanding crime as an accident of false and erroneous calculation. However, the more recent figure of *homo criminalis* envisaged crimes as indications of an evil or abnormal nature. Pasquino noted that the criminal anthropologist Enrico Ferri insisted that the criminal did not think like the normal man, if indeed he thought at all. Ferri's work was hence directed towards neutralisation of the causes of crime instead of deterrence. This involved attacking the roots of criminality through the practice of social hygiene, as well as adjusting the punishment to fit the criminal. Pasquino cited the struggle between psychiatrists and jurists over the meaning of certain monstrous crimes in the 1820s as one precursor of the figure of *homo criminalis.* He referred to Foucault's study of the case of the Norman peasant Pierre Rivière, who murdered several members of his family. This book showed the relations of power within which discourses emerged and functioned. In addition, Pasquino mentioned incorrigible children, homosexuals and the dangerous classes, as new objects of knowledge that could be seen as antecedents of *homo criminalis.* The novel personage of the criminal was hence seen by Pasquino as the product of a new kind of reflection upon how best to order society.

Some scholars have argued that the prison can be identified as a specific site from which the emergence of criminology can be traced. Marie-Christine Leps (1992) allied the history of criminology with the development of disciplinary power. However, David Garland (1992) qualified Foucault's characterisation of criminology in the late twentieth century as wholly disciplinary. Garland accepted that the term '*criminologie*' has retained a more limited psychological sense in France, explaining that the sociology of deviance remained a separate enterprise. That matter aside, Garland argued that the emergence of a critical criminology, as well as the field's diversity more generally, means that the question of criminology's relation to power is not as clear-cut as Foucault's comments might be interpreted to suggest. However, the extent to which critical criminologies have been immune from all collusion with disciplinary power is not evident.

The inspecting gaze and the panoptical society

Foucault described the Panopticon, discussed in Chapter 1 of this book, as 'a mechanism that coerces by means of observation', and demonstrated his ideas about disciplinary power by describing the operation of panopticism in the nineteenth-century penitentiary prison. The essential point about the panopticon as an ideal-typical representation of a new political technology was the principle of uncertainty that it embodied:

> The Panopticon is a machine for dissociating the see/being seen dyad: in the peripheric ring, one is totally seen, without ever seeing; in the central tower, one sees everything without ever being seen.
>
> (Foucault, 1975/1991: 202)

Foucault claimed that there had been a break away from spectacle to surveillance, writing that discipline substituted for the spectacle of public events 'the uninterrupted play of calculated gazes'. Instead of seeing Bentham's voluntaristic conception of human nature as the basis for humanitarian reform, Foucault emphasised that panopticism was a mode of subjection. Janet Semple (1992, 1993) railed against what she saw as Foucault's 'claustrophobic distrust of the world' and insisted that the Panopticon was the product of 'a realistic, kindly man looking for ways to ameliorate the lot of the poor' (Semple, 1993: 322, 314–15). Foucault's concern, however, was not with Bentham's supposed intentions, but with the political technology emblematised by the Panopticon.

Foucault claimed that this new kind of visibility constituted people as individuals who came to regulate their own behaviour. In the prison, the inmate conscious, or fearful, of being watched would come to exercise control over themselves. This idea led Foucault to assert that 'he who is subjected to a field of visibility, and who knows it . . . becomes the principle of his own subjection' (Foucault, 1975/1991: 202–3). Foucault argued that inmates became 'caught up in a power situation of which they themselves are the bearers'. Elsewhere, he wrote that surveillance was 'an inspecting gaze, a gaze which each individual under its weight will end by interiorizing to the point that he is his own overseer, each individual thus exercising this surveillance over, and against, himself' (Foucault, 1980: 155). Foucault also argued that panopticism produced distinctive modern forms of identity, because people came to think of themselves in certain ways, internalising the panoptical gaze. Taking the example of the prison, the knowledge produced about the prisoner through continual monitoring was normalising because it compared him to a standard against which his departure was to be measured. This can be seen in the examination. What was taken to be his unique individuality was actually the product of a particular way of seeing the prisoner. Foucault added to this proposition the claim that the prisoner also came to see himself in this light.

Discipline and Punish made a broader argument that modern society was disciplinary in character. Foucault contended that the organisation of a centralised police force was one of three modalities by which norms were extended throughout the social body. This was a police force occupied upon the task of exercising a 'permanent, exhaustive, omnipresent surveillance, capable of making all visible' (Foucault, 1975/1991: 214). Foucault (1997: 32) designated the period beginning in the late eighteenth century 'the age of panopticism', in which a generalised system of confinement permeated every layer of society. On several occasions, Foucault contended that capitalist societies were confinement societies. His notion of 'confinement societies' did not simply designate the segregation of criminals and the insane in closed institutions. While incarceration of that kind did take place, the more important point made by Foucault was that from the nineteenth century networks of surveillance and punishment were dispersed throughout the society, constituting a 'great carceral continuum that diffused penitentiary techniques into the most innocent disciplines . . . a subtle, graduated carceral net, with compact institutions, but also separate and diffused methods' (Foucault, 1975/1991: 297). Foucault suggested that we inhabit societies of surveillance, thoroughly suffused with penality, in which 'each subject finds himself caught in a punishable and punishing universality' (Foucault, 1975/1991: 178).

This 'punishable and punishing universality' referred to the manner in which all departures from the norm were potentially punishable, and that punishment was correctional through the imposition of gradated training practices and drills:

> Disciplinary power is exercised on the 'whole indefinite domain of the non-conforming', on the pupil's error, the soldier's lapse of concentration, the worker's absence or inefficiency, not merely on transgressions of the legal code. Thus the exercise of disciplinary power, disciplinary 'punishment', is not reducible to judicial punishment. Disciplinary power is exercised on departures from the rule, on non-observance of imposed norms.
>
> (Smart, 1983/1992: 71)

Evidently, Foucault's notion of the 'carceral archipelago' conveyed much more than the felt potential of being seen. He emphasised the respect in which inspection was the medium of a normalising judgement. This feature of Foucault's argument concerned the kind of knowledge produced about the individual. Foucault differentiated his approach from that of Durkheim by remarking that whereas the latter saw individualisation as the cause of changes in punishment (in the form of greater leniency), Foucault preferred to see processes of individualisation as one effect of the new tactics of power (Foucault, 1975/1991: 23).

From the late 1970s, scholars have employed Foucault's arguments about disciplinary power to explain the character of modes of crime control and punishment. In *Madness and Civilisation*, Foucault had depicted the striking off of the chains of the mad as the ushering in of a new kind of coercion based in moral constraint, against the conventional humanitarian account. In *Discipline and Punish* he had argued that the shift from the spectacle of gruesome bodily punishment to correctional imprisonment was an instance of a new disciplinary power. In *The Policing of Families*, Jacques Donzelot (1979) described the development of a tutelary complex in the twentieth century, which replaced stigmatising punishment with careful attention to the individual case and education. He explained how the reformers viewed this transformation of the judicial apparatus, writing that for them, 'knowledge would dissolve repressive power by opening the way to a liberating education' (Donzelot, 1979: 97). However, Donzelot pointed out that what emerged was a new landscape of supervision and the controlled 'freedom' of surveillance, replacing 'the coercion of bodies with control over relations' (Donzelot, 1979: 145).

Stan Cohen (1979) also demonstrated this scepticism towards the supposedly more benevolent. Cohen described the 'dispersal of discipline' in the move towards community corrections. He stated that rather than emphasising how decarceration brought more humane treatment and less state intervention, we should address the manner in which community control reproduced in the community the same coercive features as the previous system of confinement. This line of argument proposed that the softer ideology of community corrections concealed its actual coercive character. Cohen wrote that the segregated institution made deviance control invisible, but erected clear spatial boundaries marking off the normal from the deviant. The development of community control, however, meant that it was no longer easy to say where the prison ended and where the community began. He claimed that community control increased both the total number of deviants brought into the system and the amount of intervention directed at them once in the system. Cohen identified community corrections as a continuation of the pattern of widening of the carceral archipelago that Foucault had described in *Discipline and Punish*.

A debate ensued over the applicability of Foucault's theses to the changing penal practices of the later twentieth century. Tony Bottoms (1983) argued that the widespread use of the sanction of the fine contradicted Cohen's thesis, as it was an exemplary neo-classical form of punishment, which communicated messages about blame and the costs of wrongdoing rather than seeking to correct or retrain the offender. He stated that for Foucault the essential attribute of discipline was 'individualized soul training', that is, training exercises aimed at correcting conduct also had the effect of shaping identity. Bottoms pointed out that fines were not this kind of measure, hence a simple picture of the extension of disciplinary society must be challenged. In an essay on Disneyworld, Clifford

Shearing and Philip Stenning (1985) dissented from this view. They insisted that the most pertinent feature of Foucault's concept of discipline was embeddedness (it was integrated into social relations) and not individualised soul training. They described the features of corporate control built into the recreational facilities at Disneyworld in Orlando, Florida. These included constant instruction and omnipresent employees who corrected the slightest deviations. The pervasive control was, they wrote, also embedded in other structures and hence was both subtle and consensual. According to them, the new instrumental discipline involved prevention through the reduction of opportunities for disorder. David Nelken (1989) argued that both Cohen and Bottoms had maintained a distinction between disciplinary and juridical methods of punishment, whereas these might be mututally constitutive or supplement each other in modern social regulation. What was implicit in this debate was that different readings of Foucault were possible.

The surveillance society

In the 1990s, some scholars drew upon Foucault's ideas to understand the expansion of new visual, communication and information technologies like CCTV cameras and computerised criminal records databases. A sociology of surveillance developed. George Orwell's dystopian novel *Nineteen Eighty-Four* (1949) strongly captured the imagination of the postwar critical consciousness, with its vision of a total surveillance society. This kind of scenario was envisaged in *Private Lives and Public Surveillance* by James Rule, as a totalised and highly intrusive system of surveillance directed at everyone:

> The system would work to enforce compliance with a uniform set of norms governing every aspect of everyone's behaviour. Every action of every client would be scrutinised, recorded, evaluated both at the moment of occurrence and forever afterwards. The system would bring the whole fund of its information to bear on every decision it made about everyone. Any sign of disobedience – present or anticipated – would result in corrective action. The fact that the system kept everyone under constant monitoring would mean that in the event of misbehaviour, apprehension and sanctioning would occur immediately. By making detection and retaliation inevitable such a system would make disobedience unthinkable.
>
> (Rule, 1973: 37)

The advent of the information revolution led many commentators to warn of the likelihood of the arrival of the Orwellian nightmare. However, from the late 1970s, Foucault's analysis of the Panopticon was also drawn upon.

Scholars discussed how the development of electronic technologies vastly expanded the surveillance capacities of the state, computer-based technologies being particularly powerful in this respect. They noted that developments in information technology had expanded archive capacity and accelerated information retrieval. Studies of various kinds concluded that the ubiquity of surveillance rendered it a central feature of modern societies. The constant expansion of increasingly effective surveillance technologies was believed to make everyday life more and more transparent. Information systems were freed from the constraints of space and time. They tended to become 'information panopticons', the psychological effects of visibility alone being sufficient to ensure appropriate conduct (Zuboff, 1988: 321–2). Mark Poster (1990) contended that technological advances in communications created a 'Superpanopticon', which required as its precondition a 'disciplined self-surveillant populace'.

This discourse of the ubiquity and increasing refinement of surveillance, as well as its growing ability to shape our lives, was represented in films like *The Truman Show* and *Enemy of the State*. The 1995 film *The Net* carried the following rider:

> Like all of us, Angela Bennett [Sandra Bullock] lives in the age of information. Every trace of her existence is computerized. Everything about her is encoded somewhere on a complex network of information. It's something Angela never thought about . . . until the day she was erased.[10]

As the story goes, Angela, a computer software engineer, inadvertently accesses information that she is not supposed to have seen. Suddenly she finds that her driver's licence, credit cards, bank account, and hence her identity, has been deleted. This tale of the abuses of information was sold as straight from the headlines.

However, sometimes this literature seemed to overstate the ubiquity of surveillance. It also had scant regard for the significance of obscurities of various kinds. This was not really surprising given that, as Levin (1997) observes, Foucault did not engage in a systematic pursuit of vision's failure. One text which did take up this challenge was Alison Young's *Imagining Crime* (1996), which made an important distinction between the actual existence of the surveillance society and what she termed the 'will to watch'. The subject, Young wrote, is constantly engaged upon the activity of looking out for the criminal and imagining their crimes. She related the popularity of detective fiction to the keen desire for a transparent society in which all ambiguity would be effaced. Young also presented a fascinating analysis of how the Bulger case occasioned a 'trauma of the visible' with blind spots confounding the 'feverish desire to see all' (Young, 1996: 113).

Post-disciplinary penality and governmental rule

Foucault's notion of disciplinary power was developed through a number of arguments about an inspecting gaze in a panoptical society. An argument across a range of texts contends that we are now in a 'post-disciplinary' era of control, in which power does not reside in an alien gaze. This scholarship also contends that we are witnessing a shift away from the correctional practices associated with disciplinary penality. These accounts look to the later work of Foucault on 'governmentality' to comprehend how social regulation is currently being reconfigured.[11]

The field of governmentality that Foucault explored did not focus on objectifying technologies. Instead, these studies looked at the work done by people on themselves. The governmentality perspective holds that power works through, and by means of, an active subject. Governmental power constructs and steers individuals who are capable of action and choice. Rather than producing a regimented conformity, governmental power holds out models of the person to be adopted by willing individuals. Government does not suppress individual subjectivity, but moulds it in particular ways. Foucault's work began to address the role of power in the constitution of active subjects. This amounted to a focus on the ways in which people actively constituted themselves as the subjects of various rationalities and practices. The argument was that forms of subjectivity are not imposed upon passive subjects, but on free subjects who particip-ate knowingly in their own self-fashioning: 'power is not so much a matter of imposing constraints upon citizens as of "making up" citizens capable of bearing a kind of regulated freedom' (Rose and Miller, 1992: 174). However, Foucault stated clearly that the possible forms of this self-fashioning were supplied to the individual by their culture, society and social group.

Governmentality scholars repeat the claim that the law comes to operate as a norm. They contend that the law is incorporated into a continuum of regulatory apparatuses, as well as arguing that the legal complex is invaded by the non-legal. These ideas led Nikolas Rose and Mariana Valverde (1998) to insist that there was no unified phenomenon of 'the Law'. However, while this much would be acknowledged by contempor-ary critical legal scholars, they might also want to argue that there is something unique and specific about law or penality. The demand that we de-centre law, or the criminal justice system, from our analysis is a controversial one.

According to one of its principal exponents, governmentality schol-arship has four foci of investigation: subjectifications, normalisations, spatialisations, and authorisations (Rose and Valverde, 1998). The study of subjectifications concerns the historically specific ways in which indi-viduals are constituted as subjects by practices. Precisely, the government-ality perspective attends to particular practices of the self that consist of 'the modes of self-display and self-identification that persons are offered within those practices and of the incitements that exist to represent one-self in certain ways' (Rose and Valverde, 1998: 548). It is a matter of 'the encouragement, support and shaping of self-projects in such ways that in specific practices, these come into alignment with the diverse objectives of regulation' (Rose and Valverde, 1998: 548). The study of normalisations concerns, for instance, the respect in which legal practices have become embedded within governmental strategies. The analysis of spatialisations addresses the constitution of 'governable spaces'.

Investigating authorisations involves analysing the authority exercised over authorities, this being understood as the regulation of their exercise of power 'at a distance'. The notion of state rule 'at a distance' (Rose and Miller, 1992) employed by governmentality scholars means that the state sets an agenda which is implemented at the local level by others. The state has a steering role and a low-level monitoring role rather than one of continual and intensive intervention. This mode of operation can be seen in a trend away from state responsibility for security. An example of the use of the notion of rule 'at a distance' is to be found in Andrew Barry's essay 'Lines of Communication and Spaces of Rule' (1996). Barry emphasised that action-at-a-distance required information and communication, arguing that communications networks had become constituted as 'technologies of freedom' (Barry, 1996: 138). He illustrated his argument with the example of the telegraph which could, he claimed, facilitate the monitoring of distant events, thus obviating the need for a detailed system of surveillance. However, as Hudson (1998) points out, the state has increased its power in the field of crime, especially expanding its power to punish. Hudson writes that the state punishes more people, and also has abrogated the power to punish to itself by decreasing the discretion of intermediate experts. This at least suggests a qualification of the notion of rule 'at a distance'.

The governmentality perspective has been employed to:

1. broadly describe a new form of social control
2. explain specific crime control and penal practices.

Nikolas Rose's essay 'Government and Control' (2000) is an example of the first kind of application. Rose employs a governmentality perspective to depict a new mode of control that he claims is largely invisible, and operates through the management of risk. He argues that the new control methods can be seen as technologies of freedom because they involve action at a distance through 'the autonomous choices of relatively independent entities' (2000: 324). Rose describes control strategies that are inclusionary as well as those that are exclusionary. He claims that inclusionary control practices are designed in to everyday practices:

> [I]t is not a question of instituting a regime in which each person is permanently under the alien gaze of the eye of power exercising individualizing surveillance. . . . Conduct is continually monitored and reshaped by logics immanent within all networks of practice. Surveillance is 'designed in' to the flows of everyday existence.
>
> (Rose, 2000: 325)

Rose presents the 'securitization of identity' as central to the exercise of freedom in contemporary societies. By this phrase he denotes the flow of information into, and out of, databases concerning personal identification details. Rose points out that totalitarian control, implied by phrases like 'maximum security society' and 'electronic Panopticon', is not achieved by the new technologies for the securitisation of identity. Instead of the notion of total domination, he argues that control operates through selective access to circuits of consumption and civility. For instance, credit may be denied to risky consumers.

Moving on to strategies for the control of the excluded, Rose argues that new strategies of risk management are principally directed at those incapable of exercising responsible self-government. He employs the notion of actuarial penology, and writes that the gaze of the control professional becomes formatted by the objectives of risk management, calling this the 'risk gaze' (Rose, 2000: 332). He notes that in the penal system 'a new archipelago of confinement without reformation is taking shape' (Rose, 2000: 335). Rose's overall idea is that contemporary control strategies are posited upon the notion of a free society, and he hence describes the modes of subjectification within crime control and penal practices as problematising the infraction of freedom:

> [T]he pervasive image of the perpetrator of crime is not one of the juridical subject of the rule of law, nor that of the social and psychological subject of criminology, but of the individual who has failed to accept his or her responsibilities as a subject of moral community.
>
> (Rose, 2000: 337)

The governmentality perspective has also been taken up by scholars wishing to comprehend the character of certain crime control and penal practices. There is an expanding literature in this area, and here some work by David Garland, Adam Crawford, Malcolm Feeley and Jonathan Simon will be briefly discussed. David Garland (1996, 1997) has addressed the possibilities of a governmentality perspective for the study of crime control, writing that:

> Crime control practices embody a conception of the subjects they seek to govern. . . . The new economic rationality attempts to make up new kinds of individuals, or rather, to create and impart new forms of subjectivity, which individuals and organizations will adopt for themselves.
>
> (Garland, 1997: 190)

For instance, Garland described *homo prudens*, a security-conscious, crime preventing subject. Similarly, Adam Crawford (1998) writes that appeals to crime prevention can be seen as responsibilisation strategies. He describes how in the discourse of 'community' notions of an active citizenry constitute subjects as responsible agents in their own security.

Acknowledging their debt to Foucault's notion of power and knowledge as inseperable, Malcolm Feeley and Jonathan Simon (1992, 1994) described an emerging 'new penology', which they also denominated 'actuarial'. They held that actuarial thinking had become central to penal policy, using calculations of probabilities and statistical distributions to efficiently co-ordinate control (an actuary is an individual employed by an insurance company to calculate the probability of certain events occurring and hence the level of premium that persons should pay to offset the chance of their making a claim). According to Feeley and Simon, actuarial justice is less directed at stopping illegal activities when they occur than at reducing the probability and seriousness of offending. The new mode of control aims to regulate groups and sub-groups as a strategy of managing dangerousness, rather than focusing on the individual and hence prioritising punishment or rehabilitation. Feeley and Simon argued that contemporary correctional practices could be seen as a 'custodial continuum' rather than the 'correctional continuum' suggested by Foucault. The new penology aimed, according to them, to develop techniques of classifying and regulating groups rather than treating impaired individuals. They explained that actuarial penology held out new modes of subjectification, as individuals are constructed 'not as coherent subjects, whether understood as moral, psychological or economic agents, but as members of particular sub-populations and the intersection of various categorical indicators' (Feeley and Simon, 1994: 178).

A range of criticisms of the governmentality perspective have emerged. Kögler (1996) wrote that despite Foucault's attempts to move away from a reductionist account of the relations between subjectivity, knowledge and power, his later work remained deeply problematic in this same respect. He also commented that the individualistic self-fashioning advised by Foucault showed no concern for the oppressed other. On a similar note, Mladen Dolar wrote that the Foucauldian aesthetics of existence did not take stock of the other. Garland (1997) wrote that the idea of 'making up people' does not say much about who adopts particular personal styles or the processes through which a self-identity is taken up. Secondly, Garland notes that the governmentality scholars may acknowledge that governmental programmes are never perfectly realised in practice, but they tend to focus on depicting ideal-types rather than the pragmatics of their use. As Adam Crawford (1997: 221) points out, governmentality scholarship sometimes tends to 'conflate intentionality with effectivity'. He notes that unintended consequences might ensue and argues that we should problematise the effectiveness of governmental strategies (1997: 254). Garland writes that governmentality studies conceptualise problems through the perceptual grid of the authorities and do not present an independent analysis or alternative explanation of social reality.

A range of critics have drawn attention to the punitive turn taken in contemporary culture, and questioned the ability of Foucauldian theory to explain it. Garland writes that governmentality analyses tend to neglect the 'expressive, emotionally-driven and morally-toned currents that play such a large part in the shaping of penal policy' in their focus on the administrative and technical (Garland, 1997: 202). John Pratt (2000) suggests that a move away from the Foucauldian sociology of punishment is now timely. He writes that the Foucauldian approach made possible a critique of how apparent benevolence concealed new and more intrusive forms of social control. The 1990s, Pratt argues, saw the abandonment of any pretext of benevolence. This, he holds, means that the Foucauldian style of unmasking the concealed logics and effects of punishment is now inappropriate. Pratt calls for a transformation in our sociological frames of reference. This would entail, he explains, greater attention to the sentiments manifested in new trends as well as more concentration on the semiotics and signs of punishment.

The rise of the mass media and the power of the image

A number of scholars have recently argued that an analysis of the ways in which crime and punishment are imagined and represented is crucial to understanding the meaning of crime control and penality. Over the last two centuries, there has been a massive expansion of the circulation of information and images, with the rise of the mass media. Because Foucault argued that disciplinary power directly took hold of and shaped the body, he argued that we did not need to theorise how power was mediated through the individual's consciousness. This line of argument strongly opposed texts like Guy Debord's *Society of the Spectacle* (1967). In this provocative book, Debord argued that in modern societies 'all of life presents itself as an immense accumulation of spectacles. Everything that was directly lived has moved away into a representation' (Debord, 1967/1994: 1). Debord was a leading member of the Situationist International, a group of artists and intellectuals linked to the May 1968 revolt in France. Debord's provocative book drew attention to the important role of mediation in social relations, stating that power expands its influence through the manipulation of representations. He vigorously attacked the numbing effects of commodification and the spectacular, and suggested strategies that might go against the passive acceptance commonly seen. With the increasingly sophisticated development of electronic and communications technologies, Debord's ideas seem quite prescient. They were drawn upon by Jean Baudrillard who in a series of books theorised the manner in which the circulation of images destroys reality.

John Thompson (1995) disputed the optics of Foucault's claimed reversal of visibility. He questioned the extent to which panopticism works as a generalisable model for the exercise of power in modern societies. Thompson argued that the significance of surveillance was exaggerated by Foucault, who also overlooked the place of new forms of 'publicness' with the development of communication media. According to Thompson, these institute a new kind of mediated visibility dissociated from the situ of face-to-face interaction. Thomas Mathiesen (1997) also criticised Foucault for not giving adequate attention to the rise of technologies of the many watching the few like newspapers and television. For Mathiesen, this created another mechanism of power, parallel to the disciplinary mechanisms theorised by Foucault.

Peter Hutchings (1999) argued that Foucault's thesis in *Discipline and Punish* of a shift from public spectacle to the invisibility that comes with the hidden practices of imprisonment, should be complicated. For Hutchings, what Foucault's account missed was the transformation of the nature of spectacle with the vast proliferation of images of crime and punishment. He stated that these images, by their mediated nature, 'spectacularised' crime, by which he meant that they were not directly experienced, but are imagined. On this point, he is supported by Austin Sarat (2000: 155), who writes that 'it may very well be . . . that the more punishment is hidden, the less visible it is, the more power it has to colonize our imaginative life'. Hutchings saw the imagination of crime and punishment as central to the installation of the disciplinary regime, and wrote that surveillance was structured by elements of spectacle. He emphasised the ghostly after-life of the corporeal theatrical practices of the spectacle of punishment that Foucault saw as a thing of the past. Hutchings discussed the power of fictions to the development of the sense of interiority required by the disciplinary regime. He insisted that the maintenance of discipline worked through the constancy of demonstration, rather than following Foucault's line of argument that the reformers' dreams of theatres of exemplary punishment remained an unrealised vision.

The shape of the future and millennium blues

Foucault's provocative arguments and dazzling prose played an important part in the reinvigoration of critical criminologies during the late 1980s. For those scholars interested in exploring questions of power, his work supplied important critical tools. There is still a thriving industry in interpretation of his complex and impressively diverse range of work. From the mid-1980s, a debate began to rage concerning the question of whether Western societies might be embarking upon a new era of 'postmodernity'. This was not a problem to which Foucault had given much thought, and he died before the most important works in this genre were published. Of course even if he had lived longer, Foucault was never predictable. All that can be said is that he would have continued to ask his original, unusual, but always incisive questions in his own way.

The millennial sensibility brought a number of varieties of apocalyptic thinking, which envisaged the future as the source of considerable anxiety.

A sense of the end of history and of dark forebodings was evident in many texts of this period. Jean Baudrillard captured vividly the sense of apocalypse that haunted some of this literature:

> Time is no longer counted progressively from an origin but by subtraction, as with rocket launches or time bombs. This is a perspective of entropy. We no longer live with a vision of a world of progress and production. When you count the seconds separating you from the end, it means that everything is already at an end; we are already beyond the end.
>
> (Baudrillard, 1998: 11)

This sense of the dissolution of the modern era was reflected in the theorising of new temporalities. Foucault's notions of spatio-temporal organisation as a powerful form of control were substantially displaced by a range of scholarship which described reconfigurations of the relationship between space and time with the advent of new information and communication technologies. Paul Virilio argued that the ordering principle and orientating force shifted from time to speed at the fin de siècle, as the revolution in transmission brought a new conception of the world. This led him to elaborate a number of pessimistic thoughts:

> At the end of the century, there will not be much left of the expanse of a planet that is not only polluted but also shrunk, reduced to nothing, by the teletechnologies of generalized interactivity.
>
> (Virilio, 1995/1997: 21)

A number of scholars set out to theorise the changing existential conditions of late modernity, and it is to their work that we now turn.

Notes

1. Useful introductions to Foucault's thought in English are McNay (1994) and Dreyfus and Rabinow (1983).
2. For a discussion of the significance of Foucault's involvement with the prisoners' rights movement to his work, see Eribon (1991). Mike Fitzgerald acted as publicity officer of PROP (Preservation of the Rights of Prisoners), a UK organisation which sought to give a voice to prisoners. His discussion of prisoners' protests and their unionisation can be found in *Prisoners in Revolt* (1977).
3. On the genealogical method, see Dean (1994) and Lloyd and Thacker (1997).
4. Joe Sim (1990) saw the prison medical service as one site of the operation of disciplinary power.
5. On Marxist studies of punishment, see Garland and Young (1983/1992: 23–9).
6. On Foucault and Marxism, see Smart (1983/1992) and Poster (1984).

7. For critiques of *Punishment and Social Structure*, see Jankovic (1977), Greenberg (1977) and Garland (1990). Melossi and Pavarini (1977/1981) extended the account.
8. See also Hunt and Wickham (1994) and Dean (1999).
9. See also Butler (1997) and Copjec (1994).
10. 1995 Winkler, Columbia Pictures.
11. On the notion of governmentality, see Barry, Osborne and Rose (1996), Burchell, Gordon and Miller (1991), Dean and Hindess (1998), Hindess (1995), and Rose (1999).

Chapter 9

Crime and punishment in late modernity

> Our time is auspicious for scapegoats – be they the politicians making a mess
> of their private lives, criminals creeping out of the mean streets and rough
> districts, or 'foreigners in our midst'. Ours is a time of patented locks,
> burglar alarms, barbed-wire fences, neighbourhood watch and vigilantes;
> as well as of 'investigative' tabloid journalists fishing for conspiracies to
> populate with phantoms the public space ominously empty of actors, and for
> plausible new causes of 'moral panics' ferocious enough to release a good
> chunk of the pent-up fear and anger.
>
> (Bauman, 2000: 38–9)

During the closing decades of the twentieth century a series of social,
political, cultural and economic transformations have radically altered
the conditions of existence of millions of people. The profundity and
scope of these changes has led scholars to debate the advent of a new stage
of modernity. There has been disagreement over whether this constitutes
a qualitative break to a wholly new world of 'postmodernity', or whether
we are instead witnessing an acceleration or radicalisation of modernity
itself.[1] Scholars who prefer the latter explanation employ notions of 'late
modernity', 'high modernity' and 'second modernity'. Whichever view is
taken, the implications for our understanding of individual identity, forms
of sociality, order and social regulation, are complex. Key features of the
modern world, it seems, are being called into question. Changes that are
as rapid, deep and multiple as these give rise to both excitement and
anxiety. New freedoms, as well as new sources of uncertainty, abound.

In 1989, the fall of the Berlin Wall symbolically represented the end of
the Cold War. This event became a powerful metaphor for the removal of
barriers to the free movement of people and goods, as well as of political
reorganisation. In addition to the redrawing of the map of Europe, a new
global capitalism was taking shape, seen for example in the expansion of
massive multinational corporations like Sony and Coca-Cola. This process

has been facilitated by the development of increasingly sophisticated and widely available information and communication technologies. These technologies are noted for the instantaneity of their operation, as well as the volume of information that can be stored and analysed. They are central to a radical transformation of the spatial and temporal patterning of social practices. The concept of the internet was first advanced by the American military as part of the Arms Race in the 1950s. It was not until the 1980s, however, that the internet as we know it came into being, hailed as a quantum leap in global communications. The internet is one of the transport and communication technologies responsible for 'time–space distanciation', a phrase that designates the tendency of social systems to stretch out across space and time.[2] This is a process in which space and time are 'emptied out', becoming abstract categories without any necessary concrete referent. Space and time were once regarded as stable, uniform forces that constrained social action in fairly obvious and quantifiable ways. However, with accelerating processes of time–space distanciation, time is no longer tied to particular places. Abstract systems free activity from the constraints of local contexts. For instance, video conferencing makes it possible for three people in Sydney, Seattle and Swansea to be in mediated co-presence. Cellular telephones make communication on the move a possibility for many people. Webcams capture and encode moving images that can be sent around the world almost in real time. People can check on the snowfall in an Alpine ski resort, the level of coffee in the percolator, or – more controversially – watch live porn. Looking at the profusion of images of distant lands and other cultures, people can engage in imaginative 'virtual' travel from the comfort of their own home.

New technologies bring their contradictions, for instance, optimism about their potential to improve living conditions as well as concerns about their possible misuse. Invasive and intrusive technologies have serious implications for civil liberties. In addition, their discriminatory effect in a world that remains sexist, racist and homophobic, and the likelihood that they will magnify existing inequalities, are worrying possibilities. New crimes associated with the internet, for instance hacking, computer porn and electronic money laundering, raise challenges for regulation (Barrett, 1997; Cullen, 1997; Hamilton, 1999; Capitanchik and White, 1999; Adkeniz, Walker and Wall, 2000). Processes of globalisation more broadly undermine the forms of legitimacy and power traditionally exercised by nation-states.

An increasingly knowledge-based economy brings with it other hazards. Far-reaching changes can be seen in the sphere of work, with the emergence of post-Fordist production processes and the decline of traditional manufacturing. The term 'Fordism' denotes a modern system of mass production and consumption first developed in the automobile industry. Henry Ford introduced the first moving assembly line in 1914. Each worker performed a single, repeated, standardised task. Instead of traditional, craft-based production, Fordism was based in an intensified and unskilled division of labour. Post-Fordism requires a multi-skilled and flexible workforce. Instead of investment in heavy plant, it is based in microelectronics. Replacing Henry Ford, one might say, is Bill Gates. There are many losers in the new, global, socio-economic structure of informational capitalism. Pit closures and the cutting back of steel manufacture have brought extensive job losses to some regions. The conditions of employment are greatly changed by the increasing flexibilisation of labour, with people working from home, job sharing, or on flexitime working hours. Keeping pace with the latest skills and technologies is imperative in an information-based economy. New forms of inequalities emerge around access to the new technologies.

Inequalities are also formed around knowledge about, and proximity to, risks. There has been a widespread yet ambivalent recognition of the existence of large-scale, transnational risks caused by the use of technologies of various kinds. These risks are imperceptible to the ordinary observer and incalculable in their impact. For instance, in 1986, a reactor exploded at the Chernobyl nuclear power station in the former Soviet Union, spreading radiation over a vast area, and damaging or killing millions. The fallout from Chernobyl continues to claim new victims two decades later. To give another example, recent flooding, and a perceived increase in the occurrence of natural disasters, leads people to question whether global warming caused by the destruction of the ozone layer is already bringing damaging climate change.

If the late modern world is post-Fordist and a global risk society, it is also a society of simulations. The new technologies make possible an increasingly rapid circulation of images and signs in vast quantities. In the new era, social reproduction (information processing, knowledge industries, mass media) replaces production as the organising principle of societies. Assumptions about what is real and what is artificial are not readily sustained. As Jean Baudrillard explained, the distinction between an original and its copies is blurred with the never-ending procession of simulacra. People are caught up in a play of images and spectacles that have a diminishing relationship to an external 'reality'. Radical semiurgy, the production and proliferation of signs, has created a society of simulations governed by implosion and hyperreality. The all-pervasive images and signs give rise to a flat and fluid surface of floating signifiers. Critics worry that all distance from the text is lost. Normative distinctions, for instance true/false and good/bad evaporate. This indicates an end to the democratic belief that people can absorb and digest information critically and employ it reasonably to effect social progress. The argument is similar to that of Marcuse in *One-Dimensional Man* (1972), discussed in Chapter 6. Marcuse believed that the one-dimensionality of Western society negated the potential for resistance. Another consequence is that the ubiquity of visual technologies raises troubling questions for people's sense of identity. This process in part explains the continued widespread

fascination with the Kray twins who, as Jenks and Lorentzen (1997) explained, lived through image. They described how these notorious East
End gangsters, convicted of murder in 1969, took on a profusion of
contradictory images. The Krays engaged in a broad range of acts of
self-promotion both before and during their imprisonment. On the
demise of Reggie Kray, the media reported that he was being mourned by
vast numbers of people who had never met him.[3] Jenks and Lorentzen
argued that the legendary Krays exercised an enduring attraction because
their 'twinness' threatened the loss of identity in an era in which we must
strive constantly to constitute our identity.

Some theorists have put their faith in the advent of a new cosmopolitanism, a new mode of communication and interaction between different
peoples. Weighing against this cosmopolitanism is a surge of powerful
expressions of collective identity and explosive nationalisms. These reassert
cultural singularity and can lead to the genocidal aggression manifested
against Kurds, Kosovans and Bosnians. Late modernity sees a punitive
turn, both reflecting and reinforcing broader hostilities. Soaring rates of
imprisonment, especially in the USA, far exceed any increase in crime
rates. They indicate the use of symbolic sentencing, as well as an aggressive
use of policing and imprisonment against the poor and blacks. Differences
and inequalities become entrenched, leading Loic Wacquant (2000) to
compare the prison and the ghetto as kindred institutions of forced confinement. After its repeal around twenty-five years ago, capital punishment has made a striking return in many US states. The 'tough on crime'
stance has come to be recognised as an essential element of electoral
success. Social antagonisms and exclusionary policies are also seen in
a new perception of immigration, for instance the Maastricht Treaty,
which created the European Union in 1992, defined it as a vital matter of
security, alongside organised crime and terrorism. As Hans-Jorg Albrecht
(1997) explained, economic changes are such that whereas once immigration was seen as a positive solution to a labour shortage, it is now
portrayed as a social problem. In this context, non-European foreigners
are depicted as what Wacquant calls 'suitable enemies'.[4]

The advent of an information society, and the increasing significance
of processes of globalisation, indicate that new concepts and theories are
needed. John Urry's *Sociology Beyond Societies* (2000a) calls for a sociology
equipped to theorise the diverse mobilities of peoples, objects, images,
information and wastes, as well as their consequences. He argues that
previous sociological theories, with their central notion of the nation-state,
are inadequate to the task of engaging with the new human condition.
Instead of the ocular metaphors of works like *Discipline and Punish*, for
instance 'the eye of power', he prefers those of network, flow and travel.
The concern now is less with who can be seen than with who can move.
Other scholars have concentrated on producing a critique of the disciplines that emerged during modernity. They linked modern forms of
knowledge to the continuing subordination of certain groups in society.

This 'postmodern theory' draws attention to the way in which dominant ways of looking are constituted through an exclusion of the Other. In the latter part of this chapter, the contribution of postmodern theories to scholarship on crime, gender and sexuality will be discussed.

Theorising the contours of late modernity

Scholars like Tony Giddens (1990, 1991, 2000), Ulrich Beck (1992, 1999), Scott Lash, and John Urry (1994) believe that certain processes are changing social life to such an extent that existing social and political institutions cannot respond adequately to increasing risk and uncertainty. Each of these four scholars has played an important part in developing the concepts of 'reflexive modernisation', 'detraditionalisation' and 'ontological insecurity'.[5]

The term 'reflexive modernisation' theorises the argument that we are now facing a period typified by reflexivity. This means that increasing knowledge does not automatically produce increasing certainty. As knowledge becomes more and more specialised, an increasing reliance on experts is seen. At the same time, there is an increasing lay scepticism. The need to trust, and indeed depend upon, experts, occasions anxiety. Something of this ambivalent cultural shift is shown in media coverage of the case of 'Doctor Death', otherwise known as Harold Shipman. Shipman was convicted of the murder of fifteen elderly female patients whom he had lethally injected with diamorphine. He is suspected of 345 additional killings over many years, establishing him as the most prolific known serial killer in European history. A *Sunday Times* (7 December 2000: 11) article told readers that Shipman was not like the typical crazed serial killers of our imagination, for instance Hannibal Lecter, Peter Sutcliffe, Fred West and Dennis Nilsen. The article emphasised the mundane character of his appearance and habits, both while a prisoner and at large. This judgement did not lead the journalists to question whether normality itself was violent or repulsive, as the anti-psychiatrists Laing and Cooper discussed in Chapter 6 might have done. Instead, they appropriated the phrase 'devil in a frock coat' from the Russian author Nikolai Gogol, and informed readers that this conveyed 'the potential for evil that lurks in everyday life, all the more sinister and dangerous because it so often goes unsuspected'. The very banality of Shipman, however, makes the depiction of him as diabolical rather strained. Nevertheless, this makes the reader look even harder for the devil in him. Indeed, a large image of his bespectacled eyes is splashed across the top of the article. The article made reference to the Baker report (Department of Health, 2001), which exposed the fact that Shipman had been disciplined as long ago as 1975 for forging prescriptions to obtain excess supplies of a painkiller. The article mentioned Shipman's pride in his popularity as a doctor, having had more patients than any other GP in Greater Manchester. He was quoted as attributing his large practice to the trust invested in him by his patients. The journalists pointed out that it was this very trust that Shipman took the opportunity of abusing. The saga of 'Doctor Death' is only made more telling by the knowledge that many of Shipman's former patients have sent him letters of support, still believing in his innocence.

The term 'detraditionalisation' refers to the processes through which everyday life is becoming opened up from the hold of tradition. These give rise to a revolution in how people think of themselves, and how ties and connections are formed with others. A new individualism is associated with the declining influence of tradition and custom, but this is far from the altruistic individualism hoped for by Durkheim. The traditional parameters for fixing self-identity in modernity, for instance kinship, locality and community, break down. Individuals encounter a much wider range of ambiguous choices. They are exposed to, and actively seek out, multiple sources for establishing and maintaining a self-identity. This identity comprises an ongoing reflexive project, in that it must be created and recreated on an active basis. People have to define what kind of life they would like to live against a confusing variety of informational sources and the declining impact of tradition. Existence in such a world requires an openness to continual revision in the light of new information. There are no clear and stable social types, patterns, codes and rules to which people might conform. There are a multiplicity of patterns and configurations, often contradictory, which somewhat reduces their constraining powers. Detraditionalisation is hence both freeing and worrying. The new forms of uncertainty are a matter of not knowing the ends. The situation departs significantly from the days in which Merton depicted wealth as the universally validated goal, as discussed in Chapter 4. There is no longer a singular, or even dominant, unchanging culturally approved goal. To state the matter plainly, the goalposts keep moving.

A protective cocoon of trust is constructed, which guards the self and brackets off the anxieties occasioned by threatening events. According to Giddens, trust interacts with everyday habits and routines to generate a consistent self. This is perhaps why broken trust is so shattering, and provides some explanation for the extensive review of medical accreditation and standards of practice following in the wake of the conviction of Harold Shipman. Giddens argues that late modernity brings widespread and frequent experiences of 'ontological insecurity'. Ontological insecurity is an existential condition in which the individual experiences everyday life as a deadly threat. For the ontologically insecure, relatedness with others is not gratifying but terrifying. This destabilising experience magnifies social antagonisms.

Ontological insecurity is the normal existential condition in a risk society. The notion of risk society is most associated with the work of Ulrich Beck (1992). He argued that, due to a number of profound social changes, all areas of life become opened up to decision-making with its insecurities. He explained that the predominant logic of the risk society is one of avoidance, because the projected future is construed as threatening and hence as something to be prevented. Society is no longer organised as a class society but as a risk society, and Beck punned that it is directed at the distribution of bads and not goods (commodities). This state of affairs gives rise to a negative solidarity of fear. Describing recent changes in penal policy across European jurisdictions, Rene van Swaaningen (1997) argued that law enforcement can be seen as one of the political strategies of the risk society:

> In such a society, solidarity is no longer based on a positive feeling of connectedness, but is expressed in a negative communality of fear. The idea that something good can be done is abandoned, and cost and benefit analyses of how society can be managed in the most effective way now guide political decision-making. . . . The underlying vision of mankind has changed from the accountable citizen to the irresponsible object of control. Breaches of law are no longer judged in terms of culpability but in terms of potential risks to the social order.
>
> (van Swaaningen, 1997: 174)

New forms of social regulation and the exercise of power both arise from, and in turn shape, late modern sociality. Some recent work has drawn upon Gilles Deleuze's idea of the 'control society' (Scheerer, 1998; Jones, 1999; Haggerty and Ericson, 2000). In two essays of 1990, Gilles Deleuze claimed that with a mutation in capitalism, contemporary societies were moving towards 'control societies' beyond the earlier disciplinary forms discussed in Chapter 8. The new mode of control, he argued, operates by means of continuous regulation and instant communication instead of confinement. The predominant form is that of 'ceaseless control in open sites' (Deleuze, 1995a: 175). Deleuze explained that in the disciplinary societies of the eighteenth and nineteenth centuries described by Foucault, people were always going from one closed site to another. According to Deleuze, control is now continuous, rather than discontinuous as it was in disciplinary societies of old. Deleuze referred to the work of Paul Virilio, who posited ultrarapid forms of apparently freefloating control. Deleuze suggested electronic tagging as an example of the new control mechanisms, because it can 'fix the position of any element at any given moment' (Deleuze, 1995b: 181).

Sebastian Scheerer drew upon Deleuze's notion of the control society to argue that new forms of control were starting to supersede the traditional concept of the delinquent. He explained that disciplinary power had constructed the delinquent as an object of knowledge and a locus of control. However, the times brought a transition from the age of confinement and discipline into one of mere registration and control by the management of desires. Control strategies were aimed at the prevention, monitoring and analysis of situations, rather than the conscience and convictions of the individual. In addition, the new mode of control moved from overt, concentrated and reactive forms to covert, dissipated and proactive control. Scheerer noted that prevention is less specific than reaction, making everyone a potential offender and allocating millions to 'risk groups'. He pointed out that the exponential growth of incarceration over the last few decades in Western countries appeared to be dissonant with Deleuze's characterisation of control societies. Scheerer explained this disparity by arguing that the new covert control was only effective for cooperative individuals, who shared the value systems of the controllers. He noted a deepening gap between the very rich and the very poor, with the old techniques retained for the poor and the marginalised. The prospects for the rich and the fortunate are normalisation and de-institutionalisation. An increasing brutalisation at the margins tended to be the fate of outgroups. The marked bifurcation of control styles noted by Scheerer has been thought to be particularly visible in the late modern city.

From Chicago to LA: crime and the late modern city

Scholars have recently drawn links between the distinctive characteristics of late modernity and the forms of crime and social regulation seen in contemporary cities. They argue that the urban milieu reflects powerfully the transformations associated with the rise of late modern societies. Bottoms and Wiles (1995) related the knowledge conditions of late modernity to the development of defended spaces. They argued that with the growth of abstract systems, there is a greater dependency on reflexively acquired social knowledge rather than tradition. With reliance upon increasingly specialised experts, a delicate balancing of risk and trust becomes a common activity. This exacerbates ontological insecurity, and the reaction to this situation can be seen in the attempt to offer locations of trust, security bubbles. In 1972 the urban planner Oscar Newman published *Defensible Space*, in which he propounded the idea of controlling crime in public spaces through the creation of territories of 'natural surveillance' which could be marked off with boundaries like gates and walls. The idea that crime in public space could be 'designed out' was marketed by real estate developers, who found it attractive to their customers, with the result that 'gated communities' remodel space in terms of fear of crime and a desire for security. Scholars have described the development of new urban spaces which produce new forms of social exclusion, as they employ new kinds of policing and social regulation (South, 1997).

Over the 1990s, a Los Angeles school emerged, which depicts this Californian city as the prototype of contemporary urbanisation. They believe that changes occurring in LA are symptomatic of broader socio-geographic transformations. For these scholars, LA's polycultural condition, simultaneous deindustrialisation and reindustrialisation, ungovernable character, and profound socio-economic polarisation are emblematic of a more general urban dynamic. LA school scholars include Mike Davis, Ed Soja and Mike Dear, who hold that the Chicago school model is no longer suitable to describe the contemporary metropolitan evolution: 'they assert that Southern California is a suggestive archetype – a polyglot, polycentric, polycultural pastiche that is somehow engaged in the rewriting of the American social contract' (Dear, 2000: 21).

The most well-known text to emerge from this school of thought is *City of Quartz* (1992), in which Mike Davis described the destruction of democratic public space as it became either ghettoised or privatised. This process produced on the one hand a combination of places of total non-security, and on the other the safe defended spaces of 'Fortress LA'. The front cover of the book carried an image of the new Federal Detention Centre. This illustrated Davis' argument that the crowded state prisons could only take the most dangerous individuals, hence we were witnessing the covert imprisoning of LA as part of the postmodern built environment. After the Watts 'race riots' of the 1960s, the city's redevelopment agency began to physically segregate the core business areas from the ghettos. They employed sophisticated protective security and surveillance technologies, for instance the elevated pedways in the financial area. The overall process in the privileged areas subjected to protective surveillance constituted: 'a virtual scanscape – a space of protective visibility that increasingly defines where white-collar office workers and middle-class tourists feel safe . . . yuppies' lifestyles may soon be defined by the ability to afford electronic guardian angels to watch over them' (Davis, 1992: 5). Davis described panopticon malls, aerial surveillance over high crime areas, and the rise of new luxury developments outside the city with walls, guards and private roads.

In his later book, *The Ecology of Fear* (1999), Davis wrote that the film *Blade Runner* (Scott, 1982), a futuristic vision of a lawless LA in 2019, could be seen as a cautionary tale of what might happen to the city. He explained that this cinematic representation of hyper-violence meant that thoughts about the future of LA now generally took the dark imagery of *Blade Runner* for granted. He warned of the unchecked evolution of inequality, crime and social despair. Davis argued, however, that the picture of LA in the late 1990s was less like *Blade Runner* than a contorted form of Ernest Burgess' concentric zone model, discussed in Chapter 3 of this book. He stated that this development of spatial hierarchy could be seen in LA, but with the introduction of a decisive new factor of fear. This, he argued, could be seen in the current obsession with personal safety and social insulation. Zoning now came about, Davis contended, through the introduction of security measures, indicating a merging of the criminal code with landuse planning.

Like Davis, Ed Soja (1995) drew attention to the negative consequences of postmodernising processes for order in the city:

> The postmodern city, with all its kaleidoscopic complexities, has become increasingly ungovernable, at least within the confines of its traditional local government structures. As a result, it has become an increasingly 'carceral' city, with walled-in estates protected by armed guards, bold signs threatening that 'trespassers will be shot', panopticon-like shopping centres made safe through the most advanced forms of spatial surveillance, smart office buildings impenetrable to outsiders, neighborhood watches backed by gun-toting home owners, a proliferation of gangs equally obsessed with guarding their turf, and a police force armed with the latest advances in military technology.
>
> (Soja, 1995: 134)

Three years on from the violent urban social unrest of 1992 in LA, Soja described the city as possessing 'an incendiary urban geography' (Soja, 1995: 134). This volatile and hostile late modern urbanism is seen in the racialisation of exclusionary control. John Fiske (1998) described the racialisation of the urban scanscape. He depicted the video surveillance of the American city as a rapidly developing control mechanism directed particularly upon the black male as he moved through public space. For Fiske, surveillance is a technology of whiteness that racially zones city space by drawing lines that blacks cannot cross, and whites cannot see. These control devices were, for Fiske, an instance of the totalitarian undercurrents in late modern democracies. He argued that these developments evinced the existence of a 'non-racist racism', which may sound paradoxical, but he explained that it is a form of racism developed by white-powered nations that declare themselves non- or even anti-racist. Fiske stated that the apparent neutrality of surveillance made it a perfect technology for the exercise of non-racist racism.

Globalisation, crime and penality

The changing morphology of cities and experience of urbanism is profoundly influenced by processes of globalisation. Tony Giddens defined globalisation as 'the intensification of worldwide social relations which link localities in such a way that local happenings are shaped by events occurring many miles away and vice versa' (Giddens, 1990: 64). Most aspects of globalisation are disputed. Some reserve use of the term to describe the global economy, in which countries engage in mutual trading, and complex world financial markets operate through multiple and rapid transactions. However, globalisation does not only concern economic connections, involving a more diverse range of processes. In a multitude of ways, distant events affect us more directly and immediately than ever before. The shape and significance of the nation-state becomes radically altered. In the days of antagonistic nation-states, the other was readily identified, associated with danger, and often attacked. Citizenship was quite unproblematically the set of rights attributable to obvious categories of persons unambiguously within the nation. With processes of globalisation, boundaries of all kinds become blurred, and people's sense of belonging is less fixed.

In his trilogy *The Information Age*, Manuel Castells argued that we are witnessing the emergence of a new global order. This new order, he maintained, embodies a logic that can be characterised as a network. In *End of Millennium* (1998), Castells described the new phenomenon of global crime as an essential feature of the new global economy and of the social and political dynamics of the Information Age. In the latter part of the twentieth century, organised crime has increasingly become transnational. The diverse criminal groupings are connected in a global, diversified network that permeates national boundaries. New communication and transportation technologies permit production and management to be based in low risk areas where relative control of the institutional environment is possible. The cooperative business practice of organised crime operations with those of other countries closely follows the operational logic of the network enterprise characteristic of the Information Age, which takes the form of flexible and versatile organisation. These strategic alliances help criminal networks to evade police repression on both national and international levels. In a reaction to the threat and power of organised crime, Castells writes, democratic states adopt measures that curtail liberties. Furthermore, organised crime often uses immigrant networks with the result that the excessive association between immigration and crime is exacerbated and tolerance is undermined.

The violent and exclusionary character of contemporary processes of 'othering' has been related by Zygmunt Bauman to the existential conditions of late modernity. In *Globalization: The Human Consequences*, Bauman explores the argument that globalisation brings new kinds of stratification that result from differential access to mobilities of various kinds. He tells his reader that 'nowadays we are all on the move' (Bauman, 1998: 77). We are, he explains, either moving physically (commuting to work) or being elsewhere than home through the internet, satellite or cable television. Freedom of mobility is at the centre of contemporary polarisation, with being local signalling social deprivation and degradation (presumably with the exception of the landed aristocracy).

Some commentators have warned that the new technologies bring grave consequences for social cohesion. Bauman writes that they superimpose over the territorial and architectural space a third cybernetic space, that exceeds the material and temporal constraints of modern forms. Unlike the Chicagoan idea of the neighbourhood invested with local sentiment, discussed in Chapter 3, Bauman writes that the local area becomes denuded of its meaning-generating capacity. In the city, he contends, the pursuit of transparency by means of town planning and the shaping of functional spaces produces an artificially contrived environment in which people are deprived of the opportunity for meaning-negotiating. In homogeneous towns, uniformity breeds conformity, intolerance of difference, and a paranoiac concern with law and order. The city, originally constructed to protect those inside its walls from invaders, has in late modernity become more associated with danger. The typically urban fears of today focus on the 'enemy inside':

> The walls built once around the city now criss-cross the city itself, and in a multitude of directions. Watched neighbourhoods, closely surveilled public spaces with selective admission, heavily armed guards at the gate and electronically operated doors – are all now aimed against the unwanted co-citizens, rather than foreign armies or highway robbers, marauders and other largely unknown dangers lying in ambush on the other side of the city gates.
>
> (Bauman, 1998: 48)

Panopticon, which was the favoured modern form of social control, declines. Bauman identifies the main purpose of the Panopticon as having been one of instilling discipline and imposing uniform behaviour. He presents an argument about how prisons today are 'factories of immobility'. Imprisonment, he explains, is the most intense form of spatial confinement. The categories of criminal law are used to reduce difference and personal uniqueness to typified stranger-images, perpetuating distance. Total isolation from guards and other inmates in prisons like Pelican Bay is offered by Bauman as the ideal of this development. Here there is a near-permanent lockdown in single cells, no mingling in recreation, and no work. He differentiates prisons like Pelican Bay from the panopticon-style houses of confinement, which were designed as factories of disciplined labour. They were to correct inmates according to the norms of modern industrialised productive labour. Today, this aim of producing workers habituated to the repetitious monotony of the work ethic has disappeared in a world of mass unemployment and demands for flexible labour. Bauman writes that Pelican Bay was not designed as a factory of disciplined labour but as a factory of exclusion which brings close to perfection the technique of immobilisation. Imprisonment is used on a massive scale to neutralise threats to social orders and pacify public anxieties. Feelings of fear and anxiety are expressed in the concern with law and order. The increase of insecurity and uncertainty is perceived as a threat to personal safety. Being seen to be doing something about fighting crime that threatens personal safety has huge political appeal, in times when governments can realistically do little to control or limit insecurity and uncertainty. The spectacularity of punitive operations matters more than their effectiveness. Imprisonment is able to furnish the most popular sign that 'something has been done' because when society is stratified according to mobility, enforced immobility is a highly potent symbol of incapacitation and pain.

Punishment, explosive sociality and the politics of fear

Bauman (2000) posits that contemporary forms of individualisation indicate the disintegration of citizenship. He writes that people tend only to come together as communities of fear and hatred over particular events, on which they hang their individual anxieties for a time. Instead of the public increasingly colonising the private, a phenomenon that set the context for the labelling perspective discussed in Chapter 5, quite the reverse situation now prevails, as public space becomes the place where privatised worries are projected. For Bauman, the defensive desire for community can be seen as a form of explosive sociality.

Émile Durkheim wrote that 'punishment serves to heal the wounds inflicted upon the community'. However, the incendiary and hostile climate of the late twentieth century has led scholars to reflect upon the notion of 'wounding justice'. A powerful example of processes of legal justice that aggravated people's felt sense of injustice can be seen in the successive trials of OJ Simpson for the killing of Nicole Brown Simpson and Ronald Goldman, who were stabbed to death in June 1994. This case, like the Dreyfus affair discussed in Chapter 2, was the vehicle for broader social hostilities and resentments. OJ, a sporting legend, multi-millionaire, black American, was acquitted of the killings after a high-profile criminal trial in October 1995. In February 1997, he was found responsible for their wrongful deaths after a civil trial brought by relatives of the deceased, and ordered to pay $33 million in compensation. OJ's appeal against this verdict was denied in January 2001, and only weeks later he was convicted of a road-rage style offence. In each of these trials, much more than who did what to whom was at stake. The racist character of American society, as well as the law's inability to protect women from domestic violence, became hinges upon which OJ's guilt or innocence rested. On the one hand, evidence about OJ's prior physical and verbal abuse of Nicole Brown Simpson was a source of contestation. On the other, the racist opinions of certain Los Angeles Police Department (LAPD) officers, as well as the force's tainted record on policing black communities, were used to support the argument that OJ had been framed.

Shoshana Felman (1997) wrote that legal trials might commonly be seen as quests for finality and resolution, but the OJ case continued to haunt American culture. She explained that every trial is related to an injury or trauma which it compensates, attempts to remedy, and overcome. Yet however the OJ trial might have attempted to articulate trauma and control its damage, it had the opposite effect of aggravating the pain and injury. Felman explained that the adversarial structure of the lawyers' arguments put two traumas in competition (that of black oppression and that of women's oppression). Competing for exclusive visibility, each trauma blinded people to the significance of the other. Felman pointed up the cross-legal nature of the OJ trial, by which she meant the respect in which it referred back to the Rodney King trial of 1992, in which several LAPD officers were acquitted of offences relating to the beating of a black motorist, which had been captured on camera by an amateur and shown on TV. As Jacobs (1996) explained, the meanings attributed to the Rodney King case diverged widely among the polarised social groups of American society. Like the King case, the OJ case came to be seen as defining of racial tensions. The gendered narrative of domestic violence also took on a heavily symbolic tone. Felman argued that the jurors in the criminal trial might have looked at the image of Nicole Brown Simpson's battered face, but they did not see it. She stated that the law failed to make visible the relation between marriage and domestic violence. This led Felman to ponder whether justice is blind, in the respect that not seeing might be crucial to the practice and execution of the law. This line of thinking is supported by Sheila Jasanoff's (1999) paper on the OJ criminal case as a trial in which visual authority was hotly contested. She described the ways in which the judge's remarks and rulings established whose vision would be validated as expert. The pieces published by Felman and Jasanoff suggest that the only truth that clearly emerged from the OJ criminal case was the extent of the schism between different ways of seeing. The subsequent civil trial which found OJ responsible for the wrongful deaths, and OJ's appeal against the verdict, would probably be seen by Felman as another repetition of the trauma, with one narrative of pain battling with the other again.

Can criminal justice bring healing instead of escalating spirals of anger and pain? The last decade has brought the introduction of various forms of restorative justice, whose adherents claim that they can redress the wrongs of the past through more responsible forms of dialogue. Instead of punitive and alienating reactions to criminals that are unilaterally stigmatising, restorative justice sets out to restore harmony through dialogue between victim and offender. One of the principal advocates of restorative justice is John Braithwaite, an Australian scholar who advanced a theory of reintegrative shaming. Braithwaite's book *Crime, Shame and Reintegration* (1989), led Thomas Scheff (1990) to hail him as a 'a new Durkheim'. Why might he have received this plaudit? Braithwaite's approach sought the active participation of members of the community in the shaming and reintegration of offenders. He proposed a kind of victim–offender mediation that would follow a process of disapproval of the crime, reacceptance of the offender, and their subsequent delabelling. His point was that shaming need not be stigmatising, and could instead be restorative if a careful distinction was maintained between acts and identities. What a person had done should be located within a shaming and moralising discourse of their responsibility for their wrongful act, while conveying to them the distance between what they had done and who they were. Aware of the labelling perspective discussed in Chapter 5, which described the consolidation of deviance as master status, Braithwaite insisted that if event and perpetrator were uncoupled, the identity of the actor as a good person could be communicated to them. He also stated that the meaning of the crime should be located within an understanding of the inequalities that might have led to it. Furthermore, he advised that practical and moral support should be given to the offender in a way that enhanced their agency. Braithwaite recognised that at the end of the twentieth century, community was not spontaneously emergent, and argued that it was imperative therefore to ensure that a community of care and concern was organised around the offender. He believed that reintegrative shaming could produce interconnectedness between parties, and also be a catalyst to community problem solving.

Scholars have questioned the appeal to community seen in theories of restorative justice. For instance, Stuart Scheingold wrote that while critical criminology celebrated difference, communitarian criminology might acknowledge it, but seemed intent upon its attenuation by 'bringing people together'. He warned that although communitarians called for the toleration of difference, their schemes might turn out 'to be more about uniformity, coercion, and authoritarian rule than about difference, resistance, and democracy' (Scheingold, 2000: 874). Communitarian thought has been accused of deploying notions of 'we' that perpetuate and reinforce power differentials. Nicola Lacey foregrounded the violence inherent in the constitution of the 'we' within communitarian discourse on crime, writing that: 'amid all the welter of cosy appeals to what "we" think, do, understand or feel, there appears to be no critical space in which to reflect upon the processes of inclusion and exclusion which characterise "us"' (Lacey, 1998: 138–9). Richard Delgado pointed up the coercive quality of restorative justice practices. He objected to the power differential created in offender mediation between victim and offender, writing that, 'insofar as restorative justice aims at smoothing over the rough edges of social competition and adjusting subaltern people to their roles, it is profoundly conservative' (Delgado, 2000: 771). Kathy Daly (1999) argued that restorative justice could deliver a better kind of justice in diverse and unequal societies if it was tied to a political process. This would take the form of a process of engagement between the interests of political minority groups and governments. She emphasised that a broader engagement with the politics of race, class and culture was vital, and commented that the assimilation of minority group members into a white-centred process was not sufficient to create a better justice system. Majority group members, she warned, must also change.

How has Braithwaite responded to these criticisms? When he outlined the normative vision behind his theory of reintegrative shaming, Braithwaite announced his commitment to what he called a 'republican theory'. He affirmed his faith in the rule of law, writing that:

> The rule of law – not abolitionism or deregulation, but taking crime and regulatory law seriously – is necessary for crime prevention. The rule of law is also necessary for the preservation of freedom as non-domination on other fronts. It is therefore a central normative ideal.
>
> (Braithwaite, 2000: xviii)

This was essentially a liberal belief in rights and responsibilities based in notions of liberty, equality, fraternity and sorority (Braithwaite, 2000: xi). In lauding the rule of law and expressing faith in notions like liberty and equality, Braithwaite did not undertake the detailed answer to the many criticisms of the traditions on which he drew. Neither did he engage with the burgeoning literature that theorises contemporary forms of identities and social relations, for instance produced by scholars writing postmodern criminologies.

Postmodern theory, gender, sexuality and crime

Postmodern theorists are avowedly committed to the celebration of difference. Over the last two decades, a critique of modern ways of looking, thinking and knowing has emerged across most disciplines in the social sciences, arts and humanities. This rejects traditional assumptions about truth and reality, and in particular the faith in science and social progress associated with Enlightenment thought. There has been a rejection of modern theories as 'grand narratives' which elide difference. Criminology, as the child of modernity, must therefore transcend its modern outlines.

Postmodernist thought has provided an anti-essentialist thinking that is deeply sceptical of claims to universality. In postmodern feminist theory, a number of theorists have argued that women's identities are fragmented and multiple, and not unified by some female essence. The trait of essentialism in a work indicates that it assumes that certain categories, for instance 'woman' or 'black', have a fixed, natural or homogeneous character or essence. For instance, postmodern feminism challenges the uncritical use of the term 'woman' because it actually lacks a stable and unified referent. This is how Kerry Carrington (1998) explains essentialism:

> Essentialism is a form of analysis in which social phenomena are understood not in terms of the specific conditions of their existence, but in terms of some presumed essence or interest. . . . Thus membership of a social category (that is, women, working class) is understood to produce certain shared interests even if these are not recognised by the members themselves. Essentialism therefore imposes a unity upon its object of inquiry by assuming that members of a social group have similar interests or essences (that is, women, blacks, workers). The postmodernist critique argues that because the subject is fragmented, contingent and variable, the insistence on a fixed transcendental subject or essence is fictive and unnecessarily totalising.
>
> (Carrington, 1998: 93)

In gender essentialism it is presumed that the common experience of sex subordination among women means that one can speak transhistorically and cross-culturally about women's experience. In addition, a shared masculinist interest is attributed to all men. Postmodern feminism, however,

sees categories as historically and culturally specific, and views social identities as plural and complexly constructed. It is contended that not only
are proclaimed unities fictive, they also block difference. Notions of overall
systems of power such as patriarchy are rejected as reductive. This approach strongly challenges the notion of a unified single experience based
on women's sex.

There has been an anti-essentialist attack on the foundations of earlier
forms of feminist criminology discussed in Chapter 7. Mark Cousins (1980)
noted that early feminist criminologies had berated mainstream criminology for its neglect of the criminal woman, setting out to remember the
forgotten women. He contended that in the effort to gender a conventional androcentric social science, the same sociology was repeated at the
very same time that it was admonished. His prime example of this contradictory gesture was how Carol Smart's *Women, Crime and Criminology* (1976)
assumed that a social explanation of female criminality could not be essen-
tialist. Cousins explained that neither the category law nor the category
women were sufficiently homogeneous entities to permit the existence of
a singular relation between them. Black women, for instance, could not
be assumed to have the same relationship with law as white women.

Smart (1990) went on to develop a critique of criminology's persistent
modernism. She explained that critical criminologists had projected the
problem of positivism onto their political opponents while assuming that
their own work was free of it. She held that the main problem of positivism
was not its relationship with a conservative politics or a biological conservatism, but the fundamental assumption that verifiable knowledge about
events could be established. According to this line of thinking, positivism
was first and foremost an epistemological problem. Smart summarised the
chief outlines of postmodernist scholarship, describing how it construed
modernism as a historically specific worldview premised on a conception of
man as a knowing actor who is author of his own actions and knowledge.
Modernism, Smart explained, was a system of thought which assumed that
essential truths about human behaviour could be revealed. It was deeply
invested in the idea of progress and in the application of knowledge to
shape and transform the world. As Smart pointed out, modernism has
been seen as racist, sexist, Eurocentric, and as obsolete, hence clinging
to it must be viewed as both outdated and politically dubious.

Smart noted that feminist scholars were beginning to ask significant
questions concerning the status and power of knowledge, challenging the
assumptions of modernist philosophy and science. This especially consisted
in challenging the belief in science to supply an overall answer, a master
narrative. She wrote that feminist postmodernism rejected the notion
of the master narrative, but, unlike standpoint feminism, it did not wish
to replace this with an alternative unitary reality. Postmodernism, she
explained, did not seek to erect authentic feminist truths, instead seeing
knowledge as inextricably tied up with power. Smart gave the example of
Woodhull's (1988) critique of Brownmiller's *Against Our Will*. Woodhull

argued that in explaining rape by recourse to physiological differences between men and women, Brownmiller placed sex and biology outside the social, as preceding power relations. She stated that this approach lacked an analysis of how sexual difference was socially constructed, of how women's bodies have become endowed with certain meanings, writing that:

> [I]f we are seriously to come to terms with rape, we must explain how the vagina comes to be coded – and experienced – as a place of emptiness and vulnerability, the penis as a weapon, and intercourse as violation, rather than naturalize these processes through references to 'basic' physiology.
>
> (Woodhull, 1988: 171)

How might the practices of coding meaning be subjected to analysis? Some postmodern criminology employs the critical tools supplied by deconstruction, a critical practice associated with the French scholar Jacques Derrida. This focuses on the workings of language, and is specifically concerned to analyse how meaning is produced through a system of differences. It is argued by deconstructionists that meaning is never self-contained and complete, always referring onwards to something else that serves to define it, to give its boundary of meaning. Put simply, a term depends on its opposite term. The strategy of deconstruction hence seeks to expose the impact of dualisms on the shaping of knowledge:

> Deconstruction demonstrates that the semantic order of language is produced as an act of exclusion. The task of deconstruction, therefore, involves taking a repressed or subjugated theme . . . pursuing its various textual ramifications and showing how these subvert the very order that strives to hold them in check.
>
> (Norris, 1991: 39)

In *Femininity in Dissent* (1990), Alison Young presented an analysis of how Greenham Common Peace Camp, a women's protest at a Cruise missile base, was represented in the national press. Disarmament and nuclear policy was a central issue in the 1980s, and the Greenham camp, which began in 1981, was the most influential protest group. The camp was unique in that it linked the demand for disarmament to an indictment of patriarchy. The expansion of the military–industrial complex was linked to specifically male power. Young explained that the press discourse employed 'dichotomies such as criminal/law-abiding, mad/sane and good/evil in order to describe and evaluate social phenomena', constructing the protest through these oppositional constructs (Young, 1990: 2–3). Young also showed how the women countered these.

Queer theory is another form of postmodern scholarship supplying critical resources that enable the status of criminology as a master-narrative to be challenged. This genre of scholarship emerged during the 1990s as a critique of the identity politics and liberation paradigm seen in the gay and lesbian rights movement, which formed part of the personalising of the political discussed in Chapter 6. Queer theory draws attention to incoherencies within the terms which stabilise commonplace notions of heterosexuality and homosexuality. It seeks to subvert conventional linkings of sex, gender and sexual desire. The late 1990s has seen the tentative beginnings of a queer criminology. This critiques the fundamental heteronormativity of criminology, and calls for scholars to engage with issues of sexuality in their work. For instance, in 'Perverse Criminologies' (1999), Nic Groombridge presented a survey of the history of criminological engagement with homosexuality from the days of Lombroso to the present time. He argued that sexuality has been absent or unproblematised in most criminology, reflecting that: 'sexuality has been treated poorly in criminology. In criminology, generally, sexuality is normatively heterosexual and often explicitly possessed only by the young or black' (Groombridge, 1999: 543). The recent revival of theories of cosmopolitanism is one source from which less limited understandings might ensue, for instance the legal scholar Carl Stychin (2000) writes that this approach may yield more inclusive visions of sexual citizenship.

Towards cosmopolitan theories of crime and punishment

The preoccupation with endings that marked the scholarship of ten years ago has recently been supplanted by a notion of new beginnings, in which scholars anticipate the advent of a new global cosmopolitan society. Scholars like Beck, Urry and Giddens have outlined an optimistic view of the potential for non-hostile sociability in late modernity. They have put their faith in the advent of a new cosmopolitanism, a new mode of communication and interaction between different peoples.[6] Cosmopolitanism is an ideal; as a practice it is yet to come. What might a cosmopolitan political practice look like? In cosmopolitanism, the other is less intensely opposed, and a stance of openness towards different peoples, places and experiences is taken up. Against the attempt to impose uniformity and the desire for cultural homogeneity, the cosmopolitan is ready to acknowledge the validity of all that is different and seeks out contrasts.

What might a global civil society be like? This is not just a postnational and 'cross-borders' openness. The cosmopolitan would rigorously oppose, and seek to subvert the construction of proximate 'others' as 'enemies within' and 'intimate others'. With the recent punitive turn, furious social reaction to crimes is so widespread that the very concept of moral panic, or at least its classic outline in the work of Cohen (1973) and Hall et al. (1978) seems obsolete. The context for the new punitiveness is a surge of powerful expressions of collective identity and explosive nationalisms. This can be seen as a resurgence of 'reactionary tribalism' (Antonio, 2000), which attacks aspirations towards a multicultural nation-state and the possibility of universal citizenship. Tribalism is seen in resurgent neo-populist movements and wars. It refuses hybridity and calls for the consolidation of exclusionary monoculture. Nationalism promotes territorially based identities. In reactionary tribalism, an indictment of the failures of modernisation leads to emotive and nostalgic calls for a return to some mythical past where there was a harmonious unitary culture. A critique of modernity can form the basis for a return to pre-modern forms. A powerful example of this retrogressive tendency can be seen in the recent affirmation by the House of Lords that a purely retributive full life tariff is both lawful and appropriate for the never-ending punishment of Myra Hindley.[7]

However, the notion of cosmopolitanism must also be the subject of critical reflection. A critique of the cosmopolitan intellectual stance, in the spirit of Gouldner's essay about partisan sociology discussed in Chapter 5, might be imagined. As was discussed in Chapter 3, Chicago school scholars appealed to cosmopolitan notions of appreciating different cultures. Their stance was seen by later scholars as problematic in a number of respects, for instance Robert Park's idea of 'becoming Negro' was highly suspect. A cosmopolitan theory would undertake a permanent interrogation of its epistemology and methods. Are self-proclaimed cosmopolitans privileged mobile elites with little lasting commitment to any local struggle? Worse still perhaps, are they Bauman's (1997) tourists who trip on exciting new sensations and are actually reassured by the abject condition of others? Bauman developed the notion that globalisation produces tourists and vagabonds. Tourists, he explained, move because the world within their global reach is irresistible, whereas vagabonds move because the world within their local reach is unbearable. Bauman added that the line dividing tourist from vagabond was tenuous, unclear, and easily crossed. There is, he pointed out, no insurance policy which can protect a person against a slip into vagabondage in an uncertain world. The vagabond is hence an object of anxiety for the tourist as an image of what they themselves may become. The obsession with law and order, the confining of the vagabond in a far away ghetto, the banning of the beggar and the homeless person from the street, are attempts by the tourists to banish their fears. Advocates of cosmopolitanism claim that over parochialism, provincialism and xenophobia, the cosmopolitan is 'at home' in different places. However, respecting difference is a complex and ongoing task, and cannot be assumed to arise automatically from the adoption of a cosmopolitan stance.

Notes

1. Key works in this debate include Lyotard (1984), Jameson (1986/1991), Turner (1990), Bauman (1991, 1997) and Smart (1993).

2. See Harvey (1989), Urry (1991) and Luke (1998).
3. *The Times*, 1 September 2000, p. 5, 'World Sends its Regards to Killer Kray'.
4. See also Sarup (1996).
5. See also Beck, Giddens and Lash (1994) and Lash, Featherstone and Robertson (1995).
6. On cosmopolitanism, see Beck (1999), Urry (2000b), Cheah and Robbins (1997), Brennan (1997) and *Public Culture* 12 (3), 2001.
7. R *v* Secretary of State for the Home Department, *Ex Parte* Hindley (2000).

Bibliography

Addams, J. (1912) 'Recreation as a Public Function in Urban Communities', *American Journal of Sociology* 17 (5): 615–19.

Adkeniz, Y., Walker, C. and Wall, D. (eds) (2000) *The Internet, Law and Society*. London: Longman.

Adler, F. (1975) *Sisters in Crime*. New York: McGraw-Hill.

Adler, F. and Laufer, W.S. (eds) (1995) *The Legacy of Anomie Theory: Advances in Criminological Theory, Volume 6*. New Brunswick, NJ: Transaction.

Agnew, R. (1992) 'Foundation for a General Strain Theory of Crime and Delinquency', *Criminology* 30: 47–87.

Albrecht, H.-J. (1997) 'Minorities, Crime and Criminal Justice in the Federal Republic of Germany', in Marshall, I.H. (ed.) *Minorities, Rights and Crime: Diversity and Similarity Across Europe and the United States*. Thousand Oaks, CA and London: Sage.

Alexander, F. and Healy, W. (1935/1969) *Roots of Crime: Psychoanalytic Studies*. Montclair, NJ: Paterson Smith.

Ali, T. and Watkins, S. (1998) *1968: Marching in the Streets*. London: Bloomsbury.

Allen, J. (1989) 'Men, Crime and Criminology: Recasting the Questions', *International Journal of the Sociology of Law* 17: 19–39.

Althusser, L. (1968) 'Ideology and Ideological State Apparatuses', in *Lenin and Philosophy, And Other Essays*. London: New Left Books.

Amir, M. (1971) *Patterns in Forcible Rape*. Chicago, IL: Chicago University Press.

Anderson, N. (1923/1967) *The Hobo: The Sociology of the Homeless Man*. Chicago, IL: University of Chicago Press.

Anderson, P. (1965) 'The Left in the Fifties', *New Left Review* 29: 3–18.

Antonio, R.J. (2000) 'After Postmodernism: Reactionary Tribalism', *American Journal of Sociology* 106 (2): 40–87.

Archer, T. (1863) *The Pauper, the Thief and the Convict*. London: Groombridge & Sons.

Bailey, R. and Young, J. (eds) (1973) *Contemporary Social Problems in Britain*. Farnborough: Saxon House.

Baker, P.J. (1973) 'The Life Histories of W.I. Thomas and Robert E. Park', *American Journal of Sociology* 79 (2): 243–60.

Bankowski, Z., Mungham, G. and Young, P. (1977) 'Radical Criminology or Radical Criminologist', *Contemporary Crises* 1: 37–52.

Barrett, N. (1997) *Digital Crime: Policing the Cybernation*. London: Kogan Page.

Barry, A. (1996) 'Lines of Communication and Spaces of Rule', in Barry, A., Osborne, T. and Rose, N. (eds) *Foucault and Political Reason: Liberalism, Neo-Liberalism and Rationalities of Government*. Chicago, IL: University of Chicago Press.

Barry, A., Osborne, T. and Rose, N. (eds) (1996) *Foucault and Political Reason: Liberalism, Neo-Liberalism and Rationalities of Government*. Chicago, IL: University of Chicago Press.

Baudrillard, J. (1998) 'The End of the Millenium or the Countdown', *Theory Culture and Society* 15 (1): 1–11.

Bauman, Z. (1991) *Intimations of Postmodernity*. London: Routledge.

Bauman, Z. (1997) *Postmodernity and Its Discontents*. Cambridge: Polity.

Bauman, Z. (1998) *Globalization: The Human Consequences*. Cambridge: Polity.

Bauman, Z. (2000) *Liquid Modernity*. Cambridge: Polity.

Beccaria, C. (1764/1995) *On Crimes and Punishments and Other Writings*. Cambridge: Cambridge University Press.

Beck, U. (1992) *Risk Society: Towards a New Modernity*. London: Sage.

Beck, U. (1998) 'Politics of Risk Society', in Franklin, J. (ed.) *The Politics of Risk Society*. Cambridge: Polity.

Beck, U. (1999) *World Risk Society*. Malden, MA: Polity.

Beck, U. (2000) 'The Cosmopolitan Perspective: Sociology of the Second Age of Modernity', *British Journal of Sociology* 51 (1): 79–105.

Beck, U., Giddens, A. and Lash, S. (eds) (1994) *Reflexive Modernization: Politics, Tradition and Aesthetics in the Modern Social Order*. Cambridge: Polity.

Becker, H. and Horowitz, I.L. (1972) 'Radical Politics and Sociological Research: Observations on Methodology and Ideology', *American Journal of Sociology* 78 (1): 48–66.

Becker, H.S. (1963) *Outsiders: Studies in the Sociology of Deviance*. New York: Macmillan.

Becker, H.S. (1967) 'Whose Side Are We On?', *Social Problems* 14 (3): 239–47.

Becker, H.S. (1973) 'Labelling Theory Reconsidered', in *Outsiders: Studies in the Sociology of Deviance*. New York: Free Press.

Beirne, P. (1993) *Inventing Criminology: Essays On The Rise Of Homo Criminalis*. Albany: State University of New York.

Bellah, R. (1973) *Émile Durkheim: On Morality and Society, Selected Writings*. Chicago, IL: University of Chicago Press.

Benhabib, S., Butler, J., Cornell, D. and Fraser, N. (1995) *Feminist Contentions: A Philosophical Exchange*. New York: Routledge.

Bentham, J. (1776/1948) *A Fragment on Government*. Oxford: Blackwell.

Bentham, J. (1789/1970) *An Introduction to the Principles of Morals and Legislation*. London: Athlone Press.

Bentham, J. (1995) *The Panopticon and Other Prison Writings*. New York: Verso.

Bergreen, L. (1995) *Capone: the Man and the Era*. London: Pan.

Besnard, P. (1987) *L'Anomie: ses usages et ses functions dans la discipline sociologique depuis Durkheim*. Paris: PUF.

Bess, M.D. (1993) 'E.P. Thompson: The Historian as Activist', *American Historical Review* 98 (1): 19–38.

Bianchi, H., Simondi, M. and Taylor, I. (eds) (1975) *Deviance in Europe, Papers from the European Group for the Study of Deviance and Social Control*. London: Wiley.

Bland, L. (1984/1992) 'The Case of the Yorkshire Ripper: Mad, Bad, Beast or Male', in Radford, J. and Russell, D.E.H. (eds) *Femicide: The Politics of Woman Killing*. Buckingham: Open University Press.

Bottomore, T. (1981) 'A Marxist Consideration of Durkheim', *Social Forces* 59: 902–17.

Bottoms, A.E. (1983) 'Neglected Features of Contemporary Penal Systems', in Garland, D. and Young, P. (eds) *The Power to Punish: Contemporary Penal and Social Analysis.* London: Heinemann.

Bottoms, T. and Wiles, P. (1995) 'Crime and Insecurity in the City', in Fijnaut, C. (ed.) *Changes in Society, Crime and Criminal Justice in Europe.* The Hague: Kluwer.

Boyle, K., Hadden, T. and Hillyard, P. (1975) *Law and State: The Case of Northern Ireland.* London: Martin Robertson.

Braithwaite, J. (1989) *Crime, Shame and Reintegration.* Cambridge: Cambridge University Press.

Braithwaite, J. (2000) *Regulation, Crime and Freedom.* Dartmouth: Ashgate.

Brennan, T. (1997) *At Home in the World Cosmopolitanism Now.* Cambridge, MA: Harvard University Press.

Brownmiller, S. (1975) *Against Our Will: Men, Women and Rape.* London: Secker and Warburg.

Brownmiller, S. (2000) *In Our Time: Memoir Of A Revolution.* London: Aurum Press.

Burchell, G., Gordon, C. and Miller, P. (eds) (1991) *The Foucault Effect: Studies in Governmentality.* Chicago, IL: University of Chicago Press.

Burgess, E.W. (1925) 'The Growth of the City', in Park, R.E. and Burgess, E. (eds) *The City.* Chicago, IL: University of Chicago Press.

Burgess, E.W. (1928) 'Communication', *American Journal of Sociology* 34 (1): 117–29.

Burgess, E.W. and Bogue, D.J. (1964) 'Research in Urban Society: A Long View', in Burgess, E.W. and Bogue, D.J. (eds) *Contributions to Urban Sociology.* Chicago, IL: University of Chicago Press.

Burns, W.N. (1931) *The One-Way Ride: The Red Trail of Chicago Gangland from Prohibition to Jake Lingle.* Garden City: Doubleday.

Butler, J. (1990) *Gender Trouble: Feminism and the Subversion of Identity.* New York: Routledge.

Butler, J. (1997) *The Psychic Life of Power: Theories in Subjection.* Stanford, CA: Stanford University Press.

Cain, M. (1990) 'Towards Transgression: New Directions in Feminist Criminology', *International Journal of the Sociology of Law* 18 (1): 1–18.

Campbell, B. (1984) *Wigan Pier Revisited: Poverty and Politics in the 80s.* London: Lawrence and Wishart.

Canning, K. (1994) 'Feminist History after the Linguistic Turn: Historicising Discourse and Experience', *Signs* 19 (2): 368–404.

Capitanchik, D. and White, M. (1999) 'The Governance of Cyberspace: Racism on the Internet', in Liberty (ed.) *Liberating Cyberspace: Civil Liberties, Human Rights and the Internet.* London: Pluto.

Cardarelli, A.P. and Hicks, S.C. (1993) 'Radicalism in Law and Criminology: A Retrospective View of Critical Legal Studies and Radical Criminology', *Journal of Criminal Law and Criminology* 84 (3): 502–53.

Carlen, P. (1985) *Criminal Women: Autobiographical Accounts.* Cambridge: Polity.

Carlen, P. (1992) 'Criminal Women and Criminal Justice: The Limits to and Potential of Feminist and Left Realist Perspectives', in Matthews, R. and Young, J. (eds) *Issues in Realist Criminology.* London: Sage.

Carlen, P. (1998) 'Criminology Ltd: The Search for a Paradigm', in Walton, P. and Young, J. (eds) *The New Criminology Revisited.* Basingstoke: Macmillan.

Carmichael, S. (1968) 'Black Power', in Cooper, D. (ed.) *The Dialectics of Liberation.* Harmondsworth: Penguin.

Carrington, K. (1998) 'Postmodernism and Feminist Criminologies: Fragmenting the Criminological Subject', in Walton, P. and Young, J. (eds) *The New Criminology Revisited.* Basingstoke: Macmillan.

Castells, M. (1998) *End of Millennium.* Oxford: Blackwell.

Cheah, P. and Robbins, B. (1997) *Cosmopolitics: Thinking and Feeling Beyond the Nation.* Minneapolis: University of Minnesota Press.

Chesney-Lind, M. (1980) 'Rediscovering Lilith: Misogyny and the "New Female Criminality"', in Taylor Griffiths, C. and Nance, M. (eds) *The Female Offenders.* New York: Simon Fraser University.

Chriss, J.J. (1999) 'Role Distance and the Negational Self', in Smith, G. (ed.) *Goffman and Social Organization: Studies in a Sociological Legacy.* London: Routledge.

Clare, A. (1976) *Psychiatry in Dissent: Controversial Issues in Thought and Practice.* London: Tavistock.

Clark, J., Modgil, J. and Modgil, S. (eds) (1990) *Robert K. Merton: Consensus and Controversy.* Brighton: Falmer.

Cleaver, E. (1967/1972) *Post-Prison Writings and Speeches.* London: Panther.

Clinard, M.B. (1964) *Anomie and Deviant Behaviour: A Discussion and Critique.* New York: Free Press.

Clouston (1894) 'The Developmental Aspects of Criminal Anthropology', *The Journal of the Anthropological Institute of Great Britain and Ireland.*

Cohen, A. (1955) *Delinquent Boys: The Culture of the Gang.* New York: Free Press.

Cohen, A., Lindesmith, A. and Schuessler, K. (eds) (1956) *The Sutherland Papers.* Bloomington: Indiana University Press.

Cohen, S. (1971) *Images of Deviance.* Harmondsworth: Penguin.

Cohen, S. (1973/1976) 'Protest, Unrest and Delinquency', in Wiles, P. (ed.) *The Sociology of Crime and Delinquency in Britain,* Vol. 2, *The New Criminologies.* Oxford: Martin Robertson.

Cohen, S. (1979) 'The Punitive City: Notes on the Dispersal of Social Control', *Contemporary Crises* 3 (4): 341–63.

Cohen, S. (1981) 'Footprints on the Sand: A Further Report on Criminology and the Sociology of Deviance in Britain', in Fitzgerald, M., McLennan, G. and Pawson, J. (eds) *Crime and Society: Readings in History and Theory.* London: Routledge and Kegan Paul.

Cohen, S. (1998) 'Intellectual Scepticism and Political Commitment: The Case of Radical Criminology', in Walton, P. and Young, J. (eds) *The New Criminology Revisited.* Basingstoke: Macmillan.

Colomy, P. (1990) 'Introduction: The Functionalist Tradition', in *Functionalist Sociology.* Aldershot: Edward Elgar.

Comte, A. (1848/1865) *A General View of Positivism.* London: Trübner.

Connell, N. and Wilson, C. (1974) *Rape: The First Sourcebook For Women.* New York: Plume.

Connell, R.W. (1987) *Gender and Power: Society, the Person and Sexual Politics.* Cambridge: Polity.

Cooke, A. (1950/1968) *A Generation On Trial: USA vs Alger.* Hiss Baltimore, MD: Penguin.

Cooper, D. (1971/1973) *The Death of the Family.* Harmondsworth: Penguin.

Copjec, J. (1994) *Read My Desire: Lacan Against the Historicists.* Cambridge, MA: MIT Press.

Coser, L. (1960) 'Durkheim's Conservatism and its Implications for his Sociological Theory', in Wolff, K.H. (ed.) *Émile Durkheim, 1858–1917*. Columbus, OH: Ohio State University Press.

Cotterrell, R. (1999) *Émile Durkheim: Law in a Moral Domain*. Edinburgh: Edinburgh University Press.

Cousins, M. (1980) 'Mens Rea: A Note on Sexual Difference, Criminology and the Law', in Carlen, P. and Collison, M. (eds) *Radical Issues in Criminology*. Oxford: Martin Robertson.

Crawford, A. (1997) *The Local Governance of Crime: Appeals to Community and Partnerships*. Oxford: Clarendon.

Crawford, A. (1998) *Crime Prevention and Community Safety: Politics, Policies and Practices*. London: Longman.

Crawford, A., Jones, T., Woodhouse, T. and Young, J. (1990) *Second Islington Crime Survey*. Middlesex Polytechnic, Centre for Criminology.

Cronin, C. (1996) 'Bourdieu and Foucault on Power and Modernity', *Philosophy and Social Criticism* 22 (6): 55–85.

Crothers, C. (1987) *Robert K. Merton*. Chichester: Ellis Horwood.

Cullen, P. (1997) 'Computer Crime', in Edwards, L. and Waelde, C. (eds) *Law and the Internet: Regulating Cyberspace*. Oxford: Hart.

Currie, E. (1974) 'Beyond Criminology – a Review of the *New Criminology*', *Issues in Criminology* 9: 1.

Daly, K. (1997) 'Different Ways of Conceptualising Sex/Gender in Feminist Theory and their Implications for Criminology', *Theoretical Criminology* 1 (1): 25–51.

Daly, K. (1999) 'Restorative Justice in Diverse and Unequal Societies', *Law in Context* 17 (1): 167–90.

Daly, K. and Chesney-Lind, M. (1988) 'Feminism and Criminology', *Justice Quarterly* 5: 497–538.

Davis, M. (1992) *City of Quartz: Excavating the Future in Los Angeles*. London: Verso.

Davis, M. (1999) *The Ecology of Fear: Los Angeles and the Imagination of Disaster*. New York: Vintage.

Davis, N.J. (1975) *Sociological Constructions of Deviance: Perspectives and Issues in the Field*. Dubuque, IA: W.C. Brown Co.

Davitt, M. (1972) *Leaves From a Prison Diary*. Shannon: Irish University Press.

Dean, M. (1994) *Critical and Effective Histories: Foucault's Methods and Historical Sociology*. London: Routledge.

Dean, M. (1999) 'Normalising Democracy: Foucault and Habermas on Democracy, Liberalism and Law', in Ashenden, S. and Owen, D. (eds) *Foucault Contra Habermas: Recasting the Dialogue Between Genealogy and Critical Theory*. London: Sage.

Dean, M. and Hindess, B. (eds) (1998) *Governing Australia*. Melbourne: Cambridge University Press.

Dear, M.J. (2000) *The Postmodern Urban Condition*. Oxford: Blackwell.

Debord, G. (1967/1994) *Society of the Spectacle*. London: Rebel Press.

Deegan, M.J. (1990) *Jane Adams and the Men of the Chicago School, 1892–1918*. New Brunswick, NJ: Transaction Books.

Deleuze, G. (1995a) 'Control and Becoming', in *Negotiations 1972–1990*. New York: Columbia University Press.

Deleuze, G. (1995b) 'Postscript on Control Societies', in *Negotiations 1972–1990*. New York: Columbia University Press.

Delgado, R. (2000) 'Goodbye to Hammurabi: Analyzing the Atavistic Appeal of Restorative Justice', *Stanford Law Review* 52: 751–75.

Department of Health (2001) *Harold Shipman's Clinical Practice 1974–1998: A Clinical Audit Commissioned by the Chief Medical Officer.* London: Department of Health.

Dixon, H. (1850) *The London Prisons.* London: Jackson and Walford.

Dobash, R.E. and Dobash, R. (1979) *Violence Against Wives: A Case Against The Patriarchy.* New York: Free Press.

Dolar, M. (1998) 'Where Does Power Come From?', *New Formations* 35: 35–62.

Donzelot, J. (1975) 'The Prison Movement in France', in Bianchi, H., Simondi, M. and Taylor, I. (eds) *Deviance and Control In Europe.* London: John Wiley and Sons.

Donzelot, J. (1979) *The Policing of Families.* London: Hutchinson.

Dreyfus, H. and Rabinow, P. (1983) *Michel Foucault: Beyond Structuralism and Hermeneutics.* Chicago: Chicago University Press.

Dublin Rape Crisis Centre (1979/1981) 'First Report', in Feminist Anthology Collective (eds) (1981) *No Turning Back: Writings from The Women's Liberation Movement 1975–80.* London: The Women's Press.

Dugdale, R. (1877) *The Jukes: A Study in Crime, Pauperism, Disease, and Heredity.* New York: G.P. Putnam's Sons.

Durkheim, É. (1893/1933) *The Division of Labour in Society.* New York: Bobbs-Merrill Company.

Durkheim, É. (1894/1964) *The Rules of Sociological Method.* New York: Free Press.

Durkheim, É. (1897/1952) *Suicide: A Study in Sociology,* trans. Spaulding, J.A. London: Routledge and Kegan Paul.

Durkheim, É. (1898/1969) 'Individualism and the Intellectuals', *Political Studies* xvii (1): 19–30. This is reproduced in Bellah, R. (1973), *Émile Durkheim: On Morality and Society, Selected Writings.* Chicago, IL: University of Chicago Press.

Durkheim, É. (1901/1992) 'Two Laws of Penal Evolution', in Gane, M. (ed.) *The Radical Sociology of Durkheim and Mauss.* London: Routledge.

Durkheim, É. (1909/1987) 'Sociologie et sciences sociales', in *La Science Sociale et l'Action.* Paris: PUF.

Dyer, R. (1998) *Stars.* London: British Film Institute.

Elliott, M. (1944) 'Crime and the Frontier Mores', *American Sociological Review* 9 (2): 185–92.

Elshtain, J. (1981) *Public Man, Private Woman.* Princeton, NJ: Princeton University Press.

Eribon, D. (1991) *Michel Foucault.* Cambridge, MA: Harvard University Press.

Ewald, F. (1990) 'Norms, Discipline and the Law', *Representations* 30: 138–61.

Fanon, F. (1961/1990) *The Wretched of the Earth.* London: Penguin.

Fass, P.S. (1993) 'Making and Remaking an Event: the Leopold and Loeb Case in American Culture', *Journal of American History* 80 (3): 919–51.

Faulkner, A.S. (1921) 'Does Jazz Put the Sin in Syncopation', *Ladies' Home Journal* August: 16–34.

Feeley, M. and Simon, J. (1992) 'The New Penology: Notes on the Emerging Strategy of Corrections and its Implications', *Criminology* 30: 449–74.

Feeley, M. and Simon, J. (1994) 'Actuarial Justice: The Emerging new Criminal Law', in Nelken, D. (ed.) *The Futures of Criminology.* London: Sage.

Felman, S. (1997) 'Forms of Judicial Blindness, or the Evidence of What Cannot be Seen', *Critical Inquiry* 23: 738–87.

Fenton, S.C. (1980) 'Race, Class and Politics in the Work of Émile Durkheim', in *Sociological Theories: Race and Colonialism.* Paris: UNESCO.

Fenton, S.C. (1984) 'Race and Society: Primitive and Modern', in Fenton, S., Reiner, R. and Hamnet, I. (eds) *Durkheim and Modern Society*. Cambridge: Cambridge University Press.

Fine, B. and Millar, B. (eds) (1985) *Policing the Miners' Strike*. London: Lawrence Wishart.

Fine, B., Kinsey, R., Lea, J., Picciotto, S. and Young, J. (eds) (1979) *Capitalism and the Rule of Law*. London: Hutchinson.

Finestone, H. (1976) *Victims of Change: Juvenile Delinquents in American Society*. Westport, CT: Greenwood.

Fiske, J. (1998) 'Surveilling the City: Whiteness, the Black Man and Democratic Totalitarianism', *Theory Culture and Society* 15 (2): 67–88.

Fitzgerald, F.S. (1922/1966) *The Beautiful and Damned*. London: Penguin.

Fitzgerald, F.S. (1926/1950) *The Great Gatsby*. London: Penguin.

Fitzgerald, M. (1977) *Prisoners in Revolt*. Harmonsworth: Penguin.

Fitzpatrick, P. (1990) 'The Desperate Vacuum: Imperialism and Law in the Experience of Enlightenment', in Carty, A. (ed.) *Post-Modern Law: Enlightenment, Revolution and the Death of Man*. Edinburgh: Edinburgh University Press.

Flax, J. (1987) 'Postmodernism and Gender Relations in Feminist Theory', *Signs* 12: 621–33.

Foucault, M. (1971/1996) 'Revolutionary Action: "Until Now"', in Bouchard, D.F. (ed.) *Language, Counter-Memory, Practice: Selected Essays and Interviews by Michel Foucault*. Ithaca, NY: Cornell University Press.

Foucault, M. (1972/1996) 'Intellectuals and Power', in Bouchard, D.F. (ed.) *Language, Counter-Memory, Practice: Selected Essays and Interviews by Michel Foucault*. Ithaca, NY: Cornell University Press.

Foucault, M. (1975/1991) *Discipline and Punish: The Birth of the Prison*. London: Penguin.

Foucault, M. (1976/1990) *La Volonte de Savoir* translated into English as *The History of Sexuality*, Vol. 1. London Penguin.

Foucault, M. (1980) *Power/Knowledge: Selected Interviews and Other Writings*. Brighton: Harvester.

Foucault, M. (1981/1990) 'Practicing Criticism', in Kritzman, L.D. (ed.) *Michel Foucault: Politics, Philosophy, Culture: Interviews and Other Writings 1977–1984*. New York and London: Routledge.

Foucault, M. (1984) *The Foucault Reader*, Rabinow, P. (ed.). London: Penguin.

Foucault, M. (1996) *Foucault Live*, Lotringer, S. (ed.). New York: Semiotext(e).

Foucault, M. (1997) 'The Punitive Society', in Rabinow, P. (ed.) *Michel Foucault: Ethics, Subjectivity and Truth*. London: Allen Lane.

Fraser, N. (1989) 'Foucault on Modern Power: Empirical Insights and Normative Confusions', in *Unruly Practices: Power, Discourse and Gender in Contemporary Social Theory*. Cambridge: Polity.

Fraser, N. and Nicholson, L. (1988) 'Social Criticism Without Philosophy: An Encounter Between Feminism and Postmodernism', *Theory, Culture and Society* 5 (2/3): 373–94.

Friedan, B. (1963) *The Feminine Mystique*. London: Gollancz.

Galton, F. (1883) *Inquiries Into Human Faculty And Its Development*. London: Macmillan.

Gane, M. (ed.) (1992) *The Radical Sociology of Durkheim and Mauss*. London: Routledge.

Garfinkel, H. (1956) 'Conditions of Successful Degradation Ceremonies', *American Journal of Sociology* 61 (5): 420–4.

Garland, D. (1985) *Punishment and Welfare: A History of Penal Strategies.* Aldershot: Gower.

Garland, D. (1990) *Punishment and Modern Society: A Study in Social Theory.* Oxford: Clarendon.

Garland, D. (1992) 'Criminological Knowledge and Its Relation to Power: Foucault's Genealogy and Criminology Today', *British Journal of Criminology* 32 (4): 403–22.

Garland, D. (1994) 'Of Crimes and Criminals: The Development of Criminology in Britain', in Maguire, M., Morgan, R., and Reiner, R. (eds) *The Oxford Handbook of Criminology.* Oxford: Clarendon.

Garland, D. (1996) 'The Limits of the Sovereign State: Strategies of Crime Control in Contemporary Society', *British Journal of Criminology* 36 (4): 445–71.

Garland, D. (1997) ' "Governmentality" and the problem of crime', *Theoretical Criminology* 1 (2): 173–214.

Garland, D. and Young, P. (eds) (1983/1992) *The Power to Punish: Contemporary Penality and Social Analysis.* Aldershot: Ashgate.

Gault, R.H. (1925) 'Criminology', *The Psychological Bulletin* 22 (10): 575–91.

Gelsthorpe, L. (1997) 'Feminism and Criminology', in Maguire, M., Morgan, R. and Reiner, R. (eds) *The Oxford Handbook of Criminology*, 2nd edn. Oxford: Oxford University Press.

Giddens, A. (1972) *Émile Durkheim: Selected Writings.* Cambridge: Cambridge University Press.

Giddens, A. (1990) *The Consequences of Modernity.* Cambridge: Polity.

Giddens, A. (1991) *Modernity and Self-Identity: Self and Society in the Late Modern Age.* Stanford, CA: Stanford University Press.

Giddens, A. (2000) *Runaway World: How Globalization is Reshaping Our Lives.* New York: Routledge.

Gieryn, T.F. (ed.) (1980) *Science and Social Structure: A Festschrift for Robert K. Merton.* New York: New York Academy of Sciences.

Gilman, S. (1985) *Difference and Pathology: Stereotypes of Sexuality, Race and Madness.* Ithaca, NY: Cornell University Press.

Gilroy, P. (1982) 'Police and Thieves', in Centre for Contemporary Cultural Studies (ed.) *The Empire Strikes Back: Race and Racism in 70s Britain.* London: Hutchinson.

Gilroy, P. (1987) 'The Myth of Black Criminality', in Scraton, P. (ed.) *Law, Order and the Authoritarian State: Readings in Critical Criminology.* Milton Keynes: Open University Press.

Ginsberg, A. (1956) *Howl and Other Poems.* San Francisco, CA: City Lights Pocket Bookshop.

Gittens, J. (1994) *Poor Relations: The Children of the State in Illinois, 1818–1990.* Urbana and Chicago: University of Illinois Press.

Glover, E. (1931) *The Psycho-Pathology of Flogging.* London: Howard League for Penal Reform.

Goffman, E. (1961) *Asylums: Essays on the Social Situation of Mental Patients and Other Inmates.* Garden City, NY: Anchor Books.

Goffman, E. (1963/1990) *Stigma: Notes on the Management of Spoiled Identity.* London: Penguin.

Goring, C. (1913) *The English Convict: A Statistical Study.* London: HMSO.

Gornick, V. (1971) 'Woman as Outsider', in Gornick, V. and Moran, B.K. (eds) *Woman In Sexist Society: Studies in Power and Powerlessness.* New York: Basic Books.

Gouldner, A.W. (1968/1973) 'The Sociologist as Partisan: Sociology and the Welfare State', in *For Sociology.* London: Allen Lane.

Gouldner, A.W. (1971) *The Coming Crisis of Western Sociology.* London: Heinemann Educational Books.

Gramsci (1929/1971) *Prison Notebooks: Selections from the Prison Notebooks of Antonio Gramsci.* London: Lawrence and Wishart.

Greenberg, D. (1977) 'The Dynamics of Oscillatory Punishment Processes', *Journal of Criminal Law and Criminology* 68 (4): 643–51.

Griffin, S. (1979) *Rape: The Power of Consciousness.* New York: Harper and Row.

Griffiths, A. (1894) *Secrets of the Prison House, or Gaol Studies and Sketches,* Vol. 1. London: Chapman & Hall.

Grimberg (1928) *Emotion and Delinquency, A Clinical Study of Five Hundred Criminals in the Making.* London.

Groombridge, N. (1999) 'Perverse Criminologies: The Closet of Doctor Lombroso', *Social and Legal Studies* 8 (4): 531–48.

Guarnieri, P. (1991) 'Alienists on Trial: Conflict and Convergence Between Psychiatry and Law (1876–1913)', *History of Science* xxix: 393–413.

Habermas, J. (1987) *The Philosophical Discourse on Modernity.* Cambridge, MA: MIT Press.

Hacking, I. (1990) *The Taming of Chance.* Cambridge: Cambridge University Press.

Haggerty, K.D. and Ericson, R.V. (2000) 'The Surveillant Assemblage', *British Journal of Sociology* 51 (4): 605–22.

Hague, G. and Wilson, C. (2000) 'The Silenced Pain: Domestic Violence 1945–1970', *Journal of Gender Studies* 9 (2): 157–70.

Hahn Rafter, N. (1997) *Creating Born Criminals.* Urbana and Chicago, IL: University of Illinois Press.

Hall, S. (1974) 'Deviance, Politics and the Media', in Rock, P. and McIntosh, M. (eds) *Deviance and Social Control.* London: Tavistock.

Hall, S. (1980) *Drifting Into A Law and Order Society.* London: Cobden Trust.

Hall, S. and Jacques, M. (eds) (1983) *The Politics of Thatcherism.* London: Lawrence & Wishart.

Hall, S. and Scraton, P. (1981) 'Law, Class and Control', in Fitzgerald, M., McLennan, G. and Pawson, J. (eds) *Crime and Society: Readings in History and Theory.* London: Routledge and Kegan Paul.

Hall, S., Critcher, C., Jefferson, T., Clarke, J. and Roberts, B. (1978) *Policing the Crisis: Mugging, the State and Law and Order.* London: Macmillan.

Hamilton, A. (1999) 'The Net Out of Control – A New Moral Panic: Censorship and Sexuality', in Liberty (ed.) *Liberating Cyberspace: Civil Liberties, Human Rights and the Internet.* London: Pluto.

Hamilton, P. (1996) 'Systems Theory', in Turner, B.S. (ed.) *The Blackwell Companion to Social Theory.* Oxford: Blackwell.

Hanmer, J. (1979/1981) 'Male Violence and the Social Control of Women', in Feminist Anthology Collective (eds) (1981) *No Turning Back: Writings from The Women's Liberation Movement 1975–80.* London: The Women's Press.

Harris, R. (1990) *Murders and Madness: Medicine, Law and Society in the Fin de Siècle.* Oxford: Clarendon.

Harron, M. and Minahan, D. (1995) *I Shot Andy Warhol.* New York: Grove Press.

Hartsock, N. (1983) 'The Feminist Standpoint: Developing the Ground for a Specifically Feminist Historical Materialism', in Harding, S. and Hintikka, M.B. (eds) *Discovering Reality.* Dordrecht: Reidel.

Harvey, D. (1989) *The Condition of Postmodernity: An Enquiry Into the Origins of Cultural Change.* Oxford: Blackwell.

Healy, W. (1915) *The Individual Delinquent: A Text-Book of Diagnosis and Prognosis for all Concerned in Understanding Offenders.* Boston, MA: Little, Brown and Co.

Healy, W. (1926) *Mental Conflicts and Misconduct.* Boston, MA: Little, Brown and Co.

Healy, W. (1931) *Reconstructing Behavior in Youth: A Study of Problem Children in Foster Families.* New York: Alfred A. Knopf.

Healy, W. and Bronner, A. (1926) *Delinquents and Criminals: Their Making and Unmaking. Studies in Two American Cities.* New York: Macmillan.

Heidensohn, F. (1968) 'The Deviance of Women: A Critique and an Enquiry', *British Journal of Sociology* 19 (2): 160–75.

Hekman, S. (1997) 'Truth and Method: Feminist Standpoint Theory Revisited', *Signs* 22 (2): 431–64.

Hindess, B. (1995) *Discourses of Power: from Hobbes to Foucault.* Oxford: Blackwell.

Hirst, P. (1975a) 'Marx and Engels on Law, Crime and Morality', in Taylor, I., Walton, P. and Young, J. (eds) *Critical Criminology.* London: Routledge and Kegan Paul.

Hirst, P. (1975b) 'Radical Deviancy Theory and Marxism: A Reply to Taylor, Walton and Young', in Taylor, I., Walton, P. and Young, J. (eds) *Critical Criminology.* London: Routledge and Kegan Paul.

Hobbes, T. (1651/1991) *Leviathan: or, the matter, forme and power of a commonwealth ecclesiasticall and civil.* Cambridge: Cambridge University Press.

Hobsbawm, E. (1997) *On History.* London: Weidenfeld and Nicolson.

Honneth, A. (1991) *The Critique of Power: Stages in a Critical Social Theory.* Cambridge, MA: MIT Press.

Hooton, E.A. (1939) *The American Criminal: An Anthropological Study.* Cambridge, MA: Harvard University Press.

Horn, D. (1995) 'This Norm Which Is Not One: Reading the Female Body in Lombroso's Anthropology', in Terry, J. and Urla, J. (eds) *Deviant Bodies: Critical Perspectives on Difference in Science and Popular Culture.* Bloomington: Indiana University Press.

Horney, K. (1937) *The Neurotic Personality of Our Time.* New York: W.W. Norton and Company.

Horowitz, I.L. and Liebowitz, M. (1968) 'Social Deviance and Political Marginality: Toward a Redefintion of the Relation Between Sociology and Politics', *Social Problems* 280–96.

Hudson, B. (1998) 'Punishment and Governance', *Social and Legal Studies* 7 (4): 553–9.

Hughes, E.C., Johnson, C.S., Masovka, J., Redfield, R. and Wirth, L. (eds) (1950–55) *The Collected Papers of Robert Ezra Park.* Glencoe, IL: Free Press.

Hunt, A. (1990) 'Postmodernism and Critical Criminology', in Maclean, B.D. and Milovanovic, D. (eds) *New Directions in Critical Criminology.* Vancouver: Collective Press.

Hunt, A. and Wickham, G. (1994) *Foucault and Law: Towards a Sociology of Law as Governance.* London: Pluto.

Hutchings, P. (1999) 'Spectacularizing Crime: Ghostwriting the Law', *Law and Critique* 10: 27–48.

Isserman, M. and Kazin, M. (2000) *America Divided: The Civil War Of The 1960s.* New York: Oxford University Press.

Jacobs, R. (1996) 'Civil Society and Crisis: Culture, Discourse and the Rodney King Beating', *American Journal of Sociology* 101 (5): 1238–72.

Jagger, A. (1983) *Feminist Politics and Human Nature.* Totowa, NJ: Rowman and Allanheld.

Jameson, F. (1986/1991) *Postmodernism, Or, The Cultural Logic of Late Capitalism.* London: Verso.

Jankovic, I. (1977) 'Labour Market and Imprisonment', *Crime and Social Justice* 8: 17–31.

Jasanoff, S. (1999) 'The Eye of Everyman: Witnessing DNA in the Simpson Trial', *Social Studies of Science* 28 (5): 713–40.

Jefferson, T. (1994) 'Theorising Masculine Subjectivity', in Newburn, T. and Stanko, E.A. (eds) *Just Boys Doing Business? Men, Masculinities and Crime.* London: Routledge.

Jefferson, T. (1996) 'From "Little Fairy Boy" to "the Compleat Destroyer": Subjectivity and Transformation in The Biography of Mike Tyson', in Mac an Ghaill, M. (ed.) *Understanding Masculinities.* Buckingham: Open University Press.

Jefferson, T. (1997a) 'Masculinities and Crimes', in Maguire, M., Morgan, R. and Reiner, R. (eds) *The Oxford Handbook of Criminology*, 2nd edn. Oxford: Oxford University Press.

Jefferson, T. (1997b) 'The Tyson Rape Trial: the Law, Feminism and Emotional Truth', *Social and Legal Studies* 6 (2): 281–301.

Jenks, C. and Lorentzen, J. (1997) 'The Kray Fascination', *Theory, Culture and Society* 14 (3): 87–107.

Jensen, G.J. and Raymond, D. (1976) 'Sex Differences in Delinquency: An Examination of Popular Sociological Explantions', *Criminology* 13: 427–48.

Jensen, R.B. (1981) 'The International Anti-Anarchist Conference of 1898 and the Origins of Interpol', *Journal of Contemporary History* 16 (2): 323–47.

Jones, R. (1999) 'Digital Rule: Punishment, Control and Technology', *Punishment and Society* 2 (1): 5–22.

Jones, T., Maclean, B. and Young, J. (1986) *The Islington Crime Survey.* Aldershot: Gower.

Journal (1924) 'The Loeb–Leopold Murder of Franks in Chicago, May 21, 1924', *Journal of Criminal Law, Criminology and Police Science* 15 (3): 347–405.

Kilminster, R. and Varcoe, I. (1998) 'Three Appreciations of Zygmunt Bauman', *Theory Culture and Society* 15 (1).

Kinsey, R., Lea, J. and Young, J. (1986) *Losing the Fight Against Crime.* Oxford: Blackwell.

Kitsuse, J.J. (1962) 'Societal Reaction to Deviant Behaviour: Problems of Theory and Method', *Social Problems* 9: 247–57.

Klein, D. (1973/1996) 'The Etiology of Female Crime: A Review of the Literature', in Muncie, J., McLaughlin, E. and Langan, M. (eds) *Criminological Perspectives: A Reader.* London: Sage.

Kögler, H.H. (1996) 'The Self-empowered Subject: Habermas, Foucault and Hermeneutic Reflexivity', *Philosophy and Social Criticism* 22 (4): 13–44.

Konopka (1966) *The Adolescent Girl in Conflict.* Englewood Cliffs, NJ: Prentice Hall.

Kotowicz, Z. (1997) *R.D. Laing and the Paths of Anti-psychiatry.* London: Routledge.

Lacey, N. (1998) *Unspeakable Subjects: Feminist Essays in Legal and Social Theory.* Oxford: Hart.

Laing, R. (1965/1975) *The Divided Self.* Harmondsworth: Penguin.

Laing, R. (1968) 'The Obvious', in Cooper, D. (1968) 'Introduction', *The Dialectics of Liberation*. Harmondsworth: Penguin.

Landesco, J. (1929/1968) *Organized Crime in Chicago. Part III of the Illinois Crime Survey*. Chicago, IL and London: The University of Chicago Press.

Lash, S. (1998) 'Being after Time: Towards a Politics of Melancholy' in Lash, S., Quick, A. and Roberts, R. (eds) *Time and Value*. Oxford: Blackwell.

Lash, S. and Urry, J. (1994) *Economies of Signs and Space*. London: Sage.

Lash, S., Featherstone, M. and Robertson, R. (1995) *Global Modernities*. London: Sage.

Lea, J. and Young, J. (1984) *What is to be Done about Law and Order?* Harmondsworth: Penguin.

Lehmann, J. (1995a) 'Durkheim's Theories of Deviance and Suicide: A Feminist Reconsideration', *American Journal of Sociology* 100 (4): 904–30.

Lehmann, J. (1995b) 'The Question of Caste in Modern Society: Durkheim's Contradictory Theories of Race, Class and Sex', *American Sociological Review* 60 (4): 566–85.

Lemert, E.M. (1951) *Social Pathology*. New York: McGraw-Hill.

Lemert, E.M. (1967) *Human Deviance, Social Problems and Social Control*. Englewood Cliffs, NJ: Prentice Hall.

Leonard, E.B. (1982) *Women, Crime and Society: A Critique of Criminological Theory*. New York: Longman.

Leps, M.-C. (1992) *Apprehending the Criminal: The Production of Deviance in Nineteenth Century Discourse*. Durham, NC and London: Duke University Press.

Levin, D.M. (1997) 'Keeping Foucault and Derrida in Sight: Panopticism and the Politics of Subversion', in Levin, D.M. (ed.) *Sites of Vision: The Discursive Construction of Sight in the History of Philosophy*. Cambridge, MA: MIT Press.

Liazos, A. (1972) 'The Poverty of the Sociology of Deviance: Nuts, Sluts and Perverts', *Social Problems* 103–20.

Lilly, J.R., Cullen, F.T. and Ball, R.A. (1995) *Criminological Theory: Context and Consequences*, 2nd edn. Thousand Oaks, CA and London: Sage.

Lloyd, M. and Thacker, A. (1997) *The Impact of Michel Foucault on the Social Sciences and Humanities*. Basingstoke: Macmillan.

Lohman, J.D. (1937) 'The Participant Observer in Community Studies' *American Sociological Review* 2: 890–8.

Lombroso, C. (1911) *Criminal Man*. New York: G.P. Putnam.

Lombroso, C. and Ferreros, W. (1895) *The Female Offender*. London: Fisher Unwin.

London Rape Crisis Centre (1977/1981) 'First Report', in Feminist Anthology Collective (eds) (1981) *No Turning Back: Writings from The Women's Liberation Movement 1975–80*. London: The Women's Press.

Longino, H.E. (1993) 'Feminist Standpoint Theory and the Problems of Knowledge', *Signs* 19 (1): 201–12.

Lowman, J. and MacLean, B. (eds) (1992) *Realist Criminology*. Toronto: University of Toronto Press.

Luke, T.W. (1998) '"Moving at the Speed of Life?" A Cultural Kinematics of Telematic Times and Corporate Values', in Lash, S., Quick, A. and Roberts, R. (eds) *Time and Value*. Oxford: Blackwell.

Lukes, S. (1969) 'Durkheim's "Individualism and the Intellectuals"', *Political Studies* xvii (1): 14–19.

Lukes, S. (1973) *Émile Durkheim: His Life and Work. A Historical and Critical Study*. London: Penguin.

Lukes, S. and Scull, A. (1983) *Durkheim and the Law*. Oxford: Martin Robertson.

Lyotard, J.-F. (1984) *The Postmodern Condition: A Report on Knowledge*. Minneapolis: University of Minnesota Press.

MacDonald, A. (1893) *Abnormal Man, Being Essays on Education and Crime and Related Subjects*. Washington, DC: Government Printing Office.

MacKinnon, C. (1983) 'Feminism, Marxism, Method and the State: Towards a Feminist Jurisprudence', *Signs* 8 (4): 635–58.

Magraw, R. (1987) *France 1815–1914: The Bourgeois Century*. London: Collins.

Mannheim, K. (1929/1991) *Ideology and Utopia*. London: Routledge.

Marcuse, H. (1968) 'Liberation from the Affluent Society', in Cooper, D. (ed.) *The Dialectics of Liberation*. Harmondsworth: Penguin.

Marcuse, H. (1972) *One-Dimensional Man*. London: Abacus.

Marx, K. (1971) *Critique of Hegel's 'Philosophy of Right'*. Cambridge: Cambridge University Press.

Marx, K. and Engels, F. (1970) *The Communist Manifesto*. Harmondsworth: Penguin.

Mathiesen, T. (1983) 'The Future of Social Control Systems: The Case of Norway', in Garland, D. and Young, P. (eds) *The Power to Punish: Contemporary Penality and Social Analysis*. Aldershot: Ashgate.

Mathiesen, T. (1997) 'The Viewer Society: Michel Foucault's "Panopticon" revisited', *Theoretical Criminology* 1 (2): 215–34.

Matza, D. (1969) *Becoming Deviant*. Englewood Cliffs, NJ: Prentice Hall.

Matza, D. and Sykes, G. (1961) 'Juvenile Delinquency and Subterranean Values', *American Sociological Review* 26: 712–19.

Mayhew, H. and Binny, J. (1862) *The Criminal Prisons of London and Scenes of London Life*. Bohn: Griffin.

McKernan, M. (1925) *The Crime and Trial of Leopold and Loeb*. London: George Allen and Unwin.

McLaren, A. (1990) *Our Own Master Race: Eugenics in Canada 1885–1945*. Toronto: McClelland & Stewart.

McNay, L. (1994) *Foucault: A Critical Introduction*. Cambridge: Polity.

Mead, G.H. (1918) 'The Psychology of Punitive Justice', *American Journal of Sociology* 5: 577–602. This is reprinted in Reck (ed.) (1964) *Mead, Selected Writings*. Indianapolis and New York: Bobbs-Merill Company.

Mehrhof, B. and Kearon, P. (1973) 'Rape: An Act of Terror', in Koedt, A., Levine, E. and Rapone, A. (eds) *Radical Feminism*. New York: Quadrangle Books.

Melossi, D. (1990) *The State of Social Control: A Sociological Study of Concepts of State and Social Control in the Making of Democracy*. Cambridge: Polity.

Melossi, D. (2000) 'Changing Representations of the Criminal', *British Journal of Criminology* 40: 296–320.

Melossi, D. and Pavarini, M. (1977/1981) *The Prison and the Factory: Origins of the Penitentiary System*. London and Basingstoke: Macmillan.

Merrin, W. (1999) 'Television is Killing the Art of Symbolic Exchange: Baudrillard's Theory of Communication', *Theory, Culture and Society* 16 (3): 119–41.

Merton, R.K. (1936) 'The Unanticipated Consequences of Purposive Social Action', *American Sociological Review* 1 (6): 894–904.

Merton, R.K. (1938) 'Social Structure and Anomie', *American Sociological Review* 3: 672–82. Reprinted in Piotr Stompka (ed.) (1996) *On Social Structure and Science: Essays by Robert K. Merton*, Chicago, IL: Chicago University Press.

Merton, R.K. (1949) 'Social Structure and Anomie: Revisions and Extensions', in Anshen, R. (ed.) *The Family*. New York: Harper Brothers.

Merton, R.K. (1957) *Social Theory and Social Structure*. Glencoe, IL: Free Press.

Merton, R.K. (1995) 'Opportunity Structure: the Emergence, Diffusion, and Differentiation of a Sociological Concept, 1930s–1950s', in Adler, F. and Laufer, W.S. (eds) *The Legacy of Anomie Theory: Advances in Criminological Theory*, Vol. 6. New Brunswick, NJ: Transaction.

Merton, R.K. and Montagu, A. (1940) 'Crime and the Anthropologist', *American Anthropologist* 42: 384–408.

Messerschmidt, J. (1993) *Masculinities and Crime: Critique and Reconceptualization*. Lanham, MD: Rowman and Littlefield.

Messner, S.F. and Rosenfeld, R. (1997) *Crime and the American Dream*, 2nd edn. Wadsworth.

Mĕstrović, S. (1992) *Durkheim and Postmodern Culture*. New York: Aldine de Gruyter.

Miller, W.W. (1996) *Durkheim, Morals and Modernity*. London: UCL Press.

Millett, K. (1970) *Sexual Politics*. Garden City, NY: Doubleday.

Millman, M. (1975) 'She Did It All For Love', in Millman, M. and Kanter, R.M. (eds) *Another Voice: Feminist Perspectives in Criminology*. Garden City, NY: Anchor Press.

Mills, C.W. (1943) 'The Professional Ideology of Social Pathologists', *American Journal of Sociology* 49 (2): 165–80.

Mills, C.W. (1956) *The Power Elite*. New York: Oxford University Press.

Mills, C.W. (1969) *The Sociological Imagination*. New York: Oxford University Press.

Minda, G. (1995) *Postmodern Legal Movements: Law and Jurisprudence at Century's End*. New York and London: New York University Press.

Mitchell, J. (1971) *Woman's Estate*. Harmondsworth: Penguin.

Mongardini, C. and Tabboni, S. (eds) (1998) *Robert K. Merton and Contemporary Sociology*. New Brunswick, NJ: Transaction.

Montesquieu, Baron de (1748/1989) *Spirit of The Laws*. Cambridge: Cambridge University Press.

Moran, L. (1996) *The Homosexuality of Law*. London: Routledge.

Morrison, W. (1994) 'Criminology, Modernity and the "Truth" of the Human Condition: a Postmodern Approach to Criminological Theory', in Nelken, D. (ed.) *The Futures of Criminology*. London: Sage.

Muncie, J. (1998) 'Reassessing Competing Paradigms in Criminological Theory', in Walton, P. and Young, J. (eds) *The New Criminology Revisited*. Basingstoke: Macmillan.

Muncie, J., McLaughlin, E. and Langan, M. (eds) (1996) *Criminological Perspectives: A Reader*. London: Sage.

Mungham, G. (1980) 'The Career of a Confusion: Radical Criminology in Britain', in Inciardi, J.A. (ed.) *Radical Criminology: The Coming Crises*. Beverly Hills, CA: Sage.

Murphy, M. (1994) 'Bootlegging Mothers and Drinking Daughters: Gender and Prohibition in Butte, Montana', *American Quarterly* 46 (2): 174–94.

Murray, C. (1990) *The Emerging British Underclass*. London: Institute of Economic Affairs.

Naffine, N. (1997) *Feminism and Criminology*. Cambridge: Polity.

National Deviancy Conference (ed.) (1980) *Permissiveness and Control*. London: Macmillan.

Nelken, D. (1989) 'Discipline and Punish: Some Notes on the Margin', *The Howard Journal* 28 (4): 245–54.

Newman, O. (1972) *Defensible Space: People and Design in the Violent City*. London: Architectural Press.

Nicholson, L.J. (ed.) *Feminism/Postmodernism.* New York: Routledge.

Nordau, M. (1893/1993) *Degeneration.* London: University of Minnesota Press.

Norris, C. (1991) *Deconstruction: Theory and Practice.* London: Routledge.

Nye, R. (1985) *Crime, Madness and Politics in Modern France: The Medical Concept of National Decline.* Princeton, NJ: Princeton University Press.

O'Brien, P. (1982) *The Promise of Punishment: Prisons in Nineteenth Century France.* Princeton, NJ: Princeton University Press.

O'Reilly, K. (1982) 'A New Deal for the FBI: The Roosevelt Administration, Crime Control, and National Security', *Journal of American History* 69 (3): 638–58.

Orwell, G. (1949/1990) *Nineteen Eighty-Four.* London: Penguin.

Park, R.E. (1914) 'Racial Assimilation in Secondary Groups with Particular Reference to the Negro', *American Journal of Sociology* 19 (5): 606–23.

Park, R.E. (1915) 'The City: Suggestions for the Investigation of Human Behaviour in the City Environment', *American Journal of Sociology* 20: 577–612.

Park, R.E. (1923) 'The Natural History of the Newspaper', *American Journal of Sociology* 29 (3): 273–89.

Park, R.E. (1925) 'Community Organization and Juvenile Delinquency', in Park, R.E. and Burgess, E. (eds) *The City.* Chicago, IL: University of Chicago Press.

Park, R.E. (1928) 'Human Migration and the Marginal Man', *American Journal of Sociology* 33 (6): 881–93.

Park, R.E. (1930) 'Murder and the Case Study Method', *American Journal of Sociology* 36 (3): 447–54.

Park, R.E. (1936) 'Succession: An Ecological Concept', *American Sociological Review* 1 (2): 171–9.

Park, R.E. and Burgess, E.W. (1921) *An Introduction to the Science of Sociology.* Chicago, IL: University of Chicago Press.

Parker, D. (1936/1974) 'The Standard of Living', in *The Collected Dorothy Parker.* London: Duckworth.

Parsons, T. (1937) *The Structure of Social Action: A Study in Social Theory With Special Reference to a Group of Recent European Writers.* New York: McGraw-Hill.

Pasquino, P. (1979/1980) 'Criminology: The Birth of a Special Savoir', *Ideology and Consciousness* 7: 17–33.

Passas, N. and Agnew, R. (eds) (1995) *The Future of Anomie Theory.* Boston: Northeastern University Press.

Pavarini, M. (1994) 'Is Criminology Worth Saving?', in Nelken, D. (ed.) *The Futures of Criminology.* London: Sage.

Pearce, F. (1989) *The Radical Durkheim.* London: Unwin Hyman.

Pearson, G. (1975a) *The Deviant Imagination.* London: Macmillan.

Pearson, G. (1975b) 'Misfit Sociology and the Politics of Socialization', in Taylor, I., Walton, P. and Young, J. (eds) *Critical Criminology.* London: Routledge.

Pels, D. (1999) 'Privileged Nomads: On the Strangeness of Intellectuals and the Intellectuality of Strangers', *Theory, Culture and Society* 16 (1): 63–86.

Pick, D. (1989) *Faces of Degeneration: A European Disorder, c. 1848–1918.* Cambridge: Cambridge University Press.

Pickering, W.S.F. (1994) 'The Enigma of Durkheim's Jewishness', in Pickering, W.S.F. and Martins, H. (eds) *Debating Durkheim.* New York: Routledge.

Pitch, T. (1992) 'A Sexual Difference Approach to the Criminal Question', *Social and Legal Studies* 53 (3): 367–97.

Pitch, T. (1995) *Limited Responsibilities: Social Movements and Criminal Justice.* London: Routledge.

Platt, T. (1975) 'Prospects for a Radical Criminology in the USA', in Taylor, I., Walton, P. and Young, J. (eds) *Critical Criminology*. London: Routledge and Kegan Paul.

Poggi, G. (1993) *Money and the Modern Mind: George Simmel's Philosophy of Money*. Berkeley: University of California Press.

Porter, R. (2000) *Enlightenment: Britain and the Creation of the Modern World*. London: Penguin.

Poster, M. (1984) *Foucault, Marxism and History: Mode of Production Versus Mode of Information*. Cambridge: Polity.

Poster, M. (1990) *The Mode of Information: Poststructuralism and Social Context*. Cambridge: Polity.

Poster, M. (1996) 'Databases as Discourse; Or, Electronic Interpellations', in Lyon, D. and Zureik, E. (eds) *Computers, Surveillance and Society*. Minneapolis: University of Minnesota Press.

Pound, R. (1912) 'Social Problems and the Courts', *American Journal of Sociology* 18 (3): 331–41.

Pound, R. (1913) 'Legislation as a Social Function', *American Journal of Sociology* 18 (6): 755–68.

Pratt, J. (2000) 'The Return of the Wheelbarrow Men; Or, the Arrival of Postmodern Penality', *British Journal of Criminology* 40: 127–45.

Proal, L. (1892) *Le Crime et la Peine*. Paris: Alcan.

Radcliffe-Brown, A.R. (1935) 'On the Concept of Function in Social Science', *American Anthropologist* 37: 394–402. (This essay is reproduced in Colomy, P. (ed.) (1990) *Functionalist Sociology*, Aldershot: Edward Elgar.)

Radzinowicz, L. and King, J. (1977/1979) *The Growth of Crime: The International Experience*. Harmondsworth: Penguin.

Rafter, N.H. (1997) 'Psycopathy and the Evolution of Criminological Knowledge', *Theoretical Criminology* 1 (2): 235–59.

Rajchman, J. (1988) 'Foucault's Art of Seeing', *October* 44: 88–117.

Ransome, P. (1992) *Antonio Gramsci: A New Introduction*. London: Harvester Wheatsheaf.

Reckless, W. (1926) 'The Distribution of Commercialized Vice in the City', *Proceedings of the American Sociological Society*.

Redhead, S. (1995) *Unpopular Cultures: The Birth of Law and Popular Culture*. Manchester: Manchester University Press.

Report from Iron Mountain (1966/1968) *Report from Iron Mountain on the Possibility and Desirability of Peace*. Harmondsworth: Penguin.

Rice, M. (1990) 'Challenging Orthodoxies in Feminist Theory: A Black Feminist Critique', in Gelsthorpe, L. and Morris, A. (eds) *Feminist Perspectives in Criminology*. Milton Keynes: Open University Press.

Rock, P. (1973) *Deviant Behaviour*. London: Hutchinson.

Romilly, S. (1810) *Observations on the Criminal Law of England, as it Relates to Capital Punishments, and on the Mode in Which it is Administered*. London: T. Cadell and W. Davies.

Rose, N. (1999) *Powers of Freedom: Reframing Political Thought*. Cambridge: Cambridge University Press.

Rose, N. (2000) 'Government and Control', *British Journal of Criminology* 40 (2): 321–39.

Rose, N. and Miller, P. (1992) 'Political Power Beyond the State: Problematics of Government', *British Journal of Sociology* 43 (2): 173–205.

Rose, N. and Valverde, M. (1998) 'Governed by Law?', *Social and Legal Studies* 7 (4): 541–51.

Roughead, W. (ed.) (1910) *Trial of Oscar Slater.* Edinburgh: William Hodge.

Rule, J.B. (1973) *Private Lives and Public Surveillance: Social Control in the Computer Age.* New York: Schochen Books.

Rusche, G. and Kirkheimer, O. (1939/1968) *Punishment and Social Structure.* New York: Russell and Russell.

Ruth, D. (1996) *Inventing the Public Enemy: The Gangster in American Culture, 1918–1934.* Chicago, IL and London: The University of Chicago Press.

Sarat, A. (2000) 'The Cultural Life of Capital Punishment: Responsibility and Representation in Dead Man Walking and Last Dance', *Yale Journal of Law and the Humanities* 11: 153–90.

Sartre, J.-P. (1945/1980) *Existentialism and Humanism,* trans. Mairet, P. London: Methuen.

Sarup, M. (1996) *Identity, Culture and the Postmodern World.* Edinburgh: Edinburgh Press.

Savage, M. and Warde, A. (1993) *Urban Sociology, Capitalism and Modernity.* Basingstoke: Macmillan.

Scheerer, S. (1998) 'The Delinquent as a Fading Category of Knowledge', in Ruggiero, V., South, N. and Taylor, I. (eds) *The New European Criminology: Crime and Social Order in Europe.* London: Routledge.

Scheff, T. (1990) 'Review Essay: A New Durkheim', *American Journal of Sociology* 96: 741.

Scheingold, S.A. (2000) 'Constructing the New Political Criminology: Power, Authority, and the Post-Liberal State', *Law and Social Inquiry* 23 (4): 857–95.

Schlapp, M.G. and Smith, E.H. (1928) *The New Criminology: A Consideration of the Chemical Causation of Abnormal Behavior.* New York: Boni and Liveright.

Schlossman, S. and Sedlak, M. (1983) *The Chicago Area Project Revisited.* Santa Monica, CA: Rand.

Schur, E. (1965) *Crimes Without Victims: Deviant Behaviour and Public Policy.* Englewood Cliffs, NJ: Prentice Hall.

Schur, E. (1973) *Radical Non-Intervention: Rethinking the Delinquency Problem.* Englewood Cliffs, NJ: Prentice Hall.

Scott, J. (1996) *Only Paradoxes to Offer: French Feminists and the Rights of Man.* Cambridge, MA: Harvard University Press.

Scraton, P. and Thomas, P. (eds) (1985) *The State v the People: Lessons From The Coal Dispute.* Oxford: Blackwell.

Sedgwick, P. (1982) *Psychopolitics.* London: Pluto.

Sellin, T. (1938a) 'Culture Conflict and Crime', *American Journal of Sociology* 44 (1): 97–103.

Sellin, T. (1938b) *Culture Conflict and Crime.* New York: The Social Science Research Council, Bulletin no. 41.

Semple, J. (1992) 'Foucault and Bentham: a Defence of Panopticism', *Utilitas* 4: 105–20.

Semple, J. (1993) *Bentham's Prison: A Study of the Panopticon Penitentiary.* Oxford: Clarendon.

Sennett, R. (1977/1986) *The Fall of Public Man.* London: Faber.

Shacklady Smith, L. (1978) 'Sexist Assumptions and Female Delinquency: An Empirical Investigation', in Smart, C. and Smart, B. (eds) *Women, Sexuality and Social Control.* London: Routledge and Kegan Paul.

Shadoian, J. (1977) *Dreams and Dead Ends: The American Gangster Film.* Cambridge, MA: MIT Press.

Shaw, C.R. (1930) *The Jack-Roller: A Delinquent Boy's Own Story.* Chicago, IL: University of Chicago Press.

Shaw, C.R. and McKay, H.D. (1929) *Delinquency Areas: A Study of the Geographic Distribution of School Truants, Juvenile Delinquents and Adult Offenders.* Chicago, IL: University of Chicago Press.

Shaw, C.R. and McKay, H.D. (1942) *Juvenile Delinquency and Urban Areas.* Chicago, IL: University of Chicago Press.

Shearing, C. and Stenning, P. (1985) 'From the Panopticon to Disneyworld: the Development of Discipline', in Doob, E. and Greenspan, E.L. (eds) *Perspectives in Criminal Law.* Toronto: Canada Law Books.

Sheldon, W. (1940) *Varieties of Human Physique.* New York: Harper and Row.

Silverman, I.R. and Sinitz, D. (1974) 'Compulsive Masculinity and Delinquency: An Empirical Investigation', *Criminology* 11: 498–515.

Sim., J. (1990) *Medical Power in Prisons: The Prison Medical Service in England 1774–1989.* Milton Keynes: Open University Press.

Sim., J., Scraton, P. and Gordon, P. (1987) 'Introduction: Crime, the State, and Critical Analysis', in Scraton, P. (ed.) *Law, Order and the Authoritarian State.* Milton Keynes: Open University Press.

Simmel, G. (1900/1990) *The Philosophy of Money.* London: Routledge.

Simmel, G. (1903/1950) 'The Metropolis of Mental Life', in *The Sociology of Georg Simmel.* New York: Free Press.

Simon, R.J. (1975) *Women and Crime.* Toronto: Lexington Books.

Simon, R. (1991) *Gramsci's Political Thought: An Introduction.* London: Lawrence and Wishart.

Simon, W. and Gagnon, J.H. (1976) 'The Anomie of Affluence: a Post-Mertonian Conception', *American Journal of Sociology* 82: 356–78.

Simpson, S. (1989) 'Feminist Theory, Crime and Justice', *Criminology* 27: 605–31.

Smart, B. (1983) *Foucault, Marxism and Critique.* London: Routledge.

Smart, B. (1983/1992) 'On Discipline and Social Regulation: a Review of Foucault's Genealogical Analysis', in Garland, D. and Young, P. (eds) *The Power to Punish: Contemporary Penality and Social Analysis.* Aldershot: Ashgate.

Smart, B. (1993) *Postmodernity.* London: Routledge.

Smart, C. (1976) *Women, Crime and Criminology: A Feminist Critique.* London: Routledge and Kegan Paul.

Smart, C. (1989) *Feminism and the Power of Law.* London: Routledge.

Smart, C. (1990) 'Feminist Approaches to Criminology or Postmodern Woman Meets Atavistic Man', in Gelsthorpe, L. and Morris, A. (eds) *Feminist Perspectives in Criminology.* Milton Keynes: Open University Press.

Smart, C. (1995) *Law, Crime and Sexuality: Essays in Feminism.* London: Sage.

Smith, D. (1973) 'Women's Perspective as a Radical Critique of Sociology', *Sociological Inquiry* 14 (1): 7–13.

Smith, D. (1988) 'How to be a Successful Outsider', *Theory, Culture and Society* 15 (1): 39–46.

Snodgrass, J. (1976) 'Clifford R. Shaw and Henry D. McKay: Chicago Criminologists', *British Journal of Criminology* 16 (1): 1–19.

Soja, E.W. (1995) 'Postmodern Urbanization: The Six Restructurings of Los Angeles', in Watson, S. and Gibson, K. (eds) *Postmodern Cities and Spaces.* Oxford: Blackwell.

South, N. (1997) 'Control, Crime and "End of Century" Criminology', in Francis, P., Davies, P. and Jupp, V. (eds) *Policing Futures: The Police, Law Enforcement and the Twenty-First Century*. Basingstoke: Macmillan.

Spelman, E. (1990) *Inessential Woman: Problems of Exclusion in Feminist Thought*. London: The Women's Press.

Spencer, H. (1851/1868) *Social Statics: The Conditions Essential to Human Happiness Specified, and the First of them Developed*. London: Williams and Norgate.

Spierenburg, P. (1984) *The Spectacle of Suffering: Executions and the Evolution of Repression*. Cambridge: Cambridge University Press.

Spierenburg, P. (1991) *The Prison Experience: Disciplinary Institutions and their Inmates in Early Modern Europe*. New Brunswick, NJ: Rutgers University Press.

Spivak, G.C. (1988) 'Can the Subaltern Speak?', in Nelson, C. and Grossberg, L. (eds) *Marxism and the Interpretation of Culture*. Urbana, IL: University of Illinois Press.

Steffens, L. (1904) *The Shame of the Cities*. New York: McClure, Phillips & Co.

Steinbeck, J. (1939/1996) *The Grapes of Wrath*. New York: Library of America.

Stenson, K. and Brearley, N. (1991) 'Left Realism in Criminology and the Return to Consensus Theory', in Reiner, R. and Cross, M. (eds) *Beyond Law and Order: Criminal Justice Policy and Politics into the 1990s*. Basingstoke: Macmillan.

Stoker, B. (1897/1993) *Dracula*. London: Penguin.

Stonequist, E.V. (1937) *The Marginal Man: A Study in Personality and Culture Conflict*. New York: Charles Scribner's Sons.

Stychin, C. (2000) ' "A Stranger to its Laws": Sovereign Bodies, Global Sexualities, and Transnational Citizens', *Journal of Law and Society* 27 (4): 625–61.

Sumner, C. (1994) *The Sociology of Deviance: An Obituary*. Milton Keynes: Open University Press.

Sumner, C. (1997) 'Social Control: The History and Politics of a Concept', in Bergalli, R. and Sumner, C. (eds) *Social Control and Political Order: European Perspectives at the End of the Century*. London: Sage.

Sutherland, E. (1924/1939) *Principles of Criminology*. Chicago, IL: University of Chicago Press.

Sutherland, E. (1940) 'White-Collar Criminality', *American Sociological Review* 5: 1–12.

Sykes, G. and Matza, M. (1961) 'Juvenile Delinquency and Subterranean Values', *American Sociological Review* 26 (5): 712–19.

Szasz, A. (1961) *The Myth of Mental Illness*. New York: Harper and Row.

Sztompka, P. (1986) *Robert K. Merton: An Intellectual Profile*. Basingstoke: Macmillan.

Tame, C.R. (1991) 'Freedom, Responsibility and Justice: The Criminology of the "New Right"', in Stenson, K. and Lowell, D. (eds) *The Politics of Crime Control*. London: Sage.

Tannenbaum, F. (1938) *Crime and the Community*. New York: Columbia University Press.

Taylor, C. (1986) 'Foucault on Freedom and Truth', in Couzens Hoy, D. (ed.) *Foucault: A Critical Reader*. Oxford: Blackwell.

Taylor, I. and Taylor, L. (1968) 'We Are All Deviants Now', *International Socialism* 34.

Taylor, I. and Taylor, L. (eds) (1973) *Politics and Deviance*. London: Penguin.

Taylor, I., Walton, P. and Young, J. (1973) *The New Criminology: For a Social Theory of Deviance*. London: Routledge and Kegan Paul.

Taylor, I., Walton, P. and Young, J. (eds) (1975) *Critical Criminology*. London: Routledge and Kegan Paul.

Thomas, W.I. and Znaniecki, F. (1918) *The Polish Peasant in Europe and America.* Chicago, IL: University of Chicago Press.

Thompson, E.P. (1975) *Whigs and Hunters: The Origins of the Black Act.* Harmondsworth: Penguin.

Thompson, E.P. (1980) *Writing by Candlelight.* London: Merlin Press.

Thompson, J. (1995) *The Media and Modernity: A Social Theory of the Media.* Cambridge: Polity.

Thompson, K. (1982) *Émile Durkheim.* London: Tavistock.

Thrasher, F. (1927) *The Gang: A Study of 1,313 Gangs in Chicago.* Chicago, IL: University of Chicago Press.

Tole, L.A. (1993) 'Durkheim on Religion and Moral Community in Modernity', *Sociological Inquiry* 63 (1): 1–29.

Tolson, A (1977) *The Limits of Masculinity.* London: Tavistock.

Tombs, R. (1998) '"Lesser Breeds without the Law": The British Establishment and the Dreyfus Affair', *The Historical Journal* 41 (2): 495–510.

Torrey, E.F. (1992) *Freudian Fraud: The Malignent Effect of Freud's Theory on American Thought and Culture.* New York: HarperCollins.

Truzzi, M. (ed.) (1971) *Sociology: The Classic Statements.* New York: Random House.

Turner, B.S. (ed.) (1990) *Theories of Modernity and Postmodernity.* London: Sage.

Turner, B.S. (1995) 'Karl Mannheim's "Ideology and Utopia"', *Political Studies* 43: 718–27.

Turner, R.H. (ed.) (1967) *Robert E. Park on Social Control and Collective Behaviour.* Chicago, IL: University of Chicago Press.

Urry, J. (1991) 'Time and Space in Giddens Social Theory', in Bryant, C. and Jary, D. (eds) *Giddens' Theory of Structuration.* London: Routledge.

Urry, J. (2000a) *Sociology Beyond Societies: Mobilities for the Twenty-First Century.* London: Routledge.

Urry, J. (2000b) 'Mobile Sociology', *British Journal of Sociology* 51 (1): 185–203.

Valverde, M. (1991) 'Feminist Perspectives in Criminology', in Gladstone, J., Ericson, R.V. and Shearing, C.D. (eds) *Criminology: A Reader's Guide.* Toronto: Centre for Criminology, University of Toronto.

Van Swaaningen, R. (1997) *Critical Criminology: Visions From Europe.* London: Sage.

Veblen, T. (1899) *Theory of the Leisure Class: An Economic Study in the Evolution of Institutions.* New York: Macmillan.

Virilio, P. (1995/1997) *Open Sky.* London: Verso.

Voltaire (1763/2000) *Traité sur la tolerance à l'occasion de la mort de Jean Calas.* Cambridge: Cambridge University Press.

Vogt, W.P. (1993) 'Durkheim's Sociology of Law, Morality and the Cult of the Individual', in Turner, S. (ed.) *Émile Durkheim: Sociologist and Moralist.* London: Routledge.

Wacquant, L. (2000) 'The New "Peculiar Institution": On the Prison as Surrogate Ghetto', *Theoretical Criminology* 4 (3): 377–89.

Walklate, S. (1998) *Understanding Criminology: Current Theoretical Debates.* Buckingham: Open University Press.

Walton, P. (1998) 'Big Science: Dystopia and Utopia – Establishment and New Criminology Revisited', in Walton, P. and Young, J. (eds) *The New Criminology Revisited.* Basingstoke: Macmillan.

Ware, C. (1970) *Woman Power.* Tower Public Affairs Books.

Warrington, J. (1973) 'A Critique of R.D. Laing's Social Philosophy', *Radical Philosophy* 5: 10–16.

Weedon, C. (1987) *Feminist Practice and Poststructuralist Theory*. Oxford: Blackwell.

White, W. (1920) 'Expert Testimony in Criminal Procedure Involving the Question of the Mental State of the Defendant', *Journal of Criminal Law and Criminology* XI (4): 499–511.

White, W. (1933) *Forty Years of Psychiatry*. New York and Washington, DC: Nervous and Mental Diseases Publishing Company.

Wilkins, L. (1964) *Social Deviance: Social Policy, Action and Research*. London: Tavistock.

Wilkinson, L.R. (1992) 'The Art of Distinction: Proust and the Dreyfus Affair', *Modern Language Notes* 107 (5): 976–99.

Willrich, M. (1998) 'The Two Percent Solution: Eugenic Jurisprudence and the Socialization of American Law', *Law and History Review* 16 (1): 63–111.

Wilson, J.Q. (1975) *Thinking About Crime*. New York: Vintage.

Wilson, S. (1973) 'The Anti-Semitic Riots of 1898 in France', *Historical Journal* 16 (4): 789–806.

Wirth, L. (1936/1964) in *On Cities and Social Life*. Chicago: Chicago University Press.

Woodhull, W. (1988) 'Sexuality, Power and the Question of Rape', in Diamond, I. and Quinby, L. (eds) *Feminism and Foucault*. Boston, MA: Northeastern University Press.

Yablonsky, L. (1997) *Gangsters: Fifty Years of Madness, Drugs and Death on the Streets of America*. New York: New York University Press.

Young, A. (1990) *Femininity in Dissent*. London: Routledge.

Young, A. (1996) *Imagining Crime: Textual Outlaws and Criminal Conversations*. London: Sage.

Young, A. and Rush, P. (1994) 'The Law of Victimage in Urbane Realism: Thinking Through Inscriptions of Violence', in Nelken, D. (ed.) *The Futures of Criminology*. London: Sage.

Young, J. (1971) *The Drugtakers: The Social Meaning of Drug Use*. London: MacGibbon and Kee/Paladin.

Young, J. (1987) 'The Tasks of a Realist Criminology', *Contemporary Crises* 11: 337–56.

Young, J. (1998) 'Breaking Windows: Situating the New Criminology', in Walton, P. and Young, J. (eds) *The New Criminology Revisited*. Basingstoke: Macmillan.

Young, J. and Matthews, R. (eds) (1992) *Rethinking Criminology: The Realist Debate*. London: Sage.

Zangwill, I. (1908/1909) *The Melting Pot*. New York: Macmillan.

Zola, E. (1898/1996) 'Letter to M. Félix Faure, President of the Republic', in Pagès, A. (ed.) *The Dreyfus Affair. "J'Accuse" and Other Writings*. New Haven, CT and London: Yale University Press.

Zorbaugh, H.W. (1929) *The Gold Coast and the Slum: A Sociological Study of Chicago's Near North Side*. Chicago, IL: University of Chicago Press.

Zuboff, S. (1988) *In the Age of the Smart Machine: The Future of Work and Power*. New York: Basic Books.

Index